CHARITY LAW AND THE LIBERAL STATE

Charity Law and the Liberal State considers questions relating to state action and public discourse that are raised by the law of charity. Informed by liberal philosophical commitments and of interest to both charity lawyers and political philosophers, it addresses themes and topics such as: the justifiability of the state's non-neutral promotion of charitable purposes; the role of altruism in charity law; charity law, the tax system and the demands of distributive justice; the proper treatment of religious and political purposes in charity law; and the appropriate response of the liberal state to discrimination in the pursuit of charitable purposes.

MATTHEW HARDING is an associate professor in the Melbourne Law School, University of Melbourne.

CHARITY LAW AND THE LIBERAL STATE

MATTHEW HARDING

CAMBRIDGE
UNIVERSITY PRESS

CAMBRIDGE
UNIVERSITY PRESS

University Printing House, Cambridge CB2 8BS, United Kingdom

Cambridge University Press is part of the University of Cambridge.

It furthers the University's mission by disseminating knowledge in the pursuit of
education, learning and research at the highest international levels of excellence.

www.cambridge.org
Information on this title: www.cambridge.org/9781107022331

First published 2014

Printed in the United Kingdom by Clays, St Ives plc

A catalogue record for this publication is available from the British Library

Library of Congress Cataloguing in Publication data
Harding, Matthew, 1974- author.
Charity law and the liberal state / Matthew Harding.
pages   cm
ISBN 978-1-107-02233-1 (Hardback)
1. Charity laws and legislation.   2. Charitable uses, trusts, and foundations.
3. Charities.   I. Title.
K797.H37 2014
344.03'17632–dc23   2014014734

ISBN 978-1-107-02233-1 Hardback

CONTENTS

ACKNOWLEDGEMENTS

Some of the research for this book was funded by an Australian Research Council grant awarded to me and my colleagues Ann O'Connell and Miranda Stewart for 2010–2; I am grateful to the ARC for that support. My thanks are due to those family, friends and colleagues who helped me by providing advice, support, encouragement and wisdom: Elise Bant, Nick Beach, Natalie Burgess, Joyce Chia, Kirsty Gover, Robin Hickey, Brian Lucas, Ann O'Connell, Finola O'Sullivan, Hubert Picarda, Pauline Ridge and Andrew Robertson. I am also grateful to participants in the Melbourne Law School Legal Theory Workshop, the 2012 Not-for-Profit Conference at the University of Melbourne, the 2012 NCVO Conference at the University of Birmingham, and a 2012 seminar at the University of Liverpool (kindly organised by Debra Morris), at which ideas from this book were presented and discussed. Farrah Ahmed, Katy Barnett, Michael Bryan, Mark Burton, Chris Dent, Carolyn Evans, Dan Halliday, Tony Lee, Myles McGregor-Lowndes, Julian Sempill, Miranda Stewart, Matthew Turnour and Lael Weis all read and provided me with comments on draft materials, and in some cases on the larger part of the manuscript. Their critical and insightful attention has improved the book immensely and where my argument still falls short of the mark it is most likely because I did not heed their advice. Anna Dziedzic undertook research assistance and editorial work with great care and skill: thank you, Anna. Mathew Reiman, Cindy Bors and Joshua Keyes-Liley helped me with research assistance at the eleventh hour: thanks to all three. Rob Atkinson deserves special mention as a characteristically gracious and thoughtful reader, and more generally as an example of what an academic should be. So does Ian Malkin for his unwavering support and his friendship, so dear to me. And, of course, my wife Clare and my children Isabel and Charlie, who remind me when I most need it that there is more to life than work.

~

Introduction

Charity law is the body of law that invokes a legally understood concept of 'charity'. Through it, the state marks out for special legal treatment a range of purposes that stand to generate public benefit. Thus described, charity law is complex. In part, this is because the legal understanding of 'charity' diverges significantly from the non-legal meaning of that concept as having to do with alleviating human suffering; as we will see in this book, in addition to helping the disadvantaged, the legal understanding of 'charity' takes in a large range of public benefit purposes as diverse as founding a school, beautifying a town, or staging an opera. In part, charity law is complex because a legal understanding of 'charity' is deployed in a range of legal settings, in ascertaining the validity of trusts for purposes, in determining the availability of legal – and especially tax – privileges, and in generating a legal status that opens the door to a variety of regulatory consequences. In part, the complexity of charity law is a product of its history, as its sources may be found in hundreds of years of largely incremental, sometimes fitful, judicial activity, punctuated by occasional legislative interventions that at times have purported to restate judge-made law, at times have tinkered at the edges, and at times have effected radical change. Given the complexity of charity law, it is unsurprising that textbooks on the subject typically run to many hundreds of pages of detailed analysis;[1] nor, perhaps, is it surprising that one of the greatest charity lawyers of the twentieth century, Lord Simonds, thought that 'few, if any, subjects have more frequently occupied the time of the court'.[2]

---

[1] See, e.g., Gino Dal Pont, *Law of Charity* (LexisNexis Butterworths, Chatswood, 2010); Peter Luxton, *The Law of Charities* (Oxford University Press, 2001); Hubert Picarda, *The Law and Practice Relating to Charities* (4th edn, Bloomsbury Professional, Haywards Heath, West Sussex, 2010); Jean Warburton, Debra Morris and N.F. Riddle (eds), *Tudor on Charities* (9th edn, Sweet and Maxwell, London, 2003); Jonathan Garton, *Public Benefit in Charity Law* (Oxford University Press, 2013).
[2] *Gilmour v. Coats* [1949] AC 426 (House of Lords), 443.

If it is unsurprising that lawyers have spilt much ink over the complexities of charity law, it is perhaps more surprising that political philosophers have not done the same. Charity law, like all law, raises themes that are of interest to political philosophers – themes like the relationship of citizen and state, the distinction between public and private, the demands of social justice and the moral basis and outworkings of individual rights, to name just a few. And yet the considerable recent interest in philosophical foundations and aspects of various bodies of law, from the law of property, to the law of torts, to contract law, to the law of unjust enrichment, has not been replicated in the case of charity law. More surprising still is the lack of interest in charity law from political philosophers working in the liberal tradition,[3] for charity law raises some of the core questions in that tradition. For example, many liberals are committed to the proposition that, in some sense, the state must remain neutral with respect to contested conceptions of the good, and yet in charity law we find the state marking out certain purposes as 'charitable' according to contested conceptions of the good and then extending legal privileges to the citizens who pursue those purposes. Can this practice be justified in a way that is consistent with liberal commitments? How? To take another example, the tax privileges of charity law have distributive consequences which ought to be of interest to liberals who worry over the demands of distributive justice. When, via charity law, the state permits a rich person to deduct from her assessable income a million-dollar donation to an art gallery, is liberal distributive justice engaged? How? With what consequences? Or yet another example: one key liberal preoccupation is with the special value of political expression in light of the demands of democratic government; when the state declares that political purposes cannot be charitable in law, as is the case in a number of jurisdictions, does this interfere with political expression in a way that ought to be of liberal concern? If so, why? And what should be done about it?

The aim of this book is to contribute to rectifying the lack of liberal interest in charity law. The book will consider some questions about state action and public discourse that are raised by charity law, from a perspective informed by liberal philosophical commitments. The aim

---

[3] One notable exception is Nick Martin, 'Liberal Neutrality and Charitable Purposes' (2012) 60 *Political Studies* 936. And we should note also the important work of Rob Atkinson in the tradition of republican political philosophy: Rob Atkinson, 'Keeping Republics Republican' (2011) 88 *Texas Law Review* 235.

will not be to provide a detailed examination of every aspect of charity law; the complexity of charity law is such that any aspiration to exhaustive coverage of the legal materials must be abandoned. Nor will the aim be to provide a liberal theory of charity law that addresses every question about state action and public discourse that charity law might raise. Again, such an aim is too ambitious for one book. Rather, the book will aim to develop a theoretical framework, informed by liberal commitments, for the fruitful study of questions about state action and public discourse that are raised by charity law; it will then apply that framework in thinking about some, but not all, such questions. The selection of questions on which to focus has been guided by a sense of what liberals might find most perplexing or difficult about charity law as well as a sense of what has generated most debate and controversy among charity lawyers. To the extent that the book leaves questions about state action and public discourse in the charity law setting unaddressed, the hope is that it will at least equip readers with evaluative tools for approaching those questions themselves.

In Chapter 1, we will begin our inquiry into charity law and the liberal state by gaining an overview of the content of charity law with reference to a number of jurisdictions in which charity law may be found. In Chapter 2, we will turn to the task of selecting a liberal perspective from which to consider questions about state action and public discourse that are raised by charity law. Having selected a perspective, we will ask in Chapter 3 why the state might choose to pursue the aims of charity law via charity law and not in some other way, and we will also examine why the boundaries of that body of law might be set where they are set. Chapter 4 will focus on important questions of distributive justice that come into view once we reflect on the distributive implications of charity law, including the distributive implications of those rules of charity law extending tax privileges to citizens who pursue charitable purposes. In Chapter 5, we will take up the question of the state's use of charity law to promote religion – perhaps, from a liberal perspective, the most puzzling of charity law's dimensions. Chapter 6 will weigh up the reasons for and against charity law's longstanding rule disqualifying political purposes from being charitable, and Chapter 7 will explore the proper liberal response to discrimination, on grounds like race, sex and religion, in the pursuit of charitable purposes.

What will emerge from the various chapters is an argument for charity law in something like its current form. This argument embraces two more specific claims: first, that charity law, for all its complexity and even incoherence,[4] is broadly comprehensible and useful in light of the state aims that underpin it; and second, that the aims underpinning charity law are broadly defensible having regard to liberal commitments. These claims might strike some readers as surprising, given what others have said and thought about charity law. For example, Gino Dal Pont has argued that various state aims that are presently pursued via charity law might be better pursued by legal rules that eschew a legally understood concept of charity; Dal Pont thus calls into question the claim that charity law is useful in light of its aims.[5] Others have argued that the aims of charity law are aims that the state should not have in the first place. For instance, there is a long history of doubting the justification of the aims underpinning the state's extension of legal privileges to those who pursue charitable purposes; perhaps the most famous chapter in this history is William Gladstone's failed attempt in 1863 to impose income tax on charities.[6] Such instances of scepticism about the comprehensibility, usefulness and justification of charity law are, in large part, at odds with the conclusions of this book – conclusions suggesting that charity law makes sense and is worth having in a liberal state. That said, the book is not an uncritical apologia for modern charity law; to the extent that the content or consequences of charity law cannot be defended in light of liberal commitments, we will notice this and draw the necessary conclusions.

Before we turn to the substance of our inquiry, we should reflect for a moment on the scope of this book; doing so should clarify further the aim underpinning it. The scope of the book might be thought to be too narrow: first, in the sense that it purports to be a book about 'charity law' and yet touches on only some of the jurisdictions in which charity law may be found, viz, Australia, Canada, England and Wales, Ireland, New Zealand, Northern Ireland, Scotland and the United States; and second, in the sense that as a book about 'charity law' it chooses not to focus on bodies of law that do not invoke a legally understood concept of

---

[4] 'No-one who has been versed ... in this difficult and very artificial branch of the law can be unaware of its illogicalities': *Oppenheim* v. *Tobacco Securities Trust Co Ltd* [1951] AC 297 (House of Lords), 307 (Lord Simonds).

[5] Gino Dal Pont, 'Why Define "Charity"? Is the Search for Meaning Worth the Effort?' (2002) 8 *Third Sector Review* 5.

[6] See the account in David Owen, *English Philanthropy 1660–1960* (Belknap Press, Cambridge, MA, 1964), 330–332. For a more recent instance of scepticism about the tax privileges of charity law: Michael Chesterman, 'Foundations of Charity Law in the New Welfare State' (1999) 62 *Modern Law Review* 333.

'charity', but nonetheless serve a function of marking out for special legal treatment purposes that stand to produce public benefit, and to that extent are analogous to charity law. Such bodies of law may be found in a range of jurisdictions beyond what is typically called the common law world, in continental Europe, Asia and South America, for example.[7]

These concerns over the scope of the book should disappear once its aim is properly understood. This is a book about questions of state action and public discourse that are raised by charity law; thus, the law of particular jurisdictions is of interest to us only to the extent that it shows some of the ways in which such questions arise. That said, the charity law of jurisdictions not included in this book is in many respects similar to the charity law of jurisdictions that are included and therefore raises the questions about state action and public discourse that are addressed in the book. A similar claim may be made about jurisdictions that do not have a 'charity law' but instead mark out public benefit purposes for special treatment via a law of 'public benefit organisations' or the like. There should be much in this book of interest to readers in any jurisdiction where public benefit purposes are marked out for special legal treatment, whether via 'charity law' or in some other way. Nonetheless, in confining its inquiries to the 'charity law' of the common law world, the book aims to be sensitive to one important consideration. As we will see in what follows, one of the more noteworthy dimensions of charity law is what might be called its expressive dimension; via charity law, the state associates the pursuit of charitable purposes with a variety of public meanings, some of which are of interest from a liberal philosophical perspective. Some of these public meanings may be informed by the non-legal meaning of the concept 'charity' and, to the extent that they are, 'charity law' may have expressive effects that are absent from analogous bodies of law organised around different concepts. With these possible expressive effects in view, there are reasons to confine a study of charity law and the liberal state to jurisdictions that have 'charity law', even if many of the conclusions of such a study are applicable in jurisdictions where analogous bodies of law serve analogous state aims but are organised around different concepts.

---

[7] For overviews of many such jurisdictions, see David Moore, Katerina Hadzi-Miceva and Nilda Bullain, 'A Comparative Overview of Public Benefit Status in Europe' (2008) 11 *International Journal of Not-for-Profit Law* 5; Anne-Marie Piper (ed.), *Charity Law: Jurisdictional Comparisons* (Thomson Reuters, London, 2012).

Charity law in overview

1. Introduction

As we saw in the Introduction, this book will address questions about
state action and public discourse that are raised by charity law.
In order to set the stage for such inquiries, we should begin by looking
at our subject in overview, seeking to identify key features that tend to
characterise charity law wherever it is found, and in light of which
questions about state action and public discourse may be framed. That
is the aim of this chapter. When looked at in overview, charity law
may be divided into two broad parts: that which addresses the question whether or not a purpose is charitable in law[1] and that which
addresses the question of what legal consequences flow from the
pursuit of charitable purposes. The first part of charity law itself
breaks down into two further components: the first of these further
components consists of a set of criteria by which decision-makers
determine the charitable or non-charitable character of purposes and
the second consists of a number of rules according to which certain
purposes are disqualified from being charitable. The second broad part
of charity law consists of rules spelling out the legal consequences for
those who carry out charitable purposes; the most significant of those
consequences – at least in the context of a study of charity law and the
liberal state – are the legal privileges that charity law extends to those
with charitable purposes. With these preliminary taxonomical observations in mind, our overview of charity law in this chapter will begin
with an examination of the criteria of charity law; we will then turn to

---

[1] In most jurisdictions, charity law takes an interest in the character of purposes, rather than
in the activities that are carried out in the pursuit of purposes. The boundary between
purposes and activities is not always kept distinct, however, and in Scotland, charity law
takes an overt interest in activities. For an overview of the treatment of activities in charity
law: Jonathan Garton, *Public Benefit in Charity Law* (Oxford University Press, 2013),
[3.36]–[3.42].

some of charity law's key disqualifying rules, and we will conclude with a brief discussion of the legal privileges of charity.

2.   The criteria of charity law

The criteria of charity law are the primary means by which decision-makers – whether they be judges, regulators of the charity sector or tax officials – determine whether or not some purpose should be regarded as charitable in law. These criteria emerged gradually over time from judicial decisions in the law of trusts, the traditional home of charity law, but in modern charity law they are applied in many cases by a range of decision-makers outside the law of trusts where the question whether or not a purpose is charitable arises for consideration. For example, the criteria of charity law might be invoked by a charity regulator in deciding whether to register some entity as a charity, or by a tax official in determining whether the income of an entity is exempt from income tax. The criteria of charity law are twofold: first, in order to be charitable in law, a purpose must fall within at least one of a set of legally prescribed general descriptions of charitable purpose; and second, in order to be charitable in law, a purpose must be of public benefit. As we will see, in at least one respect the first of these criteria is best understood in light of the second, and in this sense it might be said that the only true criterion of charity law is a public benefit test. Nonetheless, for present purposes it will suffice to adhere to orthodoxy and describe the two criteria of charity law separately, even though it may in fact be possible and desirable to think of them reductively as outworkings of a single, more fundamental, concern.

A.   General descriptions of charitable purpose

One of the criteria of charity law takes the form of a requirement that, in order to be considered charitable, a purpose must fall within at least one of a set of legally prescribed general descriptions of charitable purpose. As we will see, the descriptions that make up this set vary from jurisdiction to jurisdiction, but the set is typically designed so as to incorporate two features. First, the set is usually open-ended, including a 'catch-all' description that facilitates the recognition of new types of purpose as charitable; and second, the set is usually subject to some constraint so as to ensure that the recognition of new types of purpose as charitable occurs in a controlled and (in theory at least) predictable manner.[2] General descriptions of charitable purpose typically form a starting point for analysis when the question whether or not a particular purpose is charitable is before a decision-maker. Thus, a decision-maker will typically seek to establish whether or not the purpose before her falls within one or more of the descriptions that figure in the set of descriptions in the charity law of her jurisdiction, before asking any other questions about the purpose with a view to determining whether or not it is charitable.

The best-known set of general descriptions of charitable purpose in charity law made its first appearance in counsel's argument in *Morice* v. *Bishop of Durham*,[3] but has come to be associated with the judgment of Lord Macnaghten in the celebrated case of *Commissioners for Special Purposes of Income Tax* v. *Pemsel*.[4] Until quite recently, this set – which, for convenience, we may refer to as the '*Pemsel* set' – figured in the charity law of a wide range of jurisdictions, and one consequence of this is that nearly all of the judicial decisions constituting sources of charity law since the late nineteenth century (when *Pemsel* was decided) have been decided against a legal backdrop incorporating the *Pemsel* set. As we will see shortly, in several jurisdictions the *Pemsel* set has been modified or replaced, but in Canada and New Zealand it persists,[5] and in Australia it has been replaced only for the purposes of federal law.[6] The *Pemsel* set is composed of four descriptions, also known in the distinctive terminology of charity law as the four 'heads' of charity: 'relief of poverty'; 'advancement of education'; 'advancement of religion'; and 'other purposes beneficial to the community, not falling under any of the preceding heads'.[7] The fourth 'head' of the *Pemsel* set is an open-ended 'catch-all' description, and the history of charity law shows that many new types of

---

[2] In Ireland, there would seem to be some uncertainty about whether or not the set of descriptions in section 3 of the Charities Act of 2009 is open-ended and, if it is, what constraint applies to it: Oonagh B. Breen, 'Ireland: *Pemsel* Plus' in Myles McGregor-Lowndes and Kerry O'Halloran (eds), *Modernising Charity Law: Recent Developments and Future Directions* (Edward Elgar, Cheltenham, 2010) 74.

[3] (1804) 9 Ves Jun 399; 32 ER 656 (Sir William Grant MR); (1805) 10 Ves Jun 522; 32 ER 947 (Lord Eldon LC).

[4] [1891] AC 531 (House of Lords).

[5] For the Canadian position, see *Vancouver Society of Immigrant and Visible Minority Women* v. *Minister of National Revenue* [1999] 1 SCR 10 (Supreme Court of Canada). In New Zealand, the Charities Act 2005 (NZ) s 5 'defines' charity but the 'definition' refers to judge-made law, which remains the source of the *Pemsel* set in that jurisdiction.

[6] Charities Act 2013 (Australia) s 12.

[7] [1891] AC 531 (House of Lords), 583 (Lord Macnaghten).

purpose have been found to be charitable within this 'head'. At the same time, decision-makers have often interpreted the fourth 'head' of the *Pemsel* set as subject to a constraint in the form of a requirement that a purpose within that 'catch-all' description be either listed in or analogous to a purpose listed in the preamble to a late Tudor statute, the Statute of Charitable Uses of 1601, also known as the Statute of Elizabeth.

The preamble to the Statute of Elizabeth, rendered in modern English, refers to the following purposes:

> the relief of the aged, impotent and poor people; the maintenance of sick and maimed soldiers and mariners, schools of learning, free schools and scholars in universities; the repair of bridges, ports, havens, causeways, churches, sea-banks and highways; the education and preferment of orphans; the relief, stock or maintenance of houses of correction; the marriages of poor maids, the supportation, aid and help of young trades-men, handicraftsmen and persons decayed; the relief or redemption of prisoners or captives, and the aid or ease of any poor inhabitants concerning payment of fifteens, setting out of soldiers and other taxes.

Exactly how and why this preamble came to operate as a constraint on the admission of new types of purpose to the *Pemsel* set is not well understood. The Statute of Elizabeth was enacted in order to establish a regulatory structure for the supervision of charitable trusts, against a backdrop of fraud and neglect on the part of charity trustees. The preamble was intended less as a definition of charitable purposes than as a statement of types of purposes that, to the late Tudor mind, were regarded as charitable.[8] Nonetheless, by the time of *Pemsel*, the preamble was entrenched in judge-made charity law as a sort of index to be consulted when a question was raised as to whether or not some purpose was charitable[9] and, later, reference to the 'spirit and intendment' of the preamble came to constrain the growth of the fourth 'head'.[10] That said, it must be acknowledged that there has also been a tradition of ignoring or downplaying the preamble when new types of purpose have fallen for consideration under the fourth 'head'.[11] Today, in jurisdictions whose

---

[8] On the background to the Statute of Elizabeth, see Gareth Jones, *History of the Law of Charity 1532–1827* (Cambridge University Press, 1969), ch 3.

[9] See, e.g., *Morice* v. *Bishop of Durham* (1804) 9 Ves Jun 399; 32 ER 656 (Sir William Grant MR); (1805) 10 Ves Jun 522; 32 ER 947 (Lord Eldon LC).

[10] See, e.g., *Scottish Burial Reform and Cremation Society Limited* v. *Glasgow Corporation* [1968] AC 138 (House of Lords).

[11] See, e.g., cases on purposes relating to animal welfare: *In re Wedgwood* [1915] 1 Ch 113 (Court of Appeal); *In re Grove-Grady* [1929] 1 Ch 557 (Court of Appeal); *National Anti-Vivisection Society* v. *Inland Revenue Commissioners* [1948] AC 31 (House of Lords).

charity law continues to incorporate the *Pemsel* set, the link to the preamble persists – especially in the setting of the fourth 'head'[12] – but so does the tradition of ignoring or downplaying it when the occasion suits.[13]

In the United States of America, the *Pemsel* set continues to figure in charity law, although it has been modified in certain ways. The United States Restatement (Third) of Trusts states that charitable purposes 'include' the following: 'relief of poverty'; 'advancement of knowledge or education'; 'advancement of religion'; 'promotion of health'; 'governmental or municipal purposes'; and 'other purposes beneficial to the community'.[14] This set of purposes clearly resembles, but is not identical to, the *Pemsel* set;[15] to that extent it may be viewed fairly as an American interpretation of the *Pemsel* set. As well as appearing in the Restatement, the American interpretation of the *Pemsel* set informs the authoritative treatise *Scott on Trusts*, where it is used to frame a discussion of general descriptions of charitable purpose.[16] Whether or not decision-makers in the United States follow a consistent practice of turning to the American interpretation of the *Pemsel* set when determining the charitable or non-charitable character of purposes is not easily ascertained, given the difficulty of identifying case law trends in various state courts, and the possibility must remain open that in the United States the *Pemsel* set functions more as a taxonomical tool for scholars than as a guide to the practical reasoning of decision-makers.[17] Moreover, the Restatement also states that the 'definition of charity' that will be applied in cases raising questions about the validity of trusts for purposes may not be the same as the 'definition of charity' that will be applied in cases raising questions about eligibility for tax

---

[12] See, e.g., *Vancouver Regional Freenet Association* v. *Minister of National Revenue* (1996) 137 DLR 4th 406 (Canadian Federal Court of Appeal), in which an analogy was drawn between the purpose of offering free Internet access and the 'repair of . . . highways' mentioned in the preamble.

[13] See, e.g., *Aid/Watch Incorporated* v. *Federal Commissioner of Taxation* (2010) 241 CLR 539 (High Court of Australia).

[14] US Restatement (3rd) of Trusts, § 28.

[15] It also has affinities with the general descriptions of charitable purpose given by Gray J in *Jackson* v. *Phillips* (1867) 96 Mass 539 (Massachusetts Supreme Judicial Court), 556.

[16] Austin Wakeman Scott and William Franklin Fratcher, *The Law of Trusts* (4th Edn., Little, Brown and Co, Boston, 1989) Volume IVA, §368 to §374.

[17] See John D. Colombo and Mark A. Hall, *The Charitable Tax Exemption* (Westview Press, Boulder CO, 1995), 36–38.

privileges,[18] and there is evidence that, in the tax setting, American charity law places little emphasis on general descriptions of charitable purpose and instead appeals primarily to disqualifying rules relating to 'for profit' purposes, the requirements of fundamental public policy, and political activities.[19] For these reasons, we must exercise caution when asserting that the charity law of the United States contains a criterion in the form of the (modified) *Pemsel* set.[20]

In recent years, in some jurisdictions, legislatures have introduced statutory reforms to charity law with the aim of modifying or replacing the *Pemsel* set in view of the substantial social, cultural, economic and political changes that have taken place since the late nineteenth century, when *Pemsel* was decided. These reforms have been introduced in Australia (for the purposes of federal law), England and Wales, Ireland, Northern Ireland and Scotland.[21] They entail the statutory expression of a larger number of general descriptions of charitable purpose than feature in the *Pemsel* set, although they do not depart from the *Pemsel* set altogether because they invariably include its first three 'heads', as well as a 'catch-all' description.[22] The set of descriptions in section 3(1) of the Charities Act of 2011 of England and Wales is typical of these modern statutory sets – although not identical in all respects to analogous sets in other jurisdictions – and bears setting out in full:

a. the prevention or relief of poverty;
b. the advancement of education;
c. the advancement of religion;
d. the advancement of health or the saving of lives;
e. the advancement of citizenship or community development;
f. the advancement of the arts, culture, heritage or science;
g. the advancement of amateur sport;

---

[18] US Restatement (3rd) of Trusts, § 28, comment *a*. For further discussion of the tax privileges of charity law, see below at 38–9.

[19] Miranda Perry Fleischer, 'Theorizing the Charitable Tax Subsidies: The Role of Distributive Justice' (2010) 87 *Washington University Law Review* 505; Miranda Perry Fleischer, 'Equality of Opportunity and the Charitable Tax Subsidies' (2011) 91 *Boston University Law Review* 601.

[20] See Kerry O'Halloran, *The Politics of Charity* (Routledge, London, 2011), 170–171.

[21] Charities Act 2013 (Australia) s 12; Charities Act 2011 (England and Wales) s 3; Charities Act 2009 (Ireland) s 3; Charities Act (Northern Ireland) 2008 (Northern Ireland) s 2; Charities and Trustee Investment (Scotland) Act 2005 (Scotland) s 7.

[22] Section 3 of the Charities Act 2009 (Ireland) contains a set of descriptions that is identical to the *Pemsel* set, but it also contains a subset of types of purpose that are considered to be within the fourth 'head'.

    h. the advancement of human rights, conflict resolution or reconciliation or the promotion of religious or racial harmony or equality and diversity;

    i. the advancement of environmental protection or improvement;

    j. the relief of those in need because of youth, age, ill-health, disability, financial hardship or other disadvantage;

    k. the advancement of animal welfare;

    l. the promotion of the efficiency of the armed forces of the Crown or of the efficiency of the police, fire and rescue services or ambulance services;

    m. any other purposes-

        i. that are not within paragraphs (a) to (l) but are recognised as charitable purposes by virtue of section 5 (recreational or similar trusts, etc.) or under the old law,

        ii. that may reasonably be regarded as analogous to, or within the spirit of, any purposes falling within paragraphs (a) to (l) or sub-paragraph (i), or

        iii. that may reasonably be regarded as analogous to, or within the spirit of, any purposes which have been recognised, under the law relating to charities in England and Wales, as falling within sub-paragraph (ii) or this sub-paragraph.

Paragraph (m) ensures that the set is open-ended by permitting the recognition as charitable of purposes that do not fall within paragraphs (a) to (l); it also constrains the process of recognising new types of purpose as charitable by requiring that an analogy with some extant charitable purpose be established.

One of the functions of sets of general descriptions of charitable purpose is to signal to citizens the types of purpose that decision-makers are likely to find to be charitable in law. Citizens may thus choose to pursue purposes within one or more of these descriptions with some degree of confidence that the purposes will be found to be charitable if the matter comes before a decision-maker for consideration. Given that the second criterion of charity law is a public benefit test, another way of making this point about the function of sets of general descriptions of charitable purpose is to say that they signal types of purposes that decision-makers are likely to find to be of benefit to the public. In this sense, sets of general descriptions of charitable purpose are best understood in light of the public benefit test, even though they are typically thought of as establishing an independent criterion by which it is determined whether or not purposes are charitable in law. Indeed, in his important study of the public benefit requirement of charity law, Jonathan Garton argues that sets of general descriptions of charitable purpose are actually part of the public benefit test itself; according to Garton, by indicating that purposes are charitable where they meet general descriptions such as 'relief of poverty', 'advancement of education' and 'advancement of religion', charity law lays down rules of law establishing that such purposes are of public benefit subject to evidence-based findings of fact that, in particular cases, those purposes will not generate benefit to the public if carried out. In this sense, Garton prefers to speak of a requirement of 'conceptual public benefit' rather than general descriptions of charitable purpose.[23] There is much to be said for Garton's view; nonetheless, in what follows we will adhere to orthodoxy and refer to general descriptions of charitable purpose as a criterion of charity law separate from the public benefit test.

B. *The public benefit test*

The second criterion of charity law takes the form of a requirement that a purpose must be of public benefit in order to be regarded as charitable in law. This is the 'public benefit test' of charity law. The public benefit test is typically thought to be reducible in some way, in the sense that 'public benefit' is not an irreducible concept, but there is disagreement as to the best way to break down the public benefit test into its component requirements. Recent English jurisprudence has introduced two 'senses' of public benefit;[24] recent academic work on the topic has argued that no fewer than four public benefit requirements are typically run together and referred to as the 'public benefit test'.[25] Perhaps more orthodox is the view that the public benefit test is reducible in the way suggested by its name, as a test containing a 'public' component and a 'benefit' component, each of which must be satisfied if the test is to be met. In what follows, we will follow orthodoxy and examine the 'public' and the 'benefit' components of the public benefit test in turn.

---

[23] Garton, above n 1, [2.16] and ch 3.

[24] *R (Independent Schools Council)* v. *Charity Commission for England and Wales* [2012] 2 WLR 100 (Upper Tribunal); *Attorney-General* v. *Charity Commission for England and Wales* [2011] UKUT 420 (Upper Tribunal).

[25] Garton, above n 1, esp [2.15]–[2.19].

1. The 'public' component

Generally speaking, a purpose is regarded as charitable in law only where the class of persons that it stands to benefit constitutes the public or a sufficient section of the public in some way.[26] In making this statement, it is necessary to speak in a qualified way – 'generally speaking' – because the history of charity law reveals that the 'public' component of the public benefit test is not always insisted upon. In judge-made charity law, some purposes within the description 'relief of poverty' are considered charitable even though the persons to be relieved all belong to one family group,[27] or are employees of one company,[28] or even are members of a club,[29] and thus constitute a private class.[30] In the Australian Charities Act of 2013, the 'public' character of several types of purpose based on the first three 'heads' of the *Pemsel* set is presumed in the absence of evidence to the contrary, and exemptions from the 'public' component of the public benefit test are made for purposes of relieving those in necessitous circumstances, as well as for various purposes of Indigenous groups with kinship ties, non-discriminatory 'self-help' groups and closed religious orders.[31] And in the charity law of New Zealand, in no case does a purpose fail the 'public' component of the public benefit test simply because it stands to benefit only a class of persons who are related by blood.[32] But that said, in most jurisdictions, and in most cases, a purpose will be recognised as charitable only where the class of persons who stand to benefit from it is a class with a public character. This might happen in one of two ways. Those two ways may be appreciated better in light of a distinction – most frequently invoked by economists but also of use in non-economic analyses of social phenomena – between excludable private goods and non-excludable public goods. The idea behind this distinction is that private goods – education

---

[26] *Verge* v. *Somerville* [1924] AC 496 (Privy Council), 499 (Lord Wrenbury).

[27] *Isaac* v. *de Friez* (1754) Amb 595 (High Court of Chancery); *Attorney-General* v. *Price* (1810) 17 Ves 371 (Sir William Grant MR); *In re Scarisbrick* [1951] 1 Ch 622 (Court of Appeal).

[28] *Gibson* v. *South American Stores Ltd* [1950] 1 Ch 177 (Court of Appeal); *Dingle* v. *Turner* [1972] AC 601 (House of Lords); *Jones* v. *The Executive Officers of the T Eaton Company Limited* [1973] SCR 635 (Supreme Court of Canada). Contrast *In re Drummond* [1914] 2 Ch 90 (Eve J).

[29] *Re Young's Will Trusts* [1955] 3 Ch 689 (Danckwerts J).

[30] See generally *Attorney-General* v. *Charity Commission for England and Wales* [2011] UKUT 420 (Upper Tribunal).

[31] Charities Act 2013 (Australia) ss 7–10.   [32] Charities Act 2005 (New Zealand) s 5(2)(a).

and health care are classic examples – have a character such that it is not possible for everyone to enjoy them at the same time, whereas public goods – clean air or a free society, for instance – have a character such that everyone may access and enjoy them simultaneously.[33] A purpose might benefit the public according to the public benefit test of charity law either because it entails the provision of an excludable private good to a class of persons that is in some relevant sense a public class, or because it stands to realise a non-excludable public good.

The general proposition that a purpose might satisfy the public benefit test because it entails the provision of a private good to a public class may be verified by the large number of purposes relating to the prevention and relief of poverty (where the class to be relieved is not a private group such as a family) or to social services such as education, health care or support for the disabled that are indisputably regarded as charitable in law. We should note that such purposes may satisfy the public benefit test even if the class of persons that stands to benefit from them is composed of only a few people; for the purposes of the public benefit test, the publicness of a class of persons does not turn on whether or not that class is composed of a large number of persons. There have been occasional suggestions that a purpose that stands to benefit a 'numerically negligible' class might fail the 'public' component of the public benefit test,[34] but such suggestions are difficult to reconcile with the fact that purposes that entail making private goods available to a class restricted by some personal attribute or need are routinely regarded as charitable in law, even if the personal attribute or need is possessed by only a handful of people. A trust to provide care to the sufferers of a rare disease may be offered as an example. But even if the provision of a private good to only a handful of people might satisfy the 'public' component of the public benefit test, there are at least two grounds on which a decision-maker might find that the provision of a private good is to a class lacking a sufficiently public character to satisfy that component of the test, and these grounds have generated a substantial body of case law.

---

[33] Robert Cooter and Thomas Ulen, *Law and Economics* (5th edn., Addison-Wesley, Harlow, 2008), 108; Richard Cornes and Todd Sandler, *The Theory of Externalities, Public Goods and Club Goods* (2nd edn, Cambridge University Press, 1996), 8–9.

[34] See, e.g., *Oppenheim* v. *Tobacco Securities Trust Co Ltd* [1951] AC 297 (House of Lords), 306 (Lord Simonds).

First, purposes might entail the provision of a private good to a class composed of individuals who are members of a family, employees of a company, members of an association or club or connected to each other in some other relevant way. As we saw earlier, this is not a ground for finding that the public benefit test is not satisfied in cases about purposes within the description 'relief of poverty'; nor is it such a ground to the extent that, as in Australia and New Zealand, statutory exemptions from the 'public' component of the public benefit test have been provided. However, it is a ground for refusing to find public benefit in cases about many types of purpose. For example, in *Oppenheim* v. *Tobacco Securities Trust Co Ltd*, a trust for the purpose of educating the children of employees and former employees of a group of companies was struck down on the basis that it stood to benefit a private class sharing a common connection to the group of companies in question, notwithstanding that the class numbered in the hundreds of thousands.[35] In *In re Hobourn Aero Components Limited's Air Raid Distress Fund*, employees of a certain company established a wartime fund to help those of their number who might serve in the armed forces or suffer air raid distress, but the fund was found not to be charitable because the undoubtedly great benefit it stood to realise was benefit only to contributors to the fund.[36] Similarly, in *Inland Revenue Commissioners* v. *City of Glasgow Police Athletic Association*, the House of Lords rejected the proposition that an association founded primarily for the purpose of providing recreation to its members could satisfy the public benefit test.[37]

Such cases – cases of gifts to a private class, of 'self-help' arrangements and of 'member benefit' arrangements, respectively – tend to raise subsidiary questions that give the impression that they are cases of separate and distinct types. For example, in 'member benefit' cases the primary focus of inquiry is often on a construction of the purposes of an

---

[35] [1951] AC 297 (House of Lords). See also *In re Compton* [1945] 1 Ch 123 (Court of Appeal); *In re Cox, Baker* v. *National Trust Company Limited* [1953] 1 SCR 94 (Supreme Court of Canada); *Thompson* v. *Federal Commissioner of Taxation* (1959) 102 CLR 315 (High Court of Australia); *Davies* v. *Perpetual Trustee Company Ltd* [1959] AC 439 (Privy Council); *Caffoor* v. *Commissioner of Income Tax (Colombo)* [1961] AC 584 (Privy Council); but contrast *In re Koettgen's Will Trusts* [1954] 1 Ch 252 (Upjohn J).

[36] [1946] 1 Ch 194 (Court of Appeal).

[37] [1953] AC 380 (House of Lords). See also *The Geologists' Association* v. *The Commissioners of Inland Revenue* (1928) 14 TC 271 (Court of Appeal); *The Midland Counties Institution of Engineers* v. *The Commissioners of Inland Revenue* (1928) 14 TC 285 (Court of Appeal).

association whose stated objects include both the provision of benefits to members and either the provision of private goods to a public class or the provision of non-excludable public goods.[38] Because the criteria of charity law apply only to the dominant purpose or purposes of a person or organisation, and not to subsidiary purposes, in some 'member benefit' cases it is important to ascertain whether or not the member benefit arrangements constitute the dominant purpose. Moreover, as we saw earlier, in the Australian Charities Act of 2013 purposes entailed in 'self-help' arrangements are considered to be of public benefit, implying that they are purposes of a special type.[39] However, in truth, cases of gifts to a private class, of 'self-help' arrangements and of 'member benefit' arrangements are all cases of one type: they are all cases in which purposes entail the provision of private goods to a private class, and for that reason fail the 'public' component of the public benefit test (at least in the absence of some special legislative intervention such as that relating to 'self-help' arrangements in Australia).

Second, a purpose might entail the provision of a private good exclusively to members of the public who are prepared to pay for that private good a sum of money that is beyond the means of the poor.[40] This ground for finding the 'public' component of the public benefit test not to be satisfied is most pronounced in the charity law of England and Wales, Ireland and Scotland.[41] In England and Wales, it is considered by the Charity Commission to be a ground for refusing

---

[38] In a number of cases, decision-makers have construed objects of providing private goods to a public class or providing public goods as disclosing the dominant purpose and have found member benefit arrangements to be charitable as a consequence: see, e.g., *Institution of Civil Engineers* v. *Commissioners of Inland Revenue* [1932] 1 KB 149 (Court of Appeal); *Royal College of Surgeons of England* v. *National Provincial Bank Ltd* [1952] AC 681 (House of Lords); *Guaranty Trust Company of Canada* v. *Minister of National Revenue* [1967] SCR 133 (Supreme Court of Canada); *London Hospital Medical College* v. *Inland Revenue Commissioners* [1976] 2 All ER 113 (Brightman J); *Centrepoint Community Growth Trust* v. *Commissioner of Inland Revenue* [1985] 1 NZLR 673 (Tompkins J).

[39] Charities Act 2013 (Australia) s 10(1).

[40] Of course, the scope of this dimension of the public benefit test, in jurisdictions where it is applied, depends in part on what is meant by 'the poor' for the purposes of charity law. That question has received considerable judicial attention: see Hubert Picarda, *The Law and Practice Relating to Charities* (4th Edn., Bloomsbury Professional, Haywards Heath, 2010), 41–43 for a discussion.

[41] Charities Act 2009 (Ireland) s 3(7); Charities and Trustees Investment (Scotland) Act 2005 (Scotland) s 8(2)(b). The position in England and Wales is described in the text.

to make a finding of public benefit,[42] and this has been confirmed by
the Upper Tribunal (Tax and Chancery Chamber) in *R (Independent
Schools Council)* v. *Charity Commission for England and Wales*, a case
about the extent to which private fee-charging schools should be
regarded as charitable under English law; there, the Upper Tribunal
stated that 'a trust which excludes the poor from benefit cannot be a
charity'.[43] However, excluding the poor is a controversial ground for
finding the 'public' component of the public benefit test not to be
satisfied;[44] thus, in Northern Ireland, legislative provisions stating
that the public benefit test could not be satisfied where 'unduly
restrictive' fees were charged were introduced in 2008 only to be
repealed in 2013.[45] Moreover, the Upper Tribunal in *Independent
Schools Council* stated that although the proposition that a charitable
purpose cannot exclude the poor is 'right as a matter of principle',
there is 'no case which decides [the] point'.[46] The extent to which the
proposition figures in the law of jurisdictions outside the British
Isles, and its likely future as a ground for refusing to find public
benefit in the various jurisdictions of the British Isles, must therefore
remain an open question. Echoes of the English approach to access
for the poor in the setting of the public benefit test may be found
in the tax law of the United States, where poor access was once a
requirement in order to attract the tax privileges of charity, then
was abandoned, but continues to attract political attention from
time to time.[47]

---

[42] Charity Commission for England and Wales, *Analysis of the Law Relating to Public
Benefit* (September 2013), [77]–[80].

[43] [2012] 2 WLR 100 (Upper Tribunal), [178], citing *Jones* v. *Williams* (1767) Amb 651
(Lord Hardwicke LC); *In re Macduff* [1896] 2 Ch 451 (Court of Appeal); *Taylor* v. *Taylor*
(1910) 10 CLR 218 (High Court of Australia); *In re Resch's Will Trusts, Le Cras* v.
Perpetual Trustee Co Ltd [1969] 1 AC 514 (Privy Council), although this last case does
not stand clearly for that proposition, as the text below makes clear.

[44] See Picarda, above n 40, 39D–39E; Mary Synge, 'Poverty: An Essential Element in Charity
After All?' (2011) 70 *Cambridge Law Journal* 649.

[45] Charities Act (Northern Ireland) 2008 (Northern Ireland) s 3(3), amended by Charities
Act (Northern Ireland) 2013 (Northern Ireland) s 1.

[46] *R (Independent Schools Council)* v. *Charity Commission for England and Wales* [2012] 2
WLR 100 (Upper Tribunal), [178].

[47] See generally John D. Colombo, 'The Role of Access in Charitable Tax Exemption' (2004)
82 *Washington University Law Quarterly* 343; John D. Colombo, 'The Failure of Community Benefit' (2005) 15 *Health Matrix* 29; Fleischer, 'Theorizing the Charitable Tax
Subsidies', above n 19; Fleischer, 'Equality of Opportunity and the Charitable Tax
Subsidies', above n 19.

Examples of findings of public benefit on the basis that purposes entail the provision of non-excludable public goods may be found most readily in the case law dealing with purposes under the fourth 'head' of the *Pemsel* set.[48] This case law reveals decision-makers forming the view that the public benefit test is satisfied in circumstances where purposes stand to realise public goods as diverse as a humane culture,[49] a public building,[50] advances in medical research,[51] the effective functioning of the legal system,[52] free Internet access[53] and the market economy and commercial activity.[54] In the case of *Aid/Watch Incorporated* v. *Commissioner of Taxation*, the High Court of Australia had to consider whether or not an organisation that campaigned for the reform of Australian government policy relating to foreign aid was formed for a charitable purpose.[55] A majority of the Court found that the true purpose of the

---

[48] Indeed, in *Inland Revenue Commissioners* v. *Baddeley* [1955] AC 572 (House of Lords), two members of the House of Lords (Viscount Simonds and Lord Somervell of Harrow) expressed the view that a finding of public benefit under the fourth 'head' of the *Pemsel* set ought not to be made except where public goods have been ascertained. However, Lord Reid thought that private goods made available to a public class would suffice, and the remaining two members (Lords Porter and Tucker) declined to express a view.

[49] *In re Wedgwood* [1915] 1 Ch 113 (Court of Appeal).

[50] *Monds* v. *Stackhouse* (1948) 77 CLR 232 (High Court of Australia). Note also the pre-*Pemsel* decisions recognising, as charitable, purposes of improving or preserving an urban environment: e.g., *West* v. *Knight* (1669) 1 Ch Cas 134; 22 ER 729 (Sir Harbottle Grimston MR); *Howse* v. *Chapman* (1799) 3 Ves Jr 542, 551; 31 ER 278 (Lord Loughborough LC); *Attorney-General* v. *Heelis* (1824) 2 Sim & St 67; 57 ER 270 (Sir John Leach VC).

[51] *National Anti-Vivisection Society* v. *Inland Revenue Commissioners* [1948] AC 31 (House of Lords).

[52] *Incorporated Council of Law Reporting of the State of Queensland* v. *Federal Commissioner of Taxation* (1971) 125 CLR 659 (High Court of Australia); *Incorporated Council of Law Reporting for England and Wales* v. *Attorney-General* [1972] Ch 73 (Court of Appeal); *Commissioner of Inland Revenue* v. *New Zealand Council of Law Reporting* [1981] 1 NZLR 682 (New Zealand Court of Appeal).

[53] *Vancouver Regional Freenet Association* v. *Minister of National Revenue* (1996) 137 DLR 4th 406 (Canadian Federal Court of Appeal), but contrast *News to You Canada* v. *Minister of National Revenue* [2011] FCA 192 (Canadian Federal Court of Appeal), in which the Court rejected the proposition that the provision of a free news service was a charitable purpose.

[54] *Crystal Palace Trustees* v. *Minister of Town and Country Planning* [1951] Ch 132 (Danckwerts J); *Tasmanian Electronic Commerce Centre Pty Ltd* v. *Federal Commissioner of Taxation* (2005) 142 FCR 371 (Heerey J); *Commissioner of Taxation* v. *Triton Foundation* (2005) 147 FCR 362 (Kenny J), but contrast *Canterbury Development Corporation* v. *Charities Commission* [2010] 2 NZLR 707 (Young J).

[55] (2010) 241 CLR 539 (High Court of Australia). The main interest of the case is in the High Court's rejection of the proposition that Australian charity law contains a broad

organisation was the 'generation ... of public debate ... concerning
the efficacy of foreign aid directed to the relief of poverty', that this
purpose fell within the fourth 'head' of the *Pemsel* set and that
the purpose satisfied the public benefit test in view of the importance
of public debate about political matters to Australia's system of democratic government.[56] This reasoning pointed to a public good – the public
good of a culture of free political expression – in reaching a finding of
public benefit.

Sometimes, decision-makers make findings of public benefit on the
basis that purposes entail the provision of both private goods to a public
class and non-excludable public goods.[57] And sometimes, where a purpose entails the provision of private goods to a private class but a
decision-maker thinks that the purpose also stands to realise incidental
public goods, the public component of the public benefit test will be
satisfied.[58] For example, the provision of health care by an organisation
that charges fees unaffordable to the poor may satisfy the public benefit
test on the basis that the organisation relieves the burden of health care
otherwise borne by the state, freeing up revenue to be expended in other
ways.[59] In *Neville Estates Ltd* v. *Madden*, a trust for the purposes of a
synagogue closed to the public was under consideration; in making a
finding of public benefit, Cross J said that notwithstanding that the
synagogue was closed to the public, 'some benefit accrues to the public
from the attendance at places of worship of persons who ... mix with
their fellow citizens'.[60] A similar view was expressed in *Joyce* v. *Ashfield
Municipal Council*, an Australian case about whether or not a hall used
for private worship services was used for charitable purposes; for the New
South Wales Court of Appeal, the worship services, although conducted

---

rule against political purposes. For a detailed discussion of that aspect of the case, see
Chapter 6.
[56] Ibid, [46]–[47] (French CJ, Gummow, Hayne, Crennan and Bell JJ).
[57] Arguably, *Liberty Trust* v. *Charity Commission* [2011] NZHC 577 (Mallon J) was such a
case.
[58] See Garton, above n 1, [4.03]–[4.06] for a discussion.
[59] *Re Resch's Will Trusts, Le Cras* v. *Perpetual Trustee Co Ltd* [1969] 1 AC 514 (Privy
Council), but see also the more sceptical approach in *R (Independent Schools Council)* v.
Charity Commission of England and Wales [2012] 2 WLR 100 (Upper Tribunal). 'Relief
of taxes' has been regarded as a type of charitable purpose since the time of the Statute of
Elizabeth: *Attorney-General* v. *Bushby* (1857) 24 Beav 299; 53 ER 373 (Sir John Romilly
MR); *Monds* v. *Stackhouse* (1948) 77 CLR 232 (High Court of Australia).
[60] [1962] 1 Ch 832 (Cross J), 853. This statement received qualified approval in Charity
Commission for England and Wales, *Preston Down Trust* (3 January 2014), [51].

in private, had 'public value in improving the standards of the believer in the world' and were therefore of public benefit.[61] That said, in some cases decision-makers have recognised the possibility of incidental public goods arising from the pursuit of private purposes and yet refused to make findings of public benefit;[62] and in other cases that seem analogous to *Neville Estates Ltd* v. *Madden* and *Joyce* v. *Ashfield Municipal Council*, the possibility of incidental public goods appears not even to have been considered.[63] There is thus some inconsistency of approach in charity law to the possibility of incidental public goods.

2. The 'benefit' component

Even if a purpose has a public character, it is regarded as charitable in law only where the consequences of carrying it out are likely to be beneficial to the public, as opposed to detrimental or neither beneficial nor detrimental. This general proposition underpins the 'benefit' component of the public benefit test. The 'benefit' component is not well understood, either by the decision-makers who apply it or by the commentators who study it.[64] That said, a review of the case law reveals three general characteristics of the 'benefit' component of the public benefit test – or, to be more precise, three general characteristics of the way in which decision-makers working with the 'benefit' component of the public benefit test typically go about applying that component. Such decision-makers usually adopt an attitude of objectivity when reflecting on the question of benefits and detriments that might result from purposes being carried out; they typically refuse to reason reductively about questions of benefit and detriment; and they often decline to investigate questions of fact relating to benefits and detriments and occasionally invoke a presumption of benefit in the setting of such an investigation, at

---

[61] [1975] 1 NSWLR 744 (New South Wales Court of Appeal), 751–752 (Hutley JA). An appeal to the Privy Council was dismissed: *Ashfield Municipal Council* v. *Joyce* [1976] 1 NSWLR 455 (Privy Council). For more detailed discussion of this case, and *Neville Estates Ltd* v. *Madden*, see Chapter 5.

[62] *Re Joy* (1889) 60 LTR 175 (Chitty J); *Re the Grand Lodge of Antient Free and Accepted Masons of New Zealand* CIV 2009–485–2633 (Simon France J).

[63] *Yeap Cheah Neo* v. *Ong Cheng Neo* (1875) LR 6 PC 381 (Privy Council); *Attorney-General* v. *Delaney* (1875) 10 IR (CL) 104 (Barons of the Exchequer); *Attorney-General* v. *Hall* [1897] 2 IR 426 (Irish Court of Appeal); *Re Warre's Will Trusts* [1953] 2 All ER 99 (Harman J); *In re Hetherington* [1990] 1 Ch 1 (Sir Nicolas Browne-Wilkinson VC).

[64] A point well made by a commentator who has studied it more closely than most: Garton, above n 1, [2.17] and [4.02].

least in jurisdictions where they are permitted by law to do so. We will consider each in turn.

Decision-makers mostly insist on adopting an attitude of objectivity about questions of benefit and detriment when making findings as to whether or not a purpose is of public benefit. This means that, when considering whether or not benefits or detriments are likely to flow from the pursuit of a purpose, decision-makers typically refuse to defer to the beliefs of the person or organisation whose purpose it is; instead, findings as to the benefits and detriments likely to result from the pursuit of purposes are made by decision-makers themselves, based on available evidence and arguments, without regard to the preferences of interested parties. In *National Anti-Vivisection Society* v. *Inland Revenue Commissioners*, a case about the purposes of a society formed to campaign for the banning of medical experimentation on live animals, the House of Lords endorsed an objective approach to the 'benefit' component of the public benefit test, overruling an earlier decision in which a judge had made a finding of benefit by deferring to the beliefs of the testatrix of a testamentary trust for anti-vivisection purposes.[65] This objective mindset was again on display in *Gilmour* v. *Coats*, in relation to the purposes of a Carmelite order of nuns who spent their lives in intercessory prayer and other spiritual exercises within their convent.[66] On the question whether the intercessory prayer of the nuns was of public benefit, the House of Lords had evidence from the Roman Catholic Archbishop of Westminster as to his church's teaching that such prayer generated spiritual benefit in the form of God's blessing on the whole world. Rather than defer to this teaching, their Lordships insisted that a finding of benefit was for the court itself to make, before concluding that a finding of spiritual benefit was not possible on the available evidence.[67] In *Re*

---

[65] [1948] AC 31 (House of Lords), 44–47 (Lord Wright), 65–66 (Lord Simonds). The earlier case was *In re Foveaux* [1895] Ch 501 (Chitty J). At 49, Lord Wright suggested that in forming an objective view as to benefit, at least where a claimed benefit is intangible, a decision-maker should accept only propositions that have earned 'approval by the common understanding of enlightened opinion for the time being'. This might be thought to dilute the objectivity referred to in the text. However, when we look across charity law as a whole, we find that reference to public opinion is seldom a characteristic of the inquiry into benefit. Moreover, Lord Wright endorsed reference only to 'enlightened' opinion; presumably what constitutes 'enlightened' opinion can be determined only by a decision-maker adopting an objective mindset.

[66] [1949] AC 426 (House of Lords).

[67] Ibid, 446 (Lord Simonds), 452 (Lord du Parcq), 456–460 (Lord Reid). For further discussion of this case, see Chapter 5.

Hummeltenberg, Beatty v. *London Spiritualistic Alliance*, Russell J endorsed an objective approach to benefits and detriments, stating that '[i]f a testator by stating or indicating his view that a trust is beneficial to the public can establish that fact beyond question, trusts might be established in perpetuity for the promotion of all kinds of fantastic (although not unlawful) objects, of which the training of poodles to dance might be a mild example.'[68] In *Re Pinion (deceased)*, the English Court of Appeal struck down a testamentary trust for the purpose of displaying a collection of art and furniture on the basis that, irrespective of the opinion of the testator as to the artistic and educational value of the collection, it was in fact 'junk';[69] in the same case Harman LJ expressed the view, *obiter dicta*, that a library of pornography could not be charitable, irrespective of the views of the sponsor of the library.[70]

Although an attitude of objectivity when applying the 'benefit' component of the public benefit test is the norm in modern charity law, such an attitude is not universally adopted. There is some evidence in Australian law that, at least when it comes to claims of spiritual benefit in certain 'advancement of religion' cases, courts might be prepared to defer to religious belief about the claimed benefit.[71] The United States Restatement (Third) of Trusts indicates disagreement with the insistence on objectivity that was manifested by the House of Lords in *Gilmour* v. *Coats*.[72] And in Ireland, there is a long tradition of deferring to religious beliefs in 'advancement of religion' cases. This tradition may be traced back to the decision of the Irish Court of Appeal in 1906 in *O'Hanlon* v. *Logue*,[73] a case about whether or not a trust providing for the Roman Catholic practice of saying masses for the dead was for a charitable purpose, and is also reflected today in section 3(6) of the Charities Act of 2009, which states that '[a] charitable gift for the purpose

---

[68] [1923] 1 Ch 237 (Russell J), 242.

[69] [1964] 1 All ER 890 (Court of Appeal), 893–894 (Harman LJ).

[70] Ibid, 893. See also *In re Macduff* [1896] 2 Ch 451 (Court of Appeal), 474 (Rigby LJ): 'No one will suggest, for instance, to take only one illustration, that the education of pickpockets in a thieves' kitchen to make them fit for their profession is a charity.'

[71] *Nelan* v. *Downes* (1917) 23 CLR 546 (High Court of Australia).

[72] US Restatement (3rd) of Trusts, § 28, comment i. See also the judgment of Powell J in *Bob Jones University* v. *US* 461 US 574 (1983) (US Supreme Court).

[73] [1906] 1 IR 247 (Irish Court of Appeal). See also *Attorney-General* v. *Becher* [1910] 2 IR 251 (King's Bench). *Re Cranston* [1898] 1 IR 431 (Irish Court of Appeal) is an instance of deference in the Irish case law prior to *O'Hanlon* v. *Logue*, but it was an animal welfare case.

of the advancement of religion shall have effect, and the terms on which it is given shall be construed, in accordance with the laws, canons, ordinances and tenets of the religion concerned'. So while it may be said that in modern charity law decision-makers usually adopt an objective mindset when making findings about benefit in the setting of the public benefit test, it may not be said that this is always so.

Not only do decision-makers typically adopt an attitude of objectivity when applying the 'benefit' component of the public benefit test; they also refuse to reason reductively about questions of benefit and detriment when applying that component of the test. This means that they do not frame their thinking about benefit and detriment in accordance with monistic accounts of value like utilitarianism; instead, their reasoning is consistent with the general proposition that many types of value can ground findings of benefit, and that sometimes in making findings of benefit it is necessary to choose among conflicting values.[74] As we saw earlier, one of the functions of sets of general descriptions of charitable purpose is to signal the types of purpose that decision-makers tend to regard as being of public benefit. To the extent that this is so, the fact that such sets invariably contain multiple descriptions – 'relief of poverty', 'advancement of education', 'advancement of religion', and so on – indicates in a general way an acceptance that purposes within these different descriptions are likely to realise different sorts of benefit. Moreover, the one governmental report on charity law that seeks to ground the proper development of that body of law in a philosophical theory of the good appeals not to utilitarianism or any other monistic theory, but rather to the pluralistic theory of the good of the natural law philosopher John Finnis.[75] In addition, as we have already seen, decision-makers considering the question of public benefit as an independent criterion of charity law have pointed to an array of (usually non-excludable public) goods such as a humane culture,[76] the market economy,[77] free

---

[74] This is a reason to reject Harvey Cohen's interpretation of charity law as utilitarian in inspiration: 'Charities – A Utilitarian Perspective' (1983) 36 *Current Legal Problems* 241. Donovan Waters, 'The Advancement of Religion in a Pluralist Society (Part II): Abolishing the Public Benefit Element' (2011) 17 *Trusts and Trustees* 729 has suggested that charity law ought to be reformed to bring it into closer alignment with utilitarianism; the merits of that suggestion turn ultimately on the merits of utilitarianism.

[75] Ontario Law Reform Commission, *Report on the Law of Charities: Volume 1* (1996).

[76] *In re Wedgwood* [1915] 1 Ch 113 (Court of Appeal).

[77] *Crystal Palace Trustees* v. *Minister of Town and Country Planning* [1951] Ch 132 (Danckwerts J).

political expression,[78] improved moral standards,[79] and the rule of law[80] in making findings of benefit, and – with one possible exception – they have nowhere suggested that a single currency or measure of value might animate or underpin these ostensibly diverse goods.

The possible exception is the *Anti-Vivisection* case, where the question of benefit turned on two competing propositions: one that pointed to the value of a humane culture, and one that pointed to public goods associated with advances in medical research and detriments that might be occasioned to the public should such research cease.[81] The House of Lords found that, in the circumstances of the case, the former benefit was far outweighed by the latter benefits and potential detriments, and on that basis refused to make a finding that the purposes of the anti-vivisection society were of public benefit. On one view, this preparedness to weigh competing benefits and detriments against each other and choose among them suggests a mindset that is reductive about value. There is some support for this view in the reasoning of Lord Wright, referring to 'conflicting moral and material utilities'; this reference to 'utilities' obviously suggests a monistic approach.[82] However, on another view, the choice among benefits and detriments disclosed by the reasoning in the *Anti-Vivisection* case was experienced by the judges in that case as a choice among conflicting incommensurable values, and there is also support for this view in the reasoning of Lord Wright, in a passage where he explicitly declined to form a view on whether 'utilitarian or intuitionist ethics is the truer theory'.[83] In light of the demonstrated refusal to reason reductively about questions of benefit and detriment in other cases in charity law, it is strongly arguable that this latter view of the *Anti-Vivisection* case is the more plausible one.

A third characteristic of the 'benefit' component of the public benefit test is that decision-makers often decline to investigate questions of fact relating to benefits and detriments and occasionally invoke a presumption of benefit in the setting of such an investigation. The presumption

---

[78] *Aid/Watch Incorporated* v. *Commissioner of Taxation* (2010) 241 CLR 529 (High Court of Australia).

[79] *Joyce* v. *Ashfield Municipal Council* [1975] 1 NSWLR 744 (New South Wales Court of Appeal).

[80] *Incorporated Council of Law Reporting of the State of Queensland* v. *Federal Commissioner of Taxation* (1971) 125 CLR 659 (High Court of Australia).

[81] *National Anti-Vivisection Society* v. *Inland Revenue Commissioners* [1948] AC 31 (House of Lords).

[82] Ibid, 49 (Lord Wright).   [83] Ibid, 48 (Lord Wright).

that is occasionally invoked in this setting is sometimes called a 'presumption of public benefit' but, with one exception, it is more accurately called a 'presumption of benefit' since it is employed by decision-makers when addressing the 'benefit' component of the public benefit test and not when addressing the 'public' component of that test. The exception arises in the case of Australia: under section 7 of that country's Charities Act of 2013, several types of purpose are presumed to satisfy both the 'public' and the 'benefit' components of the public benefit test. Prior to the enactment of the Charities Act, Australian decision-makers only ever presumed the benefit of certain types of purpose, but now it would seem that they are authorised and required to apply a true 'presumption of public benefit' in some cases.

It has been said that a presumption of benefit is always invoked when purposes falling within the first three 'heads' of the *Pemsel* set are in view.[84] However, the better view seems to be that the first three 'heads' of the *Pemsel* set represent rules of law to the effect that purposes within the descriptions 'relief of poverty', 'advancement of education' and 'advancement of religion' are of benefit, and that in many cases in which purposes within one of those descriptions arise for consideration, decision-makers simply apply the rules of law and decline to investigate questions of benefit as questions of fact.[85] Indeed, the case law in all jurisdictions reveals that in most cases about purposes within the first and second 'heads' of the *Pemsel* set – 'relief of poverty' and 'advancement of education' – decision-makers simply do not address factual questions about benefits and detriments; instead, they either concentrate on whether or not the purposes in question have a public character (in the case of 'advancement of education'), or refuse to inquire into public benefit altogether (in the case of 'relief of poverty'). Moreover, in the United States, there is authority indicating that decision-makers in that jurisdiction eschew treating questions of benefit as questions of fact in cases of public purposes of all types. In *Bob Jones University* v. *US*, the Supreme Court of the United States had to consider the charitable status of a university that adopted a discriminatory policy against interracial dating among its students.[86] The Court emphasised that 'sensitive determinations' to the effect that the 'benefit' component of the public benefit test is not satisfied should be made only reluctantly, 'where there is no

---

[84] Ibid, 42 (Lord Wright).   [85] Garton, above n 1, [4.19]–[4.23].

[86] 461 US 574 (1983) (US Supreme Court). We will return to this case below at 32, and again in more detail in Chapter 7.

doubt that the organization's activities violate fundamental public policy'.[87] The Court considered that racial discrimination in education was contrary to fundamental public policy, and found that the university was not a charity for federal tax purposes as a result. Notwithstanding the outcome in *Bob Jones University*, the Court's generous approach to the question of benefit indicates a broad refusal to engage with factual questions about benefits and detriments associated with purposes that have a sufficiently public character.[88]

That said, in some cases about purposes falling within the first three 'heads' of the *Pemsel* set, decision-makers do investigate questions of benefit as questions of fact. In *Gilmour* v. *Coats*, for example, the House of Lords did not apply any rule of law based on the fact that the purposes before it were clearly within the third 'head' of the *Pemsel* set, 'advancement of religion';[89] instead, their Lordships considered whether they could make findings of fact about the propensity of religious purposes to generate spiritual benefits. We will return to that aspect of the case in Chapter 5. And in cases – especially 'advancement of religion' cases – where decision-makers investigate questions of benefit as questions of fact in this way, it seems that, contrary to *Gilmour* v. *Coats*, they occasionally apply a presumption of benefit as a fact-finding tool in determining the case. For example, in *Neville Estates Ltd* v. *Madden*, the case about the closed synagogue that we encountered earlier, Cross J stated that charity law 'assumes that any religion is at least likely to be better than none' in finding the public benefit test to be satisfied.[90] In *Holmes* v. *Attorney-General*, a case about the purposes of the Christian group the Exclusive Brethren, there was some evidence before Walton J capable of supporting a finding of benefit, but also evidence that the group harmed its members in ways that pointed to a finding of detriment.[91] Walton J applied a presumption of benefit to resolve the impasse

---

[87] Ibid, 592 (Burger J).

[88] In his partly concurring judgment, Powell J went further, asserting that for a court to make a finding of 'benefit' suggests that 'the primary function of a tax-exempt organization is to act on behalf of the Government in carrying out governmentally approved policies', and that this threatens the liberal value of pluralism: ibid, 609–10. Powell J's approach arguably departs from the objectivity that typically characterises the 'benefit' component of the public benefit test.

[89] [1949] AC 426 (House of Lords).   [90] [1962] 1 Ch 832 (Cross J), 853.

[91] *The Times* (London), 12 February 1981, 8. The case was referred to Walton J by the Charity Commissioners, who had determined that certain practices of the Exclusive Brethren were contrary to the public interest but did not know whether that determination rebutted the presumption of benefit for the purposes of charity law: Peter Edge and

generated by this conflicting evidence.[92] In *Re Watson (deceased), Hobbs v. Smith*, a trust for the purpose of disseminating religious literature was under consideration; Plowman J received expert evidence that the intrinsic worth of the literature was 'nil', but nonetheless applied a presumption of benefit and consequently found that the public benefit test was satisfied.[93]

The statutory sets of descriptions that have replaced the *Pemsel* set in England and Wales and Scotland are accompanied by statutory rules providing that decision-makers may not apply a presumption of benefit in any type of case.[94] In those jurisdictions, the new rules about presuming benefit have begun to have an effect on the determination of 'advancement of religion' cases – the cases in which a presumption of benefit was sometimes explicitly invoked in the past – and may be expected to continue to do so. For example, in its 2010 decision to register the Druid Network as a charity, the Charity Commission for England and Wales considered at length a variety of propositions relating to possible benefits associated with the practice of Druidry, before concluding that the public benefit test of charity law was satisfied.[95] Similarly, in its 2014 decision to register Preston Down Trust as a charity, the Charity Commission examined in detail evidence relating to possible benefits and detriments associated with the beliefs and practices of the Plymouth Brethren Christian Church, concluding that there was sufficient evidence of benefit to satisfy the 'benefit' component of the public benefit test.[96] These decisions may be contrasted with the Charity Commissioners' 2003 decision to register Sacred Hands Spiritual Centre, decided under the old law, in which a presumption of benefit was invoked, obviating the need to consider evidence of benefit.[97]

In Ireland, the statutory successor to the *Pemsel* set is accompanied by a statutory rule requiring decision-makers in that jurisdiction to apply a

Joan Loughrey, 'Religious Charities and the Juridification of the Charity Commission' (2001) 21 *Legal Studies* 36, 48–49.

[92] *The Times* (London), 12 February 1981, 8.

[93] [1973] 3 All ER 678 (Plowman J). See also *Thornton v. Howe* (1862) 31 Beav 14; 54 ER 1042 (Sir John Romilly MR).

[94] Charities Act 2011 (England and Wales) s 4(2); Charities and Trustees Investment (Scotland) Act 2005 (Scotland) s 8(1).

[95] Charity Commission for England and Wales, *The Druid Network* (21 September 2010).

[96] Charity Commission for England and Wales, *Preston Down Trust* (3 January 2014).

[97] *Decision of the Charity Commissioners to Register Sacred Hands Spiritual Centre as a Charity* (5 September 2003).

rebuttable presumption of benefit in the case of any gift for a purpose within the description 'advancement of religion'; moreover, any regulator of charities in Ireland may not determine that a gift for such a purpose is not of benefit to the public except with the consent of the Attorney-General.[98] The Irish statute thus ensures that a presumption of benefit will continue to be applied in 'advancement of religion' cases in that jurisdiction; that said, it actually represents a weakening of commitment to the use of a presumption in such cases in Ireland, because under the Irish Charities Act of 1961, the predecessor to the current Charities Act of 2009, decision-makers were required to apply an irrebuttable presumption of benefit in 'advancement of religion' cases.[99] In Australia, on the other hand, statutory reform has reinforced any presumption of benefit that applied under the old law: there, the Charities Act of 2013 declares that a number of types of purpose are presumed to be of benefit to the public unless the contrary is proved by evidence.[100]

Earlier, we saw that one of the functions of general descriptions of charitable purpose is to signal types of purpose that decision-makers are likely to find to be of public benefit. To the extent that this is so, it is not surprising that in jurisdictions whose charity law incorporates the *Pemsel* set, decision-makers either decline to investigate factual questions relating to the benefits and detriments of purposes within the first three 'heads' of charity or apply a presumption of benefit in resolving such factual questions. With respect to jurisdictions such as England and Wales, however, where legislation sets out general descriptions of charitable purpose but at the same time prohibits decision-makers from applying a presumption of benefit in any type of case, it might be argued that the legislature sends 'mixed messages' via charity law. On the one hand, general descriptions of charitable purpose suggest that the legislature views purposes within those descriptions as beneficial to the public; on the other the legislature directs decision-makers, in individual cases, not to presume the benefit of purposes that fall within general descriptions of charitable purpose. Arguably, this apparent inconsistency of approach in jurisdictions such as England and Wales reflects, on the part of the legislature, a relatively low degree of scepticism about the general tendency of purposes of certain descriptions to benefit the public but a relatively high degree of scepticism about the tendency of specific purposes to benefit the public, even if those specific purposes are within one

---

[98] Charities Act 2009 (Ireland) s 3(4) and (5).   [99] Charities Act 1961 (Ireland) s 45(1).
[100] Charities Act 2013 (Australia) s 7.

or more of the descriptions that the legislature marks out as charitable in
a general sense. Is this combination of general acceptance of the beneficial character of certain types of purpose and scepticism about the
beneficial character of specific purposes justified? The difficulty in
coming up with a satisfactory answer to this question is one reason
why the design and application of the public benefit test in England
and Wales has, in recent years, become a matter of public controversy.[101]
It also seems to have underpinned the decision in Northern Ireland in
2013 to repeal the provisions of the Charities Act of 2008 that related to
the public benefit test.[102]

3.   Disqualifying rules

In addition to criteria by which decision-makers may determine whether
or not a purpose is charitable in law, charity law typically contains what
might be called disqualifying rules. These are rules that, if infringed,
disqualify a purpose from being charitable in law. Where decision-
makers invoke disqualifying rules, they need not make further inquiry
into whether or not purposes fall within general descriptions of charitable
purpose or are of public benefit. This is not to say that disqualifying rules
are invariably conceptually distinct from the criteria of charity law; as we
will see, there may be a case for regarding at least some of the disqualifying rules of charity law as outworkings of the public benefit test. However, even if disqualifying rules are not always conceptually distinct from
the criteria of charity law, they do perform a distinct function in the
practical reasoning of decision-makers who must determine whether or
not a purpose is charitable in law; in cases where they apply, disqualifying
rules enable decision-makers to determine that a purpose is not charitable without having to appeal to the deeper reasons – perhaps relating to
public benefit, perhaps relating to something else – justifying such a

---

[101]   For a sense of the controversy, see Peter Luxton, 'Opening Pandora's Box: The Upper
Tribunal's Decision on Public Benefit and Independent Schools' (2012) 15 *Charity Law
and Practice Review* 27; Hubert Picarda, '*Charities Act 2011*: Dog's Breakfast or Dream
Come True? A Case for Further Reform' and Christopher Decker and Matthew Harding,
'Three Challenges in Charity Regulation: The Case of England and Wales' in Matthew
Harding, Ann O'Connell and Miranda Stewart (eds), *Not-for-Profit Law: Theoretical and
Comparative Perspectives* (Cambridge University Press, 2014) 134–158 and 314–335
respectively.

[102]   Charities Act (Northern Ireland) 2008 (Northern Ireland) s 3(3), amended by Charities
Act (Northern Ireland) 2013 (Northern Ireland) s 1.

determination. In some cases, this might be an attractive option to a decision-maker: for instance, where a finding on the question of public benefit will be controversial. For present purposes, it will suffice to consider four disqualifying rules that typically figure in charity law. These are: the rule disqualifying purposes that offend public policy from being charitable; the rule disqualifying 'for profit' purposes from being charitable; the rule disqualifying certain governmental purposes from being charitable; and the rule disqualifying what in charity law are regarded as overly political purposes from being charitable. Let us call these the public policy rule, the 'not for profit' rule, the rule against governmental purposes and the rule against political purposes, respectively.

A.   The public policy rule

Purposes that are contrary to public policy are disqualified from being charitable in law. A purpose might be contrary to public policy in the setting of the public policy rule in one of several ways. Most obviously, a purpose that is illegal will be considered contrary to public policy and disqualified from being charitable as a result; this means, for example, that a trust to promote abortion or euthanasia cannot be charitable in a jurisdiction where those practices are contrary to law.[103] Moreover, since *Thornton* v. *Howe* – the celebrated nineteenth-century case about the purpose of publishing the religious writings of the *soi-disant* prophetess, Joanna Southcote – it has been established in charity law that a purpose that is 'adverse to the very foundations of all religion' or that is 'subversive of all morality' will be considered contrary to public policy and therefore disqualified from being charitable.[104] Exactly what these phrases mean remains unclear in the charity law of today, but presumably they point to the disqualification from being charitable of such purposes as running an atheistic campaign to rid society of religion or maintaining a school to teach the art of theft.[105] Another type of purpose that might be disqualified from being charitable in light of public policy considerations is a purpose that entails discrimination on

---

[103] See *Auckland Medical Aid Trust* v. *Commissioner of Inland Revenue* [1979] 1 NZLR 382 (Chilwell J), 395; *Re Collier (deceased)* [1998] 1 NZLR 81 (Hammond J), 91.

[104] (1862) 31 Beav 14; 54 ER 1042 (Sir John Romilly MR), 20. The purpose of publishing Southcote's writings fell into neither category: see further Chapter 5.

[105] The second example is drawn from *In re Macduff* [1896] 2 Ch 451 (Court of Appeal), 474 (Rigby LJ).

grounds such as race, sex or religion. In the Canadian case of *Re Canada Trust Co* v. *Ontario Human Rights Commission*, the Ontario Court of Appeal ordered a *cy-pres* scheme to vary the terms of a well-known trust established to provide scholarships for educational purposes, because the trust discriminated on various grounds.[106] The Court cited public policy considerations in ordering the scheme.[107] Although in *Canada Trust* the purpose of the trust was not disqualified from being charitable because of its discriminatory character, the willingness of the Court to order a *cy-pres* scheme to bring the trust into alignment with public policy suggests that in an appropriate case where a *cy-pres* scheme is not available, a discriminatory purpose might be disqualified, on public policy grounds, from being charitable altogether. We will return to the question of how charity law should treat discriminatory purposes in Chapter 7.

It seems strongly arguable that in many cases the public policy rule of charity law is nothing more than a proxy for the 'benefit' component of the public benefit test, serving to disqualify purposes from being charitable where, despite their public character, they are thought by decision-makers to lack a beneficial character. Earlier, we considered the case of *Bob Jones University* v. *US*, in which the US Supreme Court found a university not to be charitable on public policy grounds because those purposes entailed racial discrimination.[108] One plausible reading of *Bob Jones University* leads to the conclusion that in that case the Supreme Court found that the university was not a charity because it failed the public benefit test of charity law; it was with this reading in mind that we first considered *Bob Jones University* in the course of a discussion about the 'benefit' component of the public benefit test. However, the case is equally plausibly interpreted as one in which the Court applied a disqualifying rule and thereby avoided making the sorts of 'sensitive determinations' relating to public benefit to which the majority alluded in their judgment.[109] In some cases, though, the public policy rule seems to stand apart from an inquiry into benefit; arguably, this is the case where the rule is invoked to disqualify illegal purposes from being charitable without regard to whether or not the purposes in question, despite being illegal, might benefit the public. (An illegal purpose might benefit the

---

[106] (1990) 69 DLR (4th) 321 (Ontario Court of Appeal).

[107] Ibid, 334–335 (Robins JA). Contrast *Re Lysaght* [1966] Ch 191 (Buckley J), in which a *cy-pres* scheme was ordered even though the judge declined to find that the discriminatory purpose was contrary to public policy.

[108] 461 US 574 (1983) (US Supreme Court).   [109] Ibid, 598 (Burger J).

public where the law under which it is illegal is an unjust law warranting civil disobedience.) In these cases, the public policy rule is more truly a disqualifying rule, disqualifying purposes on account of some quality they possess unrelated to the consequences that they are likely to bring about.

B. The 'not for profit' rule

The 'not for profit' rule is engaged in cases where the purpose of an organisation is the making of profit, usually for founders or stakeholders of the organisation or for related parties. Such purposes are disqualified from being charitable in law, even if, as a consequence of carrying them out, public benefit will be realised.[110] The justification of the 'not for profit' rule is a large and interesting question that we will explore in Chapter 3. However, that question tends to arise only rarely in the setting of charity law cases in which decision-makers are asked to apply the 'not for profit' rule. Much more frequent are disputes over whether or not, on the facts of a particular case, an organisation has a 'for profit' or a 'not for profit' purpose; such disputes tend to arise where an organisation has two or more purposes, at least one of which aims at the generation of profit and at least one of which aims at the provision of private goods to a public class or the provision of public goods. The disqualifying rules of charity law, just like the criteria of charity law, apply only to the dominant purpose of an organisation and not to its subsidiary purposes. So, as happens in the 'member benefit' cases that we encountered earlier, in cases where the question is whether an organisation has a 'for profit' or a 'not for profit' purpose, decision-makers must construe the objects of the organisation in question and form a view, in light of those objects, as to which of the organisation's purposes is dominant and which are subsidiary. If the objects of an organisation reveal that it has both 'for profit' and 'not for profit' purposes, and a 'not for profit' purpose is the dominant purpose, then the 'not for profit' rule is satisfied by the only purpose that matters to charity law. In this regard, it is instructive to contrast two cases. In *R* v. *The Assessors of the Town of Sunny Brae*, a society distributed the profits of its laundry and dry-cleaning business for

---

[110] *Incorporated Council of Law Reporting of the State of Queensland* v. *Federal Commissioner of Taxation* (1971) 125 CLR 659 (High Court of Australia); *Incorporated Council of Law Reporting for England and Wales* v. *Attorney-General* [1973] Ch 72 (Court of Appeal). See also Charities Act 2009 (Ireland) s 3(10)(a).

the advancement of religion; the Supreme Court of Canada found that the society had a purpose of advancing religion but also a purpose of running the business for profit and that the latter purpose was neither charitable nor subsidiary to the first, undoubtedly charitable, purpose.[111] In contrast, in *Federal Commissioner of Taxation* v. *Word Investments Ltd*, a corporation distributed the profits of its funeral business for the advancement of religion; the High Court of Australia construed the objects of the corporation as disclosing a dominant purpose of advancing religion, and found that the 'for profit' funeral business was simply a means by which the corporation pursued its charitable purpose.[112]

Cases like *Sunny Brae* and *Word Investments* show that the application of the 'not for profit' rule does not turn on whether an organisation makes a profit in the pursuit of its purposes; it turns on whether the making of that profit is the dominant purpose of the organisation. In circumstances where an organisation has a dominant purpose of making a profit for founders, stakeholders or related parties, the dominant purpose of that organisation may fairly be said to be private in the sense that it aims at the generation of a private good – profit – to be enjoyed by a private class constituted by the founders, stakeholders or related parties in question. We saw earlier that purposes fail to satisfy the 'public' component of the public benefit test where they entail the delivery of private goods to a private class; we are now in a position to see that purposes that fall foul of the 'not for profit' rule do so for the same reason. Given that the 'public' component of the public benefit test and the 'not for profit' rule both appear to be directed against purposes entailing the provision of private goods to a private class, we may fairly conclude that the 'not for profit' rule is in fact an outworking of the 'public' component of the public benefit test, even though it is spoken of and utilised as a freestanding rule.[113] This connection between the 'not for profit' rule and the 'public' component of the public benefit test will be evident once again in Chapter 3, where we will consider how the state uses both elements of charity law to draw boundaries around legal charity in the pursuit of a single aim.

---

[111] [1952] SCR 76 (Supreme Court of Canada).
[112] (2008) 236 CLR 204 (High Court of Australia).
[113] See, e.g., Garton, above n 1, [2.19] and ch 6.

C. The rule against governmental purposes

In a number of cases in different jurisdictions, decision-makers have refused to recognise purposes as charitable in law on the basis that the purposes in question have been, in some sense, purposes of government. There is, to this extent, a disqualifying rule against governmental purposes in charity law.[114] However, trying to isolate precisely the sorts of purposes against which the rule is aimed, thus moving beyond a vague sense that they involve government in some way, proves difficult. As we saw earlier, in the United States of America, the Restatement (Third) of Trusts explicitly states that 'governmental or municipal purposes' are prima facie charitable in the setting of trusts law,[115] suggesting either that a rule against governmental purposes does not apply in the United States in respect of trusts law or that in that jurisdiction such a rule is conceptualised idiosyncratically. Moreover, case law in other jurisdictions reveals that it is unclear exactly what sort of government involvement in purposes will cause them to infringe the rule against governmental purposes. In some cases, the fact of government control seems to have been thought sufficient to render purposes non-charitable; nonetheless, other cases indicate that it is not desirable in the setting of the rule to draw a general distinction between purposes that are carried out under the control of government and purposes that are not.[116] Neither is it possible to draw a distinction between purposes that are carried out by government on the one hand and purposes that are not carried out by government on the other; a number of cases indicate that in certain circumstances – most notably where gifts are made to government to benefit the inhabitants of a locality – purposes carried out by government are regarded as charitable in law.[117]

---

[114] See also Charities Act 2013 (Australia) ss 4 and 5(d).

[115] US Restatement (3rd) of Trusts, § 28.

[116] Compare *Construction Industry Training Board* v. *Attorney-General* [1973] 1 Ch 173 (Court of Appeal), in which the question of control was regarded as determinative, and *Central Bayside General Practice Association Limited* v. *Commissioner of State Revenue* (2006) 228 CLR 168 (High Court of Australia), in which members of the High Court of Australia doubted the sufficiency of a control test.

[117] See *Thellusson* v. *Woodford* (1799) 4 Ves Jr 227; *Newland* v. *Attorney-General* (1809) 3 Mer 684 (Lord Eldon LC); *Mitford* v. *Reynolds* [1835–42] All ER Rep 331 (Lord Lyndhurst LC); *Nightingale* v. *Goulbourn* (1848) 2 Ph 594 (Lord Cottenham LC); *Goodman* v. *Mayor of Saltash* (1882) 7 App Cas 633 (Lord Selborne LC, Earl Cairns, Lord Watson); *Commissioners for Special Purposes of Income Tax* v. *Pemsel* [1891] AC 531 (House of Lords); *Robinson* v. *Stuart* (1891) 12 LR (NSW) Eq 47 (Owen CJ in Eq); *In re Tetley* [1923] 1 Ch 258 (Russell J and Court of Appeal); *In re Smith* [1932] 1 Ch 153

A more promising distinction is between purposes that are both carried out by government and realise collective decisions made through the institutions of the political community on the one hand, and purposes that, whether or not they are carried out by government, realise decisions made in the exercise of individual autonomous choice on the other. Such a distinction would explain, for example, why the purposes of a statutory body are not charitable, while a gift to government to benefit the inhabitants of a locality is charitable.[118] It would also appear to be consistent with the apparent acceptance of governmental purposes as charitable in the trusts law setting in the United States; in every case where a trust is settled for governmental purposes the trust is the product of individual autonomous choice, even if the carrying out of the purpose is a matter of government administration. Yet exceptions may be found even to this distinction, such as in the case of the British Museum, established under an act of parliament in the eighteenth century and nonetheless found to have charitable purposes in the early nineteenth century.[119] That charity law contains a rule against governmental purposes seems clear enough. But, given the uncertainty in charity law about the parameters of the rule, the circumstances in which a decision-maker will consider a purpose governmental and therefore disqualified from being charitable in law cannot be predicted with confidence.

D. The rule against political purposes

In the charity law of a number of jurisdictions, there exists a rule disqualifying from being charitable in law any purpose that seeks to bring about change to, or even in some circumstances to defend or justify, law or government policy, or that entails lobbying government, engaging in party politics or agitating for a particular point of view on a social issue. Such a broad rule against political purposes may be traced back to 1917 and the decision of the House of Lords in

---

(Court of Appeal); *Monds* v. *Stackhouse* (1948) 77 CLR 232 (High Court of Australia); possibly also *Bathurst City Council* v. *PWC Properties Pty Ltd* (1998) 195 CLR 566 (High Court of Australia).

[118] For fuller discussion: Matthew Harding, 'Distinguishing Government from Charity in Australian Law' (2009) 31 *Sydney Law Review* 559, 570–577.

[119] *Trustees of the British Museum* v. *White* (1826) 2 Sim & St 594; 57 ER 473 (Sir John Leach VC). The British Museum was established under the British Museum Act 1753 (26 Geo 2 c 22).

Bowman v. *Secular Society Ltd*,[120] and it has been adopted and endorsed in Canada, England and Wales, and New Zealand numerous times since.[121] In other jurisdictions, however, the rule against political purposes has not had such prominence; for example, in the United States, decision-makers have not been reluctant to recognise political purposes as charitable,[122] although the tax law has imposed restrictions on charities engaging in political activities.[123] And in Scotland the rule against political purposes is not applied, although under the Charities and Trustee Investments (Scotland) Act of 2005, political parties and those who seek to advance political parties may not be charities.[124] In Australia, a broad rule against political purposes was accepted by decision-makers – with some degree of reluctance[125] – until the landmark decision of the High Court of Australia in 2010 in a case that we encountered earlier in the context of a discussion of the 'benefit' component of the public benefit test, *Aid/Watch Incorporated* v. *Federal Commissioner of Taxation*.[126] In that case, the Court declared that a broad rule against political purposes no longer formed part of Australian charity law, thus setting the Australian treatment of political purposes on a new course.[127] The fact that, in 2012, the New Zealand Court of Appeal reaffirmed the applicability of a broad rule against political purposes for that jurisdiction despite being asked to endorse the reasoning of the High Court of Australia in *Aid/Watch* indicates as well as anything could that the question whether or not the rule is warranted in modern charity law is not one that admits of an easy answer.[128] In Chapter 6, we will return to this difficult question.

---

[120] [1917] AC 406 (House of Lords).

[121] The case law is discussed in detail in Chapter 6.

[122] *Taylor* v. *Hoag* 116 A 826, 828 (Frazer J) (Pa, 1922).

[123] For an overview, see Nina J. Crimm and Laurence H. Winer, 'Dilemmas in Regulating Electoral Speech of Non-Profit Organisations' in Matthew Harding, Ann O'Connell and Miranda Stewart (eds), *Not-for-Profit Law: Theoretical and Comparative Perspectives* (Cambridge University Press, 2014) 61–86.

[124] Charities and Trustee Investment (Scotland) Act 2005 (Scotland) s 7(4)(c).

[125] *Royal North Shore Hospital of Sydney* v. *Attorney-General (NSW)* (1938) 60 CLR 396 (High Court of Australia); *Public Trustee* v. *Attorney-General (NSW)* (1997) 42 NSWLR 600 (Santow J); *Victorian Women Lawyers' Association Inc* v. *Federal Commissioner of Taxation* (2008) 170 FCR 318 (French J).

[126] (2010) 241 CLR 539 (High Court of Australia).

[127] And see now Charities Act 2013 (Australia) s 12(1)(l).

[128] *In re Greenpeace of New Zealand Incorporated* [2012] NZCA 533 (Court of Appeal). At the time of writing, the case had been appealed to the Supreme Court of New Zealand but no decision had been handed down.

4.   The privileges of charity law

For those with charitable purposes, charity law makes available a range of privileges that would not otherwise be available. Many of these privileges may be found in that part of charity law that also forms part of the law of trusts. It is a well-known rule that, subject to certain limited exceptions, trusts for purposes are not valid and enforceable in law unless the purposes in question are charitable.[129] It was not always thus: according to the Mortmain Act of 1736, testamentary trusts of land for charitable purposes were invalid, as were *inter vivos* dispositions of land for charitable purposes made in contemplation of death.[130] The Mortmain Act was enacted to thwart the practice of devising land to the church upon death; it was the product of state concerns about the manipulation of testators by churchmen and the perceived need to protect the interests of heirs. It shows that in the eighteenth century charity law rendered it difficult, even impossible, to settle trusts of land for charitable purposes. But the Mortmain Act, like the testamentary practice that inspired it, disappeared many years ago,[131] and its strategy of withholding facilities from those with charitable purposes is foreign to the charity law of today. As well as enabling trusts for purposes, charity law extends a variety of privileges to those creating or managing charitable trusts, in the form of perpetuity, flexible rules of construction and interpretation, statutory powers authorising courts to give effect – for charitable purposes – to what would otherwise be invalid trusts for a mixture of charitable and non-charitable purposes, and *cy-pres* schemes enabling charitable trusts that are impossible or impractical to carry out to be refashioned for analogous purposes.[132]

The best-known of the privileges of charity law are the tax privileges. These fall into two broad categories. First, there are direct privileges in the form of exemptions from income and other taxes for those with

---

[129]   *Morice* v. *Bishop of Durham* (1804) 9 Ves Jun 399; 32 ER 656 (Sir William Grant MR); (1805) 10 Ves Jun 522; 32 ER 947 (Lord Eldon LC); *Re Endacott* [1960] Ch 232 (CA). Some have argued for the legal validity of a wider class of purpose trusts: see Nigel P. Gravells, 'Public Purpose Trusts' (1977) 40 *Modern Law Review* 397; Gino Dal Pont, 'Why Define "Charity"? Is the Search for Meaning Worth the Effort?' (2002) 8 *Third Sector Review* 5.

[130]   On the Mortmain Act, see Jones, above n 8, 109–119, 128–133.

[131]   The Mortmain Act was not repealed until the passage of the Charities Act 1960, but it was substantially relaxed by the Mortmain and Charitable Uses Act 1891.

[132]   Gino Dal Pont, *Law of Charity* (LexisNexis Butterworths, Chatswood, 2010), ch 6.

charitable purposes.[133] In all jurisdictions, such privileges are extended not only to those with charitable purposes but also to some who pursue non-charitable purposes that are 'not for profit' purposes; nonetheless, to the extent that direct tax privileges are extended to those with charitable purposes, they may be said to be part of charity law. Second, there are indirect privileges in the form of state support for those who make gifts to organisations with charitable purposes. The precise nature of this state support varies from jurisdiction to jurisdiction: in Australia and the United States of America it takes the form of a deduction when assessing the taxable income of charitable donors;[134] in Canada and New Zealand it takes the form of a tax credit for individual donors and a deduction for corporate donors;[135] in the United Kingdom it takes the form of a scheme known as 'Gift Aid', according to which a donor declares a charitable gift and the donee then receives a payment from the state calculated with reference to tax payable by the donor on the gift.[136] In Australia, the class of organisations that qualifies for these indirect tax privileges overlaps with, but is not the same as, the class of organisations with charitable purposes. In Canada, New Zealand and especially the United States, the qualifying class is wider than those with charitable purposes. In the United Kingdom, it is restricted to those with charitable purposes. It must therefore be said that, except in the United Kingdom, the rules of the tax law extending indirect tax privileges to those with charitable purposes are strictly speaking not part of charity law; they do not employ the category of 'charity' in the legal sense, utilising instead overlapping or broader categories. However, these overlapping or broader categories invariably capture a large number of those whose purposes are regarded as charitable in law. To this extent, we may speak of an association of charity law and indirect tax privileges, even in jurisdictions where the trigger for those indirect tax privileges is not the pursuit of charitable purposes *qua* charitable.

---

[133] See, e.g., the following provisions relating to income tax: Income Tax Assessment Act 1997 (Australia) Division 50; Income Tax Act 1985 (Canada) s 149; Taxes Consolidation Act 1997 (Ireland) ss 207 and 208; Income Tax Act 2007 (NZ) ss CW 41 and CW 42; Income Tax Act 2007 (UK) Part 10 and Corporation Tax Act 2010 (UK) ss 478–489; Internal Revenue Code (US) § 501.

[134] Income Tax Assessment Act 1997 (Australia) Division 30; Internal Revenue Code (US) § 170.

[135] Income Tax Act 1985 (Canada) ss 110.1 and 118.1; Income Tax Act 2007 (NZ) ss LD1 and DB41.

[136] Finance Act 1990 (UK) ss 25–26, as amended by Finance Act 2000 (UK) ss 39–40.

Another, arguably more diffuse, privilege of charity law is extended to those with charitable purposes via findings that their purposes are 'charitable'. By recognising purposes as 'charitable', decision-makers express the state's endorsement of those purposes,[137] and this endorsement may help to generate public trust and confidence in the people and organisations whose purposes they are.[138] Endorsement is expressed, in part, through the choice of the language of 'charity' to describe the purposes to which the state wishes to extend the privileges of charity law. The non-legal meanings of the word 'charity' lend to that word a strong expressive quality as a result of which the word, however it is used, typically connotes worthiness and virtue.[139] Decision-makers draw on this expressive quality when they deploy the word 'charity' in charity law. Of course, it would be possible for the state to express its endorsement of charitable purposes through different terminology; indeed it has been argued that the use of the language of 'charity' in charity law is apt to mislead because of the substantial differences between its legal and non-legal meanings, and that the state should cease to use the word 'charity' in charity law as a result.[140] As we saw in the Introduction to this book, in many jurisdictions outside the common law world, different terminology is used, and functional equivalents of charity law take the form of the law of 'public benefit organisations' or the like. On the other hand, as was alluded to in the Introduction, the expressive effects of charity law may depend in some ways on the non-legal meaning of the concept of charity, and abandoning the language of 'charity' might have undesirable expressive

---

[137] There is a large academic literature on the expressive function of law: see Matthew D. Adler, 'Expressive Theories of Law: A Skeptical Overview' (2000) 148 *University of Pennsylvania Law Review* 1363 for a detailed and critical overview of much of this literature.

[138] In England and Wales, many charitable organisations that need not be registered with the Charity Commission because their annual income is under £5,000 choose to remain on the register, arguably indicating that they value the state endorsement that charitable status signals. The register may be viewed and searched at the website of the Charity Commission.

[139] For some, 'charity' (in the non-legal sense) connotes something patronising and demeaning to those who 'benefit' from it. If that view were to gain widespread support, the expressive function of charity law would be compromised. For reasons why such a negative view of charity in the non-legal sense might be mistaken: John Gardner, 'The Virtue of Charity and Its Foils' in Charles Mitchell and Susan R. Moody (eds), *Foundations of Charity* (Hart Publishing, Oxford, 2000) 1–27.

[140] Paul Valentine, 'A Lay Word for a Legal Term: How the Popular Definition of Charity Has Muddied the Perception of the Charitable Deduction' (2010) 89 *Nebraska Law Review* 997.

consequences for charity law. Either way, questions about whether or not the expressive effects of charity law might affected in undesirable ways by the abandonment of the language of 'charity' may be put to one side for present purposes; the point to note for now is that in describing purposes as 'charitable', the state expresses endorsement of them, and there are reasons to think that this endorsement functions as one of the privileges of charity law.

Arguably, the expressive function of charity law extends to the state practice of 'recognising', 'endorsing' or 'registering' organisations with charitable purposes as 'charities'. This practice varies from jurisdiction to jurisdiction: in some, charities are recognised or endorsed by tax authorities to signal their eligibility for particular tax privileges;[141] in others, a regulator registers charities for some or all legal purposes.[142] In broad terms, these acts of endorsement or registration reveal a state practice of conferring the status of 'charity' on organisations. This practice of conferring charitable status would appear to have several functions. Some relate to administrative ease and efficiency; there can be little doubt that the administration of tax law, for example, is made easier when tax authorities can make decisions based on the fact that some organisations enjoy a certain status while others do not. Others have to do with ensuring that those who manage resources for charitable purposes are subjected to appropriate legal duties.[143] But it is also arguable that among the functions of the state's practice of conferring charitable status on organisations with charitable purposes is the expression of endorsement not only of charitable purposes but also of those who carry them out. To the extent that this argument holds, the conferral of charitable status may be counted among the privileges of charity law.

5. Conclusion

The aim of this chapter has been to enable us to gain a sense of the content of charity law in overview, so that we may think through questions of state action and public discourse as they relate to charity law in an informed and meaningful way. In the next chapter, we will turn to those questions of state action and public discourse; this will demand that we abstract considerably from the details of charity law and think

---

[141] See, e.g., Income Tax Act 1985 (Canada) s 149.1(1).
[142] See, e.g., Charities Act 2011 (England and Wales) ss 1 and 30.
[143] See Garton, above n 1, [3.07]–[3.18] and passim.

philosophically about the territory that we have traversed so far. But as we direct our thinking away from the content of the law to the philosophical questions that it raises, it will be helpful to have the building blocks of charity law before us: general descriptions of charitable purpose such as the *Pemsel* set; the public benefit test with its 'public' and 'benefit' components; disqualifying rules such as the public policy rule, the 'not for profit' rule and the rules against governmental and political purposes; and, last but by no means least, the legal privileges that are extended to those who pursue charitable purposes – privileges that arise in the law of trusts, tax law and regulatory law. We will have occasion to return to each of these elements, in some cases on a number of occasions, as we think through questions relating to charity law and the liberal state in the chapters to come.

2

Towards a liberal theory of charity law

1. Introduction

In this chapter, we will take up some philosophical questions relating to state action and public discourse that are raised by charity law. We will do so from a perspective informed by the liberal tradition of political philosophy. The liberal tradition is a rich one, and there are many perspectives within it from which to choose in developing a liberal theory of charity law. Thus, the chapter will begin by considering briefly some liberal perspectives that might be viewed as candidates to ground a liberal theory of charity law. We will see that one central feature of charity law is that through charity law the state promotes charitable purposes. We will also see that in light of this central feature of charity law, there are reasons to think that what we will call 'autonomy-based' liberalism is a more attractive candidate in which to ground a liberal theory of charity law than some alternatives. We will then sketch the outlines of autonomy-based liberalism with reference to the work of its leading exponent, Joseph Raz. Next, from the perspective of autonomy-based liberalism, we will consider some questions that arise when we inquire into the extent to which the state's promotion of charitable purposes might be justified and desirable. Finally, we will introduce the idea of autonomy-based aspirations for public discourse and we will consider how, in light of those aspirations, we might evaluate the reasoning of decision-makers when applying the 'benefit' component of the public benefit test. The conclusions of this chapter will lay the groundwork for the more detailed consideration of questions of state action and public discourse in the charity law setting with which we will be occupied in the remainder of this book. To this extent, even though the chapter will not provide us with a complete liberal theory of charity law, it will assist us in moving us closer to the goal of developing such a theory.

2. Choosing a liberal perspective

In choosing a liberal perspective to ground a liberal theory of charity law, our starting point will be to notice a central feature of charity law that emerged from the overview of charity law in Chapter 1. Recall from that chapter that through charity law the state ascertains whether or not purposes are charitable according to certain criteria and disqualifying rules, and extends certain legal privileges to those whose purposes are recognised as charitable in this way. In particular, via charity law the state confers validity, perpetuity and associated advantages on charitable trusts, makes available a range of direct and indirect tax exemptions and subsidies to those with charitable purposes and expresses endorsement of charitable purposes and those who carry them out. To this extent, charity law entails what might be called facilitative, incentive and expressive strategies. These facilitative, incentive and expressive strategies are most plausibly understood as directed to ensuring that citizens are able to and will pursue charitable purposes and to ensuring that the incidence of this pursuit is at least maintained and most likely also augmented over the course of time. In other words, in light of the facilitative, incentive and expressive strategies of charity law, it is reasonable to assert that a central feature of charity law is that the state uses it to promote charitable purposes.

A liberal theory of charity law should have something to say about the state's promotion of charitable purposes. With this theoretical aim in mind, some liberal accounts of state action and public discourse seem more promising than others as candidates in which to ground a liberal theory of charity law. For example, John Rawls's celebrated theory of social justice seems ill suited to tackling key questions that are raised by the state's promotion of charitable purposes.[1] For one thing, Rawls's theory of justice is an ideal theory, aiming to specify principles of justice for the well-ordered society as a whole rather than for particular institutions and arrangements within it; as such, the theory may not deliver prescriptions for state action specific enough to be applicable in the charity law setting. We will return to this point in Chapter 4, where we will see that the requirements of principles of distributive justice for society – one of which is Rawls's famous 'difference principle' – are insufficiently fine-tuned to evaluate the tax privileges of charity law. At the same time, Rawls's theory of justice aims to specify ways in which the

---

[1] See John Rawls, *A Theory of Justice* (rev. paperback edn., Oxford University Press, 1999).

'basic structure' of society should be ordered so as to extend rights and duties to citizens and distribute the fruits of social co-operation in certain ways.[2] This is hardly surprising, insofar as Rawls's theory is a theory of *justice*: justice, as Rawls himself tells us, is a matter of rights and distribution.[3] As a theory of justice, then, Rawls's theory is capable of grounding only those theoretical approaches to charity law whose central focus is an inquiry into rights and distribution.[4]

Questions about rights and distribution can be formulated with regard to the state's promotion of charitable purposes. Indeed, Leslie Green suggests that the recognition of a purpose as charitable is itself a distributable social good, implying that the promotion of charitable purposes cannot but be viewed as a matter of distribution.[5] But although it is possible to think about the state's promotion of charitable purposes in terms of rights and distribution, in a sense questions about rights and distribution seem to be the wrong sort of questions to ask about that promotion; more obvious appropriate questions seem to relate to whether or not there is something special or worthy about charitable purposes that warrants their promotion by the state, irrespective of the implications of that promotion for rights and distribution. In other words, the state's promotion of charitable purposes is not obviously first and foremost a matter of justice, even if it has implications in justice. And to the extent that the state's promotion of charitable purposes is not a matter of justice, Rawls's theory of social justice is not interested in it.

Other candidates in which to ground a liberal theory of charity law may be found in various liberal accounts of state action or public discourse that appeal to a principle of neutrality, whether in aim,

---

[2] Ibid, 6–10.

[3] Ibid, 3–6. See also H.L.A. Hart, 'Justice' (1953) 28 *Philosophy* 348; John Gardner, 'The Virtue of Justice and the Character of Law' in his *Law as a Leap of Faith* (Oxford University Press, 2012) ch 10. It may be more accurate to say that justice is a matter of rights-based claims than that it is a matter of rights: see John Gardner, 'The Virtue of Charity and Its Foils' in Charles Mitchell and Susan R. Moody (eds), *Foundations of Charity* (Hart Publishing, Oxford, 2000) 1, 13–15. In the text, we will refer, for convenience, to 'rights'.

[4] This assumes that charity law is part of the basic structure of society. Rawls himself is famously cryptic as to the content of the basic structure (see, e.g., *A Theory of Justice*, above n 1, 6–8) but there are reasons to think that it should be understood broadly, in which case charity law is within it: for a broad understanding of the basic structure, see Kok-Chor Tan, *Justice, Institutions and Luck: The Site, Ground and Scope of Equality* (Oxford University Press, 2012), 34–38.

[5] Leslie Green, 'The Germ of Justice', available on SSRN, abstract id 1703008.

justification, effect or treatment.[6] One such is Rawls's account of political liberalism.[7] Political liberalism is a theory about the proper conduct of public discourse in a political community; its gist is that in certain respects, citizens ought to exercise restraint in offering their conceptions of the good as reasons for political action, and that the public life of a political community should be characterised by neutrality of justification to that extent.[8] At first glance, the principle of neutrality in justification embedded in Rawls's political liberalism seems to constitute an evaluative tool for thinking about the public discourse of decision-makers who promote charitable purposes, but on closer inspection this turns out not to be the case. According to Rawls, political liberalism is a theory only about the conduct of public discourse touching on certain topics of central importance to the political community, viz, 'constitutional essentials' and 'matters of basic justice'.[9] When citizens engage in public discourse on other topics, whether or not they offer their conceptions of the good as reasons for political action is not of interest from the perspective of political liberalism, according to Rawls. Thus, the principle of neutrality at the heart of political liberalism is narrow in scope. The difficulty that arises when public discourse in the charity law setting is evaluated in light of political liberalism is that much of that discourse appears not to be about 'constitutional essentials' or 'matters of basic justice'. In particular, there are reasons to think that decision-makers do not typically approach the promotion of charitable purposes with a mindset focused on questions of rights or distribution,[10] the mindset

---

[6] For this taxonomy of types of neutrality see Alan Patten, 'Liberal Neutrality: A Reinterpretation and Defence' (2012) 20 *The Journal of Political Philosophy* 249.

[7] See John Rawls, *Political Liberalism* (expanded edn., Columbia University Press, New York, 2005); John Rawls, 'The Idea of Public Reason Revisited' in his *The Law of Peoples, with 'The Idea of Public Reason Revisited'* (Harvard University Press, Cambridge, MA, 1999) 129.

[8] The central cases of conceptions of the good are comprehensive ethical worldviews such as utilitarianism, Roman Catholicism and Islam; however, a conception of the good might also be unsystematised and diffuse, such as a belief that art is intrinsically good or that a life of action is the best sort of life. See further Ronald Dworkin, 'Liberalism' in his *A Matter of Principle* (Harvard University Press, Cambridge, MA, 1985) 181, 191.

[9] Rawls, *Political Liberalism*, above n 7, 1 and passim; Rawls, 'Idea of Public Reason Revisited', above n 7, 133 and passim. See also Martha Nussbaum, 'Rawls's *Political Liberalism*: A Reassessment' (2011) 24 *Ratio Juris* 1, 12: 'It is extremely important to recognize how specific and how narrow the range of issues that trigger [political liberalism] is.'

[10] Although occasionally they do: see *AYSA Youth Soccer Association* v. *Canada Revenue Agency* [2007] 3 SCR 217 (Supreme Court of Canada).

that, as we have just seen, is characteristic of those who would do justice. To the extent that this is true, the principle of neutrality embedded in political liberalism offers little to a liberal theory of charity law that seeks to understand and evaluate the public discourse entailed in the state's promotion of charitable purposes.

Liberal neutrality-based theories that are broader in scope than Rawls's political liberalism are likely to fare better as candidates in which to ground a liberal theory of charity law.[11] Nick Martin, for example, has argued that a principle of neutrality of justification, applicable to public discourse on a wide range of topics and not only when constitutional essentials or matters of basic justice are in view, can be deployed in developing a liberal theory of charity law.[12] With such a broad principle of neutrality of justification in view, Martin argues that there are reasons for the state to confine itself to promoting only those charitable purposes that stand to produce outcomes that all reasonable people would agree are good.[13] If the state is to confine itself in this way, according to Martin, charity law will have to change; decision-makers will have to refrain from promoting religious purposes and other purposes the value of which reasonable people disagree on.[14] Similarly, a broad liberal principle of neutrality of treatment of those who pursue different conceptions of the good, along lines proposed by Alan Patten, might be deployed in insightful ways in thinking about the promotion of charitable purposes.[15] From this perspective, according to Patten, the state should aim at policies that are equally accommodating of different conceptions of the good; such an aim may be pursued effectively via strategies of withdrawing from the regulation of conceptions of the good altogether, regulating only goods that figure in all or most conceptions of the good, or supporting different conceptions of the good in an even-handed way, for example by subsidising them all equally.[16] In light of a broad principle of neutrality of

---

[11] Some may not. For example, Steven Lecce argues that a principle of neutrality in justification should apply in every case of public discourse about the deployment of the coercive power of the state. This widens the scope of such a principle considerably in comparison to Rawlsian political liberalism, but Lecce's account still may not fare better as a candidate for a liberal theory of charity law, for the reason that much public discourse in the charity law setting is not about the deployment of state coercion. Steven Lecce, *Against Perfectionism: Defending Liberal Neutrality* (University of Toronto Press, 2008), 230–237.

[12] Nick Martin, 'Liberal Neutrality and Charitable Purposes' (2012) 60 *Political Studies* 936, 943.

[13] Ibid, 948–950.   [14] Ibid.   [15] Patten, above n 6.   [16] Ibid, 259–261.

treatment, the promotion of charitable purposes ought to be of concern; the facilitative, incentive and expressive strategies of charity law seem at odds with the strategies of accommodation that, according to Patten, are outworkings of the demands of a broad principle of neutrality of treatment. To this extent, a broad principle of neutrality of treatment, like a broad principle of neutrality of justification, seems to demand the reform of charity law.

Liberal theories that appeal to a broad principle of neutrality are able to say more than Rawls's political liberalism about the state's promotion of charitable purposes, because they apply to a wider range of state action and public discourse. However, as Martin suggests in his careful treatment of liberal neutrality-based theories and charity law, whether such theories are narrow or broad in scope, their demands cannot be reconciled with the fact that in promoting charitable purposes, the state is non-neutral in every relevant sense towards different conceptions of the good.[17] The only purposes that are promoted as charitable in law are purposes that satisfy the criteria and disqualifying rules of charity law, and those criteria – especially the 'benefit' component of the public benefit test – are applied in a non-neutral way as between different conceptions of the good, whether neutrality is understood as neutrality of aim, justification, effect or treatment. The promotion via charity law of religious purposes, purposes relating to elite arts and purposes relating to animal welfare may be offered as examples. So may the refusal, in some jurisdictions at least, to recognise as charitable purposes relating to amateur sports. Thus, when liberal accounts based on principles of neutrality are applied to charity law, their conclusions are likely to include that charity law is to a degree misguided and should be reformed in some way. There is of course no reason to think that such conclusions must be wrong, but for the theorist who has a conviction that there is value and purpose in the non-neutral traditions of charity law, and who wishes to develop a liberal theory of charity law that is consistent with that conviction, neutrality-based accounts are likely to lead to unsettling conclusions.[18]

---

[17] Martin, above n 12, 950.

[18] Ibid, 936–937, 950–951. In his well-known account of 'reflective equilibrium', Rawls argues that propositions in political philosophy should be tested for plausibility against 'considered convictions' about social institutions. To the extent that those propositions are inconsistent with those convictions, Rawls argues that it may be necessary to revise the propositions (and vice versa): Rawls, *A Theory of Justice*, above n 1, 17–18, 40–46. As Martin suggests, those who: (a) endorse Rawls's method; (b) endorse a principle of

Rawls's theory of justice seems to suggest that the state's promotion of charitable purposes is irrelevant to political morality except to the extent that it raises questions of justice. Liberal theories that appeal to a principle of neutrality seem either to have nothing to say about the state's promotion of charitable purposes or to yield the conclusion that to some degree that promotion is misguided. These conclusions do not augur well for developing a liberal theory of charity law. There is, however, a liberal perspective that enables us to inquire into the state's promotion of charitable purposes without reducing that inquiry to an inquiry into social justice, and at the same time enables us to avoid committing ourselves to the view that the promotion of charitable purposes is misguided insofar as it is non-neutral. This perspective, often associated with the work of Joseph Raz,[19] is the perspective of autonomy-based liberalism. Autonomy-based liberalism appeals to a distinctly liberal conception of the good, at the heart of which is a distinctly liberal ideal – the ideal of personal autonomy. This ideal has been understood, within the tradition of autonomy-based liberalism, in terms of self-authorship,[20] self-determination,[21] self-transformation,[22] self-disclosure,[23] self-creation,[24] control over one's destiny[25] and the fashioning of one's life through successive decisions of one's own.[26] Autonomy, thus understood, is a species of freedom; it is the sort of freedom that is sometimes described in the liberal tradition as 'positive liberty' and it may be distinguished from the conception of freedom as 'negative liberty', according to which a person is free to the extent that she occupies a zone or sphere of non-interference.[27] Understood in its positive or its negative

---

neutrality; and (c) have a considered conviction that the state's non-neutral promotion of charitable purposes via charity law is broadly justified may have reasons to rethink the plausibility of the principle of neutrality that they endorse.

[19] The main works are Joseph Raz, *The Morality of Freedom* (Clarendon Press, Oxford, 1986); Joseph Raz, 'Autonomy, Toleration and the Harm Principle' in Ruth Gavison (ed), *Issues in Contemporary Philosophy: The Influence of HLA Hart* (Clarendon Press, Oxford, 1987) 313–333; Joseph Raz, 'Facing Up: A Reply' (1989) 62 *Southern California Law Review* 1153.

[20] Raz, *Morality of Freedom*, above n 19, 204, 369.

[21] Raz, 'Autonomy, Toleration and the Harm Principle', above n 19, 323; Stephen Macedo, *Liberal Virtues: Citizenship, Virtue and Community in Liberal Constitutionalism* (Clarendon Press, Oxford, 1990), 204.

[22] Macedo, above n 21, 204.

[23] Jeremy Waldron, 'Autonomy and Perfectionism in Raz's *Morality of Freedom*' (1989) 62 *Southern California Law Review* 1097, 1110.

[24] Raz, *Morality of Freedom*, above n 19, 204.   [25] Ibid, 369.   [26] Ibid.

[27] Isaiah Berlin, 'Two Concepts of Liberty' in his *Liberty* (Henry Hardy ed, Oxford University Press, 2002) 166–217.

sense, freedom is a core value in the liberal tradition. Thus, an account of political morality that is grounded in the value of autonomy may be described fairly as an instance of liberalism.

Autonomy-based liberalism is broad in scope; it is not preoccupied solely with the justice of the basic structure of society and can therefore conceive of the state's promotion of charitable purposes in ways other than by posing questions about the implications of that promotion for rights and distribution. Autonomy-based liberalism asks questions about the ways in which the state can and should promote a conception of the good grounded in the ideal of autonomy; in its interest in questions about what the state ought to promote and why, autonomy-based liberalism seems attuned to analysing and evaluating the state's promotion of charitable purposes. Moreover, autonomy-based liberalism is not built on any notion that, when deciding what to promote and why, the state ought to aim at or achieve some sort of neutrality towards different conceptions of the good. In autonomy-based liberalism, the state ought to promote autonomy; to the extent that this requires non-neutral engagement with citizens' different conceptions of the good, whether in aim, justification, effect or treatment, so be it. Again, in its acceptance that the state may deal with citizens' different conceptions of the good in a non-neutral way, autonomy-based liberalism equips us with theoretical tools to think sensitively about the non-neutral character of the state's promotion of charitable purposes, rather than compelling us to argue that insofar as charity law entails non-neutral strategies it is misguided, thereby shutting down further inquiry into charity law's non-neutral dimensions. For these reasons, we will employ autonomy-based liberalism in working towards a liberal theory of charity law.

3.   Autonomy-based liberalism

An autonomy-based account of state action and public discourse begins with an account of the nature and value of autonomy. Autonomy is, in a sense, a personal achievement,[28] and the extent to which a given life is an autonomous one depends in part on the extent to which the person whose life it is exercises her will in self-determining ways. Such self-determining exercises of the will typically, and centrally, take the form of choices; thus, a person who never made any choices and preferred to drift

---

[28] See Raz, *Morality of Freedom*, above n 19, 204.

on life's currents could not be said to have achieved autonomy. However, it is important to notice that, even though choice is central to autonomy, voluntary activity not amounting to choice can also contribute to self-determination in just the ways that manifest the value of autonomy.[29] To take two of many possible examples, a person may deliberately detach or distance herself from certain beliefs and commitments and try from that position to understand herself in relation to those beliefs and commitments, perhaps with a view to making a choice in the future; or she may subject to scrutiny what she feels to be unchosen claims upon her – say, the claims of family – and may respond to those claims in some voluntary way, whether by identifying with them and 'owning' them, or by rejecting them, or by adopting a more nuanced stance towards them. Raz, the key exponent of autonomy-based liberalism, writes at times as though voluntary activity not amounting to choice cannot be described as autonomous;[30] however, there appears to be no reason to think that choice exhausts autonomy to the exclusion of other voluntary activity, rather than constituting autonomy's typical and central case.

While autonomy depends on self-determining exercises of the will, an autonomous life can also be achieved only where certain conditions obtain, and it is these conditions that make the ideal of an autonomous life an ideal of interest not only as a matter of personal ethics but also as a matter of political morality. In his work, Raz arranges the conditions of autonomy into three categories. First, in order to be autonomous, a person must have, develop and maintain what Raz calls 'inner capacities' that are necessary to autonomy; these capacities include a certain standard of physical health and robustness, some degree of intellectual ability, predispositions to have and manifest certain beliefs, attitudes, emotions and other character traits and the ability to form intentions, plan (even in a modest way), make commitments and reflect on one's life.[31] Second, in order to be autonomous, a person must live a life that is, to some sufficient degree, free of the coercion and manipulation of others, including of course the state.[32] As Raz argues, not only do coercion and

---

[29] See Macedo, above n 21, 220 and 225; George Sher, *Beyond Neutrality: Perfectionism and Politics* (Cambridge University Press, 1997), 47; Leslie Green, 'What Is Freedom For?' available on SSRN, abstract id 2193674.

[30] See Raz, *Morality of Freedom*, above n 19, 369, distinguishing between 'willingly endorsed pursuits' and 'free choice of goals and relations'.

[31] Ibid, 372–373; Raz, 'Autonomy, Toleration and the Harm Principle', above n 19, 323–324.

[32] Raz, *Morality of Freedom*, above n 19, 148–157, 205; Raz, 'Autonomy, Toleration and the Harm Principle', above n 19, 323–324.

manipulation interfere with the free choice that is characteristic of autonomous living; they also express contempt for the autonomy of the person at whom they are directed, and this in itself interferes with that autonomy.[33]

Third, and most importantly for present purposes, in order to be autonomous a person must have options to choose from in forging a path of self-determination in the world.[34] As choice is central to autonomy, and as choice can only be exercised between or among options, the availability of options is critical to autonomy. In Raz's view, it is not necessary to a person's autonomy that the range of options among which that person may choose be as large as possible, nor is it necessary (in ordinary cases) that any particular option be available to choose.[35] Instead, Raz argues that a person's autonomy depends on her having an 'adequate range' of options to choose from.[36] It seems clear enough that in circumstances where a person suffers significant hardship and, as a consequence, must make great physical and/or mental efforts in order just to cope from day to day, an adequate range of options is not available to that person.[37] But where such circumstances of hardship do not obtain, the question whether or not a range of options is adequate depends on a number of variables, including the character of the options,[38] the general social environment in which they are available[39] and whether the options in question make possible the pursuit of goals of central importance in a person's life or whether they are options of lesser significance to a person's overall well-being.[40]

In autonomy-based liberalism, autonomy is the core value but it is not the only value, nor is it the ultimate value. Raz describes autonomy as an 'enabling' value, the point of which is to 'enable people to engage with other values'.[41] The goodness of enabling values such as autonomy is

---

[33] Raz, *Morality of Freedom*, above n 19, 378.

[34] Ibid, 372; Raz, 'Autonomy, Toleration and the Harm Principle' above n 19, 324.

[35] Raz, *Morality of Freedom*, above n 19, 410–411.   [36] Ibid, 372.

[37] Ibid, 155, 205, 373–374. See also Jeremy Waldron, 'Homelessness and the Issue of Freedom' in his *Liberal Rights: Collected Papers 1981–1991* (Cambridge University Press, 1993) 309–338 and G.A. Cohen, 'Freedom and Money' in his *On the Currency of Egalitarian Justice and Other Essays in Political Philosophy* (Princeton University Press, 2011) 166–199, arguing that some forms of hardship deny people even negative liberty.

[38] Raz, *Morality of Freedom*, above n 19, 381.   [39] Ibid, 375.   [40] Ibid, 374, 376–377.

[41] Joseph Raz, *The Practice of Value* (with Christine Korsgaard, Robert Pippin and Bernard Williams, ed. R Jay Wallace, Oxford University Press, 2003) 36. See also Waldron, 'Autonomy and Perfectionism', above n 23, 1128–1129, discussing the 'aspiration to value' that is implicit in autonomous choices.

derivative; they derive their goodness from the values that they enable engagement with.[42] In the case of autonomy, its value is derived from the value of options chosen or voluntarily engaged with in other ways. In light of an understanding of autonomy as an enabling value, we may draw out three important elements of the conception of the good that is implied by autonomy-based liberalism. First, as it is only possible to conceive of an enabling value such as autonomy if one accepts the existence of values other than autonomy – for how else can autonomy serve its point of enabling engagement with such other values? – it is clear that autonomy is not a matter of unfettered choice or the satisfaction of personal preferences.[43] Instead, autonomy is a matter of self-directed engagement with goods whose goodness is established independently of their being chosen. Thus, the conception of the good implied by autonomy-based liberalism depends on the existence of what Derek Parfit calls 'facts about value';[44] it depends on objectivity in matters of value.[45] A second, related, element of an autonomy-based conception of the good also comes into relief in light of an understanding of autonomy as an enabling value: the derivative value of autonomy means that the autonomy of a person who chooses valueless or base options is itself without value to that extent. It follows that an adequate range of options need never include such valueless or base options, and this has implications for both personal ethics and political morality.[46]

A third element of an autonomy-based conception of the good that emerges from an understanding of autonomy as an enabling value is a commitment to value pluralism. Value pluralism, as a philosophical position, is associated with acceptance of two related propositions: first, that there are many distinct types of value; and second, that values can sometimes conflict, in the sense of being incompatible and

---

[42] Raz, *Morality of Freedom*, above n 19, 16–17, 380–381; Raz, 'Autonomy, Toleration and the Harm Principle', above n 19, 325–326; Raz, *Practice of Value*, above n 41, 35–36.

[43] See Sher, above n 29, ch 3.

[44] Derek Parfit, *Reasons and Persons* (Clarendon Press, Oxford, 1984), 499.

[45] Raz's own thinking on objectivity and value is more complex than this statement might suggest, largely on account of his beliefs about the social dependence of value: see Raz, *Practice of Value*, above n 41; Joseph Raz, *Engaging Reason: On the Theory of Value and Action* (Oxford University Press, 1999) chs 6–9; Joseph Raz, *Between Authority and Interpretation: On the Theory of Law and Practical Reason* (Oxford University Press, 2009), 305–306. Nonetheless, Raz's account of autonomy as an enabling value depends on there being facts about value, even if those facts are (as Raz thinks they are) heavily qualified by social contingencies.

[46] Raz, *Morality of Freedom*, above n 19, 381.

incommensurable with each other.[47] Thus understood, value pluralism may be contrasted philosophically with monism about value, which entails acceptance of the proposition that all values are to be understood as instances of some master value, as well as the proposition that values can never be incompatible or incommensurable. Perhaps the best-known examples of monist theories of value are the various strands of utilitarianism, according to which all questions of value may be reduced to questions about utility understood in one way or another.[48] In contrast, value pluralism characterises a range of theories of the good, from natural law theories, to objective list theories of other kinds, to Raz's liberal conception of the good. Acceptance of value pluralism is necessary to understanding how autonomy works as an enabling value;[49] it is only in light of value pluralism that a person can ever stand to make true choices among genuine options, as opposed to illusory choices among what are only ostensibly options. A person whose only options were to realise one master value in a variety of ways would lack an adequate range of options; indeed, in a sense she would lack any options at all.[50]

An appreciation of autonomy as a political ideal begins with the proposition that, in light of the value of autonomy, everyone has reasons to assist in bringing about and maintaining the conditions of autonomy. These reasons are reasons not only to refrain from coercing or manipulating others in ways that interfere with their negative liberty; they are also reasons to take positive or proactive steps to ensure that the conditions of autonomy are created and persist.[51] In other words, they are reasons to promote the conditions of autonomy. In Raz's thinking, reasons appealing to the ideal of autonomy can ground duties, owed by citizens to each other, to promote the conditions of autonomy; moreover, Raz thinks that such duties are owed by the state, constituted by the institutional arrangements of the political community, as much as they

---

[47] See generally Isaiah Berlin, 'The Decline of Utopian Ideas in the West' and 'Alleged Relativism in Eighteenth Century European Thought', both in his *The Crooked Timber of Humanity: Chapters in the History of Ideas* (ed Henry Hardy, Pimlico, London, 2003) 20–48 and 70–90 respectively; Charles Taylor, 'The Diversity of Goods' in his *Philosophy and the Human Sciences: Philosophical Papers 2* (Cambridge University Press, 1985) 230–247; Raz, *Practice of Value*, above n 41.

[48] For a monist theory of value that is not utilitarian: Ronald Dworkin, *Justice for Hedgehogs* (Belknap Press, Cambridge, MA, 2011).

[49] Raz, *Morality of Freedom*, above n 19, 161, 398–399.

[50] Ibid, 376. See also Berlin, 'Two Concepts of Liberty', above n 27, 166, 216–217.

[51] Raz, *Morality of Freedom*, above n 19, 407–408.

are owed by any citizen in that community.[52] Thus, for Raz, autonomy both justifies and demands state action.

That said, state action in order to promote the conditions of autonomy is subject to constraints.[53] For Raz, certain of these constraints arise in light of John Stuart Mill's celebrated 'harm principle': 'the only purpose for which power can be rightfully exercised over any member of a civilized community, against his will, is to prevent harm to others.'[54] Raz interprets the harm principle in light of the ideal of autonomy, so that it specifies constraints on state action whose true basis in political morality is to be found in the demands of that ideal.[55] According to Raz's interpretation, the harm principle specifies that the state may not deploy coercive power against a citizen except where this is necessary either in order to prevent that citizen from diminishing the autonomy of others or, in certain cases, in order to compel that citizen to take actions that are necessary to improve the conditions of autonomy for others.[56] In Raz's view, one can harm another either by making her worse off through impairing her autonomy or by failing in a duty to make her better off by furthering her autonomy, and the harm principle endorses coercive state action to prevent either type of harm.[57] By reinterpreting the harm principle in light of the demands of autonomy, Raz shows that that ideal illuminates both the point and the limits of state action, and to that extent grounds a unified conception of political morality.

4.   Charity law and the ideal of autonomy

As we saw earlier, it is reasonable to assume that the state uses charity law to promote charitable purposes. From the perspective of autonomy-based liberalism, one obvious question to ask about charity law is that of the extent to which the state's promotion of charitable purposes is justified and desirable in light of the political ideal of autonomy. And the answer to this question turns on the answers to at least two more specific questions. First, to what extent does the promotion of charitable purposes have the consequence of promoting the conditions of autonomy?

---

[52] Ibid, 407–408, 416, 417–418.
[53] One set of constraints, which will not be pursued further here, arises because of the limits of state authority: for Raz's account, see ibid, chs 2–4; Joseph Raz, 'The Problem of Authority: Revisiting the Service Conception' (2006) 90 *Minnesota Law Review* 1003.
[54] See John Stuart Mill, *On Liberty* (Longmans, Green & Co, London, 1865), 6.
[55] Raz, *Morality of Freedom*, above n 19, 412–424.   [56] Ibid, 415–417.   [57] Ibid.

To the extent that promoting charitable purposes does have such a consequence, then, all else being equal, charity law would seem to be both justified and desirable in light of the demands of autonomy. Second, to what extent, if at all, does the promotion of charitable purposes violate the harm principle, interpreted along Razian lines in light of the value of autonomy? To the extent that the harm principle, so understood, rules out the promotion of charitable purposes, charity law is unjustified in light of the demands of autonomy and should probably be discontinued. Let us consider each of these questions in turn.

A. Charitable purposes and the conditions of autonomy

We can only know the extent to which charity law is justified and desirable in light of the demands of autonomy once we know the extent to which the promotion of charitable purposes promotes the conditions of autonomy. In thinking about the extent to which the promotion of charitable purposes promotes the conditions of autonomy, several questions arise for consideration. Among them are questions about the extent to which promoting charitable purposes presents a more effective or more efficient way of promoting the conditions of autonomy than alternative strategies do. Will the conditions of autonomy be enhanced more by the promotion of charitable purposes than by the promotion of purposes of other types? Will those conditions be enhanced more by promoting charitable purposes via the facilitative, incentive and expressive strategies of charity law than via 'tax and spend' means? Are the conditions of autonomy more likely to be augmented by strategies that do not entail the promotion of purposes of any type but rather entail the state distributing resources to citizens to spend on such purposes as they please? These are questions about the choice and the boundaries of charity law, a topic that we will take up in Chapter 3. But before we can turn to the question of the extent to which the promotion of charitable purposes is an apt strategy for promoting the conditions of autonomy when compared with alternatives, we must first address a prior question: to what extent do the purposes that are identified as charitable in law themselves contribute to the conditions of autonomy?

Clearly, to the extent that charitable purposes make no contribution to the conditions of autonomy, promoting them via charity law can hardly be said to be autonomy-promoting, even if it is not – at least in the absence of any infringement of the harm principle – autonomy-hindering. If this is the case, then there seems little point in asking questions about whether promoting charitable purposes might be a better strategy than alternatives for promoting the conditions of autonomy. On the other hand, to the extent that charitable purposes do make a contribution to the conditions of autonomy, there is a prima facie case for thinking that promoting charitable purposes does promote the conditions of autonomy, subject to further inquiries into the effectiveness and efficiency of the state's promotion of charitable purposes as opposed to alternative strategies for promoting the conditions of autonomy. So in trying to ascertain the extent to which charity law is justified and desirable in light of the demands of autonomy, we should begin by reflecting on various types of charitable purpose and on the various goods – both private and public – that those different types of purpose are likely to realise, and we should then consider the ways in which those goods might contribute to the conditions of autonomy. Considering the question of the justification and desirability of charity law in light of the demands of autonomy thus requires, among other things, that we test the extent of connections between charitable purposes, goods and the conditions of autonomy.[58]

In this regard, the first point to note is that connections between charitable purposes, goods and the conditions of autonomy are more easily established in relation to some types of charitable purpose than they are in relation to other types of charitable purpose. There can be little doubt that purposes within the description 'relief of poverty' tend to generate substantial goods, and that these goods contribute to the conditions of autonomy in substantial ways, for example by ensuring that people can maintain the physical and mental capacities that are among the fundamental conditions of autonomy or by enabling people to be free from want and fear and thus situated so as to choose among options. Equally, purposes within the description 'advancement of education' tend to generate goods associated with the acquisition of knowledge and skills that are necessary in order both to access and to respond to options, and also help to constitute some options, such as being a student or a teacher. These are all substantial contributions to the conditions of autonomy. On the other hand, the connections between purposes within the description 'advancement of religion', goods and the conditions of autonomy are less clear, not least in light of the view expressed by some

---

[58] It also requires that we test such connections in respect of purposes that are not regarded as charitable in law but might come to be: see further the discussion of charity law's treatment of political purposes in Chapter 6.

philosophers that religious lives cannot be autonomous.[59] This is not to say that 'advancement of religion' describes purposes that make no contribution to the conditions of autonomy; indeed, as we will see in Chapter 5, quite the contrary is the case. It is simply to say that such connections as there are between religious purposes and the conditions of autonomy are not obvious or easily established. Similarly, it may prove difficult to establish connections between at least some purposes within the description 'promotion of . . . equality and diversity' in section 3(1) of the English Charities Act of 2011 and the conditions of autonomy. This is because it is conceivable that the promotion of equality and diversity might to some extent detract from the conditions of autonomy, say where it entails the promotion of non-autonomous ways of living.[60]

Because connections between charitable purposes, goods and the conditions of autonomy are more easily established in the case of some types of purpose than in the case of others, a consideration of the justification and desirability of charity law with the demands of autonomy in view may choose to pay particular attention to those types of purpose in respect of which the connections are not easily established, and may choose to pay less attention to the types of purpose in respect of which the connections are clear. This is the method that we will adopt in this book. We will assume that purposes to do with the relief and prevention of poverty, education, health care and support for the disabled and other disadvantaged people clearly contribute in substantial ways to the conditions of autonomy; the connections between such purposes, goods and the conditions of autonomy are sufficiently clear that the burden of argument falls on those who would deny them. Rather than focusing

---

[59] See, e.g., Michael J. Sandel, 'Religious Liberty – Freedom of Conscience or Freedom of Choice?' [1989] *Utah Law Review* 597; Michael J. Sandel, *Democracy's Discontent: America in Search of a Public Philosophy* (Belknap Press, Cambridge, MA, 1996), 65–71; Rex Ahdar and Ian Leigh, *Religious Freedom in the Liberal State* (Oxford University Press, 2005), 60–61; Sonu Bedi, 'Debate: What Is So Special About Religion?' (2007) 15 *The Journal of Political Philosophy* 235.

[60] See *Walz v. Tax Commission of the City of New York* 397 US 664 (1970) (US Supreme Court), 689 (Brennan J); *Bob Jones University v. US* 461 US 574 (1983) (US Supreme Court), 609 (Powell J); Rob Reich, 'Towards a Political Theory of Philanthropy' in Patricia Illingworth, Thomas Pogge and Leif Wenar (eds), *Giving Well: The Ethics of Philanthropy* (Oxford University Press, 2011) 177–195, for arguments suggesting that diversity might be the key value underpinning not-for-profit law (including charity law). From the perspective of autonomy-based liberalism, the diversity that charity law undoubtedly promotes is good only to the extent that it promotes the overarching liberal ideal of autonomy.

on cases where charitable purposes are obviously autonomy-promoting, we will concentrate on cases where the propensity of charitable purposes to promote the conditions of autonomy is not obvious. It is in these latter cases that an account of the justification and desirability of charity law informed by autonomy-based liberalism promises to do the most work. To this end, in Chapters 5 and 7, we will consider connections between charitable purposes, goods and the conditions of autonomy with reference to two types of purpose often identified as charitable in law and promoted on that basis, but not obviously autonomy-promoting: religious purposes and purposes that entail discrimination on grounds such as race, sex and religion.

One further point of a general nature might be made about the connections between charitable purposes, goods and the conditions of autonomy. As we have seen, the conditions of autonomy include an adequate range of options to choose from in living a self-determining life. The goods that help to constitute such options are in part excludable private goods such as education, employment, health care, books, holidays abroad, fine wines and so on. However, as Raz emphasises in his work, non-excludable public goods also make an important contribution to constituting an adequate range of options to choose from in living autonomously. As Raz points out, many options are simply inconceivable except against a rich backdrop of cultural institutions, practices, meanings and arrangements, many of which entail public goods going to the 'general character of . . . society'.[61] Such cultural public goods are numerous; they range from goods associated with living in a social setting in which there are institutions and arrangements such as the family, friendship and marriage, to goods associated with a culture of progress and achievement in science, the humanities and the arts, to goods associated with the existence of various professions, occupations, forms of association and leisure activities, to goods as elevated as a tolerant, respectful or educated society. The importance of cultural public goods to the provision and maintenance of an adequate range of options to choose from, and therefore to the conditions of autonomy, cannot be overstated. Such goods generate social meaning, help to condition and define more

---

[61] Raz, *Morality of Freedom*, above n 19, 199, 205–207, 308–313 (the quotation is at 198–199). See also Joseph Chan, 'Legitimacy, Unanimity and Perfectionism' (2000) 29 *Philosophy and Public Affairs* 5, 29, describing the dependence of many options on social conditions as a 'sociological truism'.

specific instances of value[62] and make available ways in which to engage with particular goods.[63] On this view, the very existence of many options as more or less individuated objects of choice is largely contingent on cultural public goods; 'being a dentist', 'following opera', 'playing football' and 'being politically active' are all examples of options that are contingently related to cultural public goods in this way. Indeed, in Raz's thinking, the importance of cultural public goods leads him to the limits of liberalism: he goes so far as to elevate 'common culture' alongside 'individual action' in the 'shaping of the moral world'.[64]

In light of the significant contribution that cultural public goods make to the conditions of autonomy, the general point to be made about the connections between charitable purposes, goods and the conditions of autonomy is this: many of the purposes that are regarded as charitable in law seem to generate cultural public goods, and to the extent that these cultural public goods play a role in the framing and constitution of options that may be the subject of autonomous choice, a connection between many charitable purposes, goods and the conditions of autonomy may be established. To the extent that charitable purposes generate cultural public goods, we might view the state's promotion of charitable purposes as a contribution to the liberal project of building and maintaining a certain sort of society, viz, a society with an autonomy-promoting culture. Indeed, if charitable purposes invariably generate cultural public goods, then from a perspective informed by autonomy-based liberalism, there may be some unity to charity law in the sense that it is justified and desirable as a matter of political morality because of a particular contribution that it makes to an autonomy-promoting society. In order to adopt this view of charity law, it would be necessary to construct convincing arguments drawing connections between different types of charitable purpose and cultural public goods. There will not be space enough in this book to explore such arguments in respect of all the different types of charitable purpose. However, the prospect of mounting such arguments successfully seems not to be a remote one.

A brief look at section 3(1) of the English Charities Act of 2011 – a typical modern statutory expression of general descriptions of charitable

---

[62] Including the value of autonomy itself: see Charles Taylor, 'Atomism' in his *Philosophy and the Human Sciences: Philosophical Papers 2* (Cambridge University Press, 1985) 187–210, esp 204–205.

[63] Raz, *Morality of Freedom*, above n 19, 198–199, 207, 247, 250, 254–255.

[64] Ibid, 193.

purpose – should help us to think through the prospects for arguments connecting different types of charitable purpose and cultural public goods. Among the general descriptions to be found there are 'advancement of citizenship or community development', 'advancement of the arts, culture, heritage or science', 'advancement of amateur sport', 'advancement of . . . conflict resolution or reconciliation or the promotion of religious or racial harmony' and 'advancement of environmental protection or improvement'. These types of purpose relate in a fairly direct way to the general character of society; they contribute to the creation and maintenance of the sorts of cultural institutions, practices and other arrangements that themselves create social meaning and give form and content to individuated options in other ways. They are, to this extent, likely to generate the cultural public goods on which the conditions of autonomy depend.[65] On the other hand, the propensity of some types of charitable purpose listed in section 3(1) of the English Charities Act to generate cultural public goods seems obscure; for example, 'advancement of animal welfare' appears not to relate to goods for human beings at all. In other cases, the autonomy-promoting character of types of charitable purpose in section 3(1) seems to be grasped most directly by focusing on private goods that they yield. For example, purposes within the description 'relief of poverty' contribute to the conditions of autonomy most obviously by making a difference to the lives of the poor; similarly, there are direct connections between educational purposes, goods and the conditions of autonomy via the substantial private goods that education entails. And in other cases again, the autonomy-promoting character of purposes in section 3(1) is at least partly a matter of their propensity to generate non-cultural public goods; for example, the purposes within the description 'promotion of the efficiency of the armed forces of the Crown or the efficiency of the police, fire and rescue services or ambulance services' are most obviously autonomy-promoting via the production of non-cultural public goods such as safety and security.

At first glance, then, the prospects for arguments drawing connections between different types of charitable purposes and cultural public goods seem mixed. However, we should remember that to discern the autonomy-promoting character of a type of charitable purpose without

---

[65] See also the argument in Rob Atkinson, 'Re-Focusing on Philanthropy: Revising and Re-Orienting the Standard Model' (2012) 4 *William and Mary Policy Review* 1, 2, asserting that philanthropy's 'most distinctive function' is 'providing global value systems'.

pointing to cultural public goods is not to rule out the possibility that cultural public goods stand to be produced by that type of charitable purpose. Indeed, there are reasons to think that there are cultural public goods associated with many types of charitable purpose that also generate autonomy-promoting private goods or non-cultural public goods. For example, there is an argument that relieving people from poverty or educating people contributes to the creation of social conditions that benefit all members of society and not only those whose poverty is relieved or who receive the education in question;[66] similarly, the armed forces and various emergency services are public institutions and as such it is arguable that their operations stand to produce cultural public goods in addition to the non-cultural public goods that are their raison d'être. In addition, we should be sensitive to the possibility that a purpose that appears not to generate autonomy-promoting goods at all might, on closer inspection, turn out to generate public goods that are both autonomy-promoting and cultural in character. Thus, while purposes within the description 'advancement of animal welfare' seem not to generate goods that are autonomy-promoting in any obvious way, it is arguable that such purposes contribute to the development and maintenance of a public good in the form of a culture of humanity,[67] and that such a cultural public good makes an important contribution to the conditions under which people may exercise autonomy or even simply enjoy negative liberty.

B.   Charity law and the harm principle

From the perspective of autonomy-based liberalism, the state's promotion of charitable purposes is justified only to the extent that it does not violate the harm principle as interpreted along Razian lines in light of the demands of autonomy. To the extent that the state's promotion of charitable purposes is within the range of state action that is prohibited by the harm principle, so understood, charity law is unjustified in view of the liberal ideal of autonomy – even if, apart from violating the harm principle, the promotion of charitable purposes can be shown to promote

---

[66] See, in respect of the relief of poverty, Liam Murphy and Thomas Nagel, 'Taxes, Redistribution, and Public Provision' (2001) 30 *Philosophy and Public Affairs* 53, 64; Liam Murphy and Thomas Nagel, *The Myth of Ownership: Taxes and Justice* (Oxford University Press, 2002), 87.

[67] This is recognised in charity law: *In re Wedgwood* [1915] 1 Ch 113 (Court of Appeal).

the conditions of autonomy. So it is important to know, with the demands of autonomy in view, the extent to which – if at all – the harm principle constrains the state's promotion of charitable purposes. When considering the sorts of state action entailed in charity law in light of the harm principle, the first point to note is that the harm principle, as understood by Raz and also by Mill, is a principle about the circumstances in which the state is justified in deploying coercive power against citizens. Thus understood, the harm principle has nothing to say about state action that is not coercive; it does not rule out any state action which adopts non-coercive strategies.[68] This is significant when thinking about the likely application of the harm principle to charity law, because the promotion of charitable purposes that is at the core of charity law occurs in accordance with strategies that are non-coercive in character. In a sense, of course, all state action may be said to be coercive, in that the state could not exist except for its coercive powers. However, while this is true in a general and ultimate sense, in the setting of the day-to-day engagement of the state and its citizens it is possible, indeed helpful, to draw a meaningful distinction between state actions that are coercive in aim and state actions that are not coercive in aim.[69] It is in light of this distinction that it may be said that the core project of charity law occurs in accordance with non-coercive strategies. We encountered these strategies in Chapter 1: they are the facilitative, incentive and expressive strategies entailed in the extension of legal privileges of various sorts to those with charitable purposes. To the extent that charity law works by such facilitative, incentive and expressive strategies, the harm principle, understood as a constraint on coercive state action, has nothing to say about it.

It might be objected that this dispenses with matters a little too quickly. Consider the tax privileges of charity law. As we have seen, by extending these privileges to those who pursue charitable purposes, the state may fairly be taken to aim to provide incentives to citizens, in the sense of giving citizens reasons to choose to pursue charitable purposes that they would otherwise lack.[70] The provision of these incentives is a

---

[68] Raz, *Morality of Freedom*, above n 19, 417–418. Of course, state action might be ruled out for other reasons, say because it exceeds the limits of state authority.

[69] See H.L.A. Hart, *The Concept of Law* (3rd edn, Clarendon Press, Oxford, 2012) ch 3.

[70] In fact, historically, it would seem to be far from clear what aims law-makers have consciously had in mind when making available the tax privileges of charity law: see Ann O'Connell, 'Charitable Treatment? – A Short History of the Taxation of Charities in Australia' in John Tiley (ed), *Studies in the History of Tax Law: Volume 5*

non-coercive strategy and, to that extent, it does not seem to violate the harm principle, conceptualised along Razian lines. However, it might be objected that coercive action is not the only sort of action in which the harm principle should take an interest, and that the provision of incentives in the form of the tax privileges of charity law is an instance of the sort of non-coercive action which ought to be of concern in light of the harm principle. In a critical review of Raz's book, *The Morality of Freedom*, Jeremy Waldron writes that 'an autonomous decision may be undermined not only by overt coercion from the outside, but also by interfering with the way people form their beliefs about value. Messing with options that one faces, changing one's pay offs can be seen as manipulation along these lines'.[71] In other words, for Waldron, autonomy is impaired not only by coercion but also by manipulation of an autonomous person's self-directed engagement with value in the form of interference with her reasons; indeed, Raz also recognises this in his discussion of the conditions of autonomy, when he discusses freedom from coercion *and* manipulation as an important dimension of those conditions.[72]

If autonomy is impaired by manipulation in the way Waldron describes, then any interpretation of the harm principle that grounds it in the demands of autonomy ought to construe it as a principle that constrains state action that is either coercive or manipulative. The problem for the state's provision of incentives in the form of the tax privileges of charity law is that this appears to be an instance of manipulation along the lines described by Waldron. Those incentives, insofar as they constitute state-given reasons to pursue charitable purposes, have a tendency to interfere with or distort the process by which citizens choose whether or not to pursue charitable purposes in light of the independent reasons for and against doing so. If autonomy is impaired by manipulation as well as by coercion, the harm principle should rule out the state's use of such incentives, unless this is necessary to prevent those who might, in the absence of the incentives, choose not to pursue charitable purposes from thereby harming others either by diminishing their autonomy or by

---

(Hart Publishing, Oxford, 2012) 91–124. That said, if we are to make sense of those tax privileges within a liberal theory of charity law, we must try to attribute some aim or aims to those who legislated to bring them about and, as was suggested earlier in this chapter, it seems reasonable to attribute an incentive aim to them.

[71] Waldron, 'Autonomy and Perfectionism', above n 23, 1145. For a similar argument see Lecce, above n 11, 122–123.

[72] Raz, *Morality of Freedom*, above n 19, 377–378.

failing in a duty to promote their autonomy. As it seems implausible to suggest that a person's failure to pursue charitable purposes constitutes either a diminution of the autonomy of others or a failure to discharge a duty to promote the autonomy of others, this leaves the incentives of charity law in violation of the harm principle.

Do the incentives of charity law really manipulate citizens in the way Waldron describes? At least two arguments might be made to cast doubt on the idea that those incentives manipulate citizens and therefore to cast doubt on the idea that at least some of the non-coercive strategies of charity law entail the sort of state action that should attract the harm principle. First, it might be argued that when a person is incentivised to do something that she has independent reasons to do, it does not necessarily follow that she has not acted for those independent reasons. She may have acted for reasons generated by the incentive as well as independent reasons. Indeed, an incentive may prove efficacious precisely because it causes a person to be more responsive to independent reasons than she would otherwise have been, say because it motivates her to overcome dispositions – such as laziness or indifference – that might have interfered with her responsiveness to independent reasons.[73] Second, it might be argued that, even if it is accepted that incentives might have some effect on the responsiveness to independent reasons that is characteristic of autonomy, incentives also tend to encourage people to act such that they come to be in positions from which they are better able to understand and engage with independent reasons that apply to them.[74] A person might initially get involved in the pursuit of some charitable purpose because of the incentives of charity law but, as she pursues the purpose in question over time, she may come to appreciate and act for independent reasons to pursue the purpose – reasons that may be largely to do with the values that pursuing the purpose is likely to realise. In circumstances like these, the argument goes, far from interfering with the process by which a person who chooses to pursue a charitable purpose engages in a self-directed way with the values associated with that pursuit, the incentives of charity law facilitate that engagement.

---

[73] See Thomas Hurka, *Perfectionism* (Oxford University Press, New York, 1993), 159–160, 189. Indeed, Waldron seems to concede this point in part: Waldron, 'Autonomy and Perfectionism', above n 23, 1147.

[74] An argument to this effect is made by Sher, above n 29, 63–64.

If it turns out that the state action entailed in charity law violates the harm principle by manipulating citizens, that part of charity law that extends various legal privileges to those who pursue charitable purposes should be reformed. The incentives of charity law, most notably the tax privileges of charity law, should be abolished. The practice of expressing endorsement of charitable purposes and those who carry them out might also require close scrutiny, for, as well as having expressive value, such endorsement may itself serve as an incentive to those deciding whether or not to pursue charitable purposes. The rules conferring validity, perpetuity and other advantages on trusts for charitable purposes, on the other hand, might not require reform; rather than constituting state-given reasons to pursue charitable purposes, such facilitative rules enable those who have already determined that the balance of reasons is in favour of pursuing charitable purposes to do so in specific ways. If nothing else, if it is possible that the incentives of charity law manipulate citizens in violation of the harm principle, we should probably think about the state action entailed in charity law as divided into two categories: the promotion of charitable purposes by facilitative and expressive means that do not violate the harm principle, and the promotion of charitable purposes by incentive means that do violate that principle. This would enable us to isolate and deal with the dimensions of charity law that are of concern from a liberal point of view without at the same time jeopardising those dimensions of charity law that are both justified and desirable from a liberal point of view. But, of course, any such reconsideration of the state action entailed in charity law rests on the assumption that charity law, via its incentive strategies, does manipulate citizens in violation of the harm principle; if the arguments canvassed earlier about the role that incentives play in practical reasoning are sound, this is an assumption that we may not have to make.

5.   Public discourse, autonomy and 'benefit' in charity law

So far, we have been thinking about charity law from the perspective of autonomy-based liberalism by thinking about questions relating to the justification and desirability of the state action entailed in the design and administration of that body of law. With the demands of autonomy in view, such questions are preoccupied with the effects or consequences of charity law: the social consequences, understood in terms of autonomy, that flow from the state's promotion of charitable purposes on the one hand and the individual consequences, again understood in terms of autonomy, that result from the impact of the facilitative, expressive and incentive strategies of charity law on those who would pursue purposes of various descriptions on the other. Up to this point, we have not considered from the perspective of autonomy-based liberalism the question of the justification and desirability of the content of charity law, and in particular of the criteria by which it is determined whether or not a purpose is charitable in law and the rules that disqualify certain purposes from being charitable. In order to think about the content of charity law, we must shift our focus away from the effects or consequences of charity law and towards the reasoning in which decision-makers engage when deciding whether or not – and, most importantly, why or why not – some purpose or type of purpose is charitable in law. This, in turn, demands that we develop a sense, from the perspective of autonomy-based liberalism, of aspirations for public discourse – aspirations against which the reasoning of decision-makers in the charity law setting may be evaluated.

Liberal aspirations for public discourse are often associated with John Rawls's account of political liberalism, which we touched on earlier in this chapter. In political liberalism, aspirations for public discourse take the form of an ideal that Rawls calls 'public reason'; this ideal entails a 'duty of civility' in accordance with which citizens refrain from offering, as reasons for political action, reasons that may be accepted only by the holders of one or some, as opposed to all, conceptions of the good.[75] As we saw earlier in the chapter, Rawls's ideal of public reason applies only to public discourse on the topics of 'constitutional essentials' and 'matters of basic justice' and thus appears to have little to say about much of the reasoning of decision-makers in the charity law setting. But the fact that Rawls's account of political liberalism is largely irrelevant to charity law does not mean that liberal aspirations for public discourse have no potential as evaluative tools when considering the content of charity law. Indeed, autonomy-based liberalism would seem naturally to deliver just such aspirations. After all, the value of autonomy gives us all reasons to promote it; one way of promoting autonomy is to express respect for it when offering to other people reasons for those of our actions that might affect their autonomy in some way, and one way of expressing this sort of respect for autonomy is to offer, as reasons for our autonomy-affecting actions, reasons that reflect a conception of the good grounded in the value of autonomy. At the very least, the value of autonomy demands

---

[75] For Rawls's fullest statement of the ideal of public reason see Rawls, 'Idea of Public Reason Revisited', above n 7.

that we refrain from expressing disrespect for autonomy by offering, as reasons for our autonomy-affecting actions, reasons that undermine or are inconsistent with an autonomy-based conception of the good. The reasons we all have to express respect for the value of autonomy, when giving reasons for our autonomy-affecting actions, apply no less to the giving of reasons by office-holders in the institutions of the political community than they do to individual citizens in their private inter-actions with each other. In other words, they apply no less to public discourse than to private discourse.

In light of these autonomy-based aspirations for public discourse, decision-makers in the charity law setting have reasons to express respect for autonomy in their reasoning, and that reasoning stands to be evalu-ated, in light of the demands of autonomy, with reference to the extent to which it expresses or fails to express such respect. One way of carrying out such an evaluative exercise might be to ask: to what extent is the reasoning of decision-makers in the charity law setting consistent with an understanding that the liberal justification and desirability of the state's promotion of charitable purposes turns, at least in part, on the propensity of those purposes to promote the conditions of autonomy? Given that reasoning in the charity law setting is largely about whether or not the criteria of charity law are met on the facts of an individual case or whether or not some disqualifying rule applies to the purpose of an organisation, such inquiries should focus on the reasons given for making decisions about whether or not purposes are charitable in law in accordance with those criteria and rules. Obviously, given that decision-makers are not typically political philosophers, we should not be looking for reasoning in charity law cases that explicitly makes the sorts of connections between charitable purposes, goods and the condi-tions of autonomy that we have been exploring in this chapter. Instead, we might rest satisfied that such reasoning expresses respect for auton-omy where it reflects the general contours or architecture of a liberal conception of the good grounded in the value of autonomy, or where it makes connections between charitable purposes and goods that, once subjected to philosophical scrutiny, turn out to make a contribution to the conditions of autonomy in one way or another.

The overview of charity law presented in Chapter 1 was hopefully sufficient to demonstrate that decision-makers' reasoning about the criteria and disqualifying rules of charity law is rich in content. In the case of the criteria of charity law, decision-makers have engaged in careful and sustained reasoning on numerous occasions as to: the reasons why certain general descriptions of purpose should be regarded as charitable while others should be excluded from sets of general descriptions of charitable purpose; the types of case in which factual inquiries should be eschewed or presumptions applied when working with the criteria of charity law; whether or not, and why, some purpose or type of purpose might fall within or outside one or another general description of charitable purpose; the meaning of 'public' and 'benefit' in the setting of the public benefit test of charity law; and whether or not a particular purpose satisfies the 'public' or the 'benefit' component of the public benefit test, among other matters. Moreover, much ink has been spilt by decision-makers in dealing with questions relating to disqualifying rules, such as the justification and proper parameters of the rule against political purposes and how to distinguish between government and charity for the purposes of charity law. Decision-makers' reasoning on any one of these topics would provide fruitful material for an evaluative exercise in light of autonomy-based aspirations for public discourse. For now, let us pursue just one aim: that of exploring the extent to which the content of charity law, insofar as it relates to questions of 'benefit', appears to be consistent with liberal aspirations for public discourse understood with reference to the value of autonomy. Let us do so by making three observations of a general nature about the reasoning of decision-makers on the topic of the 'benefit' component of the public benefit test. This will be far from an exhaustive treatment of the extent to which the content of the 'benefit' component of the public benefit test is consistent with autonomy-based aspirations for public discourse, but hopefully it will perform some of the groundwork for a liberal theory of 'benefit' in the charity law setting with reference to such aspirations. We will have occasion to return to liberal aspirations for public discourse in the setting of the 'benefit' component of the public benefit test in Chapters 5 and 7.

The first observation assumes, with Raz, that autonomy is an 'enabling' value, the point of which is to enable engagement with other values. Recall from earlier in the chapter that three elements of an autonomy-based conception of the good flow from the recognition of autonomy as an 'enabling' value: first, objectivity about value; second, a commitment to the proposition that an adequate range of options need never include valueless or base options; and finally, a commitment to value pluralism. With autonomy-based aspirations for public discourse in view, we might wish to know the extent to which the reasoning of decision-makers in the charity law setting reflects or is consistent with these three elements of an autonomy-based conception of the good. To the extent that there is such consistency, it would seem that decision-makers in the charity law setting reason about value in ways that are apt to promote the conditions of autonomy – assuming that autonomy is an 'enabling' value – and to this extent, we might conclude that there are reasons to think that the reasoning of decision-makers in the charity law setting in some respects lives up to liberal aspirations for public discourse.

To what extent does the reasoning of decision-makers in the charity law setting reflect the three elements of an autonomy-based conception of the good that emerge from the recognition of autonomy as an 'enabling' value? Based on the overview of charity law that was presented in Chapter 1, there are reasons to think that, when designing and applying charity law, decision-makers reason in ways that are substantially consistent with all three elements of such a conception of the good. To begin with, as we saw in Chapter 1, decision-makers mostly insist on adopting an attitude of objectivity when making findings of benefit in the setting of the public benefit test; this objectivity is manifested in the refusal of decision-makers to defer to the beliefs about benefit of those who would do charity. Moreover, the objectivity of decision-makers when considering the question of benefit sometimes leads them to find that a purpose is not charitable because it stands to generate disvalue; this sort of reasoning is consistent with the proposition that certain purposes are likely to produce consequences that should not be promoted by the state in view of the demands of autonomy. For example, in Chapter 1 we saw that in the case of *Re Pinion (deceased)*, the English Court of Appeal refused to recognise a testamentary trust as charitable because its purpose was to display to the public a collection of art and furniture that was in the opinion of Harman LJ 'junk';[76] we also saw that in the same case Harman LJ expressed the view, *obiter dicta*, that a library of pornography could not be charitable.[77] And finally the refusal of decision-makers to reason reductively about benefit when designing and applying charity law – a refusal that, as we saw in Chapter 1, characterises even the *Anti-Vivisection* case in which Lord Wright toyed with utilitarian thinking[78] – is consistent with value pluralism. These characteristics of decision-makers' reasoning when working with the 'benefit' component of the public benefit test indicate that, in important ways, the content of

---

[76] [1964] 1 All ER 890 (Court of Appeal), 893–894 (Harman LJ).   [77] Ibid, 893.

[78] *National Anti-Vivisection Society* v. *Inland Revenue Commissioners* [1948] AC 31 (House of Lords), 48–49 (Lord Wright).

charity law reflects thinking about value that is consistent with autonomy-based aspirations for public discourse.

A second observation relates to the fact that, as we saw in Chapter 1, in at least some cases, and in certain jurisdictions in many cases, decision-makers either decline to investigate questions of benefit as questions of fact or apply a presumption of benefit when making findings on the question of benefit in the setting of the public benefit test. These techniques indicate a relatively low level of scepticism on the part of the state that the purposes to which they are applied are likely to generate benefit. In cases about purposes within the descriptions 'relief of poverty' or 'advancement of education', the application of such techniques is arguably consistent with aspirations for public discourse informed by the value of autonomy, because the propensity of such purposes to generate autonomy-promoting goods is clear. However, it is also arguable that where decision-makers refuse to investigate questions of benefit as questions of fact or apply a presumption of benefit in 'advancement of religion' cases, their techniques are less readily justifiable in light of autonomy-based aspirations for public discourse.

In Chapter 1, we encountered the case of *Holmes* v. *Attorney-General*, in which Walton J applied a presumption of benefit in finding that the purposes of the Exclusive Brethren were charitable, notwithstanding that there was some evidence before him that the group harmed its members in certain ways.[79] We also noted the 2014 decision of the Charity Commission for England and Wales to register Preston Down Trust as a charity, a decision in which the Charity Commission was not permitted to apply any presumption of benefit and therefore considered evidence of possible benefits and detriments associated with the beliefs and practices of the Plymouth Brethren Christian Church (a denomination historically connected with the Exclusive Brethren), before concluding that there was sufficient evidence of benefit to satisfy the 'benefit' component of the public benefit test.[80] The application of a presumption of benefit in *Holmes* v. *Attorney-General*, in place of a more detailed consideration of the available evidence including the evidence of harm, may have been inconsistent with a liberal conception of the good grounded in the value of autonomy; it is, after all, possible that the evidence of harm was evidence that the group interfered with its members in ways that diminished their autonomy. In contrast, the detailed consideration of evidence

---

[79] *The Times* (London), 12 February 1981, 8.
[80] Charity Commission for England and Wales, *Preston Down Trust* (3 January 2014).

of benefits and detriments in *Preston Down Trust* seems consistent with an autonomy-based conception of the good, especially as much of the evidence of detriment in that case was evidence that the beliefs and practices of the Plymouth Brethren Christian Church interfered in different ways with the autonomy of its past and present members. Thus, we have reasons to think that the reasoning in *Preston Down Trust* is more easily justified than the reasoning in *Holmes* v. *Attorney-General* in light of liberal aspirations for public discourse, because it expressed greater respect for the value of autonomy. At the same time, however, both *Holmes* v. *Attorney-General* and *Preston Down Trust* suggest that from the perspective of autonomy-based liberalism, the question of the justification of eschewing factual inquiries into or presuming benefit in 'advancement of religion' cases is likely to be a difficult one, demanding close study of the ways in which religion promotes the conditions of autonomy and the ways in which it does not. We will return to this difficult question in Chapter 5.

Finally, in Chapter 1 we saw that decision-makers in the charity law setting consider that the public benefit test is satisfied where purposes stand to produce either (or both) of two types of goods: excludable private goods, so long as they are available to a public class, and non-excludable public goods. In that chapter, we examined the jurisprudence establishing the link between the production of non-excludable public goods and satisfaction of the public benefit test in the course of a discussion about the 'public' component of that test. Now it is time to draw out another dimension of that jurisprudence: where the jurisprudence reveals decision-makers making findings of public benefit on the basis that purposes stand to realise public goods, it often reveals reasoning about the 'benefit' component of the public benefit test that seems consistent with a liberal conception of the good grounded in the value of autonomy. Recall that, in such a conception of the good, cultural public goods – non-excludable goods going to the general character of society – make a significant contribution to the conditions of autonomy, and in particular make a significant contribution to constituting the options on which autonomy depends. Where findings of public benefit in charity law appeal to public goods, they are often the product of reasoning as to benefit that is consistent with the view that cultural public goods make this significant contribution to the conditions of autonomy. In Chapter 1, we encountered findings of public benefit under the fourth 'head' of the *Pemsel* set that appealed to cultural public goods such as a culture of humanity,[81] advances in medical research,[82] the effective functioning of the legal system[83] and the market economy and commercial activity.[84] Recognition of such cultural public goods may also be discerned in the case law about purposes falling under other general descriptions of charitable purpose; for example, in *Royal Choral Society* v. *Inland Revenue Commissioners*, an 'advancement of education' case, Lord Greene MR found the Society to be charitable on the basis that it was 'established for the purpose of raising the artistic taste of the country'.[85] To the extent that cultural public goods do in fact contribute to the conditions of autonomy – and in the case of each of the examples just given, there are reasons to think that they do – the reasoning of decision-makers who ground findings of public benefit in those public goods is consistent with what autonomy-based liberalism has to say about the conditions of autonomy.

Before concluding this brief consideration of the 'benefit' component of the public benefit test in light of the demands of autonomy-based aspirations for public discourse, we should return to a type of case that we first encountered in Chapter 1: the case where a purpose entails the provision of private goods to a private class and, to that extent, does not benefit the public, but also stands to realise incidental public goods. As we saw in Chapter 1, in some cases of this type, the public benefit test of charity law has been satisfied based on the perceived propensity of the purpose in question to generate such incidental public goods: cases such as *Re Resch's Will Trusts* and *Neville Estates Ltd* v. *Madden* would appear to constitute examples.[86] And in some of these cases, the incidental public goods have been cultural public goods. With autonomy-based aspirations for public discourse in view, then, and given that the

---

[81] *In re Wedgwood* [1915] 1 Ch 113 (Court of Appeal).

[82] *National Anti-Vivisection* Society v. *Inland Revenue Commissioners* [1948] AC 31 (House of Lords).

[83] *Incorporated Council of Law Reporting of the State of Queensland* v. *Federal Commissioner of Taxation* (1971) 125 CLR 659 (High Court of Australia).

[84] *Crystal Palace Trustees* v. *Minister of Town and Country Planning* [1951] Ch 132 (Danckwerts J).

[85] [1943] 2 All ER 101 (Court of Appeal), 105. See also *Re Delius' Will* [1957] 1 All ER 854 (Roxburgh J).

[86] *Re Resch's Will Trusts, Le Cras* v. *Perpetual Trustee Co Ltd* [1968] 1 AC 514 (Privy Council); *Neville Estates Ltd* v. *Madden* [1962] 1 Ch 832 (Cross J). It is appropriate to speak here of 'perceived' propensity because, as we will see in Chapter 5, in the case of *Neville Estates Ltd* v. *Madden* it is unlikely that the perceived public goods in question were goods at all.

production and subsistence of cultural public goods are of great importance to ensuring that the conditions of autonomy obtain in a society, we
might hope to see decision-makers in the charity law setting exhibiting a
willingness to find purposes charitable, notwithstanding that they entail
the provision of private goods to a private class, in circumstances where
they stand to realise cultural public goods. Moreover, any augmentation
of this willingness that might be detected over the course of time might
be considered to be a welcome development in charity law. In this regard,
it is noteworthy that in its recent decision in the *Independent Schools
Council* case, the Upper Tribunal (Tax and Chancery) for England and
Wales exhibited scepticism towards the argument that the purpose of
educating children of the rich, even if it is a purpose entailing the
provision of private goods to a private class, might nonetheless generate
incidental cultural public goods associated with an educated popula-
tion.[87] From a perspective that is sensitive to the great contribution of
cultural public goods to the conditions of autonomy for all of the
members of a community, this scepticism towards the wider or indirect
benefits of education seems at least questionable, raising the possibility
that in light of liberal aspirations for public discourse, the reasoning of
the Upper Tribunal on the question of 'benefit' in the *Independent
Schools Council* case might – in one respect at least – have fallen short
of the mark.

6. Conclusion

In Chapter 1 we saw that charity law is complex, addressing questions
about the character of purposes and the status of organisations in
accordance with criteria and rules, as well as the legal consequences of
carrying out purposes of one type or another; we saw that charity law
entails facilitative, incentive and expressive strategies, found in the law of
trusts, tax law and regulatory law, deployed in the service of an overarching project of promoting charitable purposes. Now we are in a position to
see that a liberal theory of charity law must be complex as well, navigating and responding to the complexity of its subject matter. Ideally, such a
theory should not confine itself to questions of social justice as they arise
in the charity law setting; rather, it should be responsive to the state's
promotion of charitable purposes irrespective of consequences in justice.

---

[87] R *(Independent Schools Council)* v. *Charity Commission for England and Wales* [2012] 2
WLR 100 (Upper Tribunal), [111]–[112].

Nor should a liberal theory of charity law respond to charity law's non-neutral character by declaring it misguided, at least to the extent that we think there is sufficient value in charity law's non-neutral aspects to hold open the question of their justification *qua* non-neutral. In this chapter we have seen that, in light of these theoretical aims, autonomy-based liberalism is an attractive candidate in which to ground a liberal theory of charity law. We have also done some of the work of developing such a theory by considering questions about charitable purposes, goods and the conditions of autonomy and charity law and the harm principle, and by applying autonomy-based aspirations for public discourse to the reasoning of decision-makers who work with the 'benefit' component of the public benefit test. But most importantly, we now have a liberal perspective to work with in addressing the many questions about charity law and the liberal state that this chapter has left unanswered. Addressing some of those questions will be our task in the remainder of this book.

3

The choice and the boundaries of charity law

1. Introduction

As the title of Chapter 2 suggested, the arguments of that chapter worked towards a liberal theory of charity law, rather than constituting such a theory. Those arguments pointed to some considerations that ought to be taken into account when thinking, from a liberal perspective, about the extent to which the state's promotion of charitable purposes is justified and desirable as a matter of political morality; moreover, they appealed to liberal aspirations for public discourse that may be deployed in evaluating the reasoning of decision-makers on the question of 'benefit' in the setting of the public benefit test. However, the arguments of Chapter 2 had little to say about why the state might choose to promote charitable purposes via the facilitative, incentive and expressive strategies of charity law and not in some other way, for example by direct 'tax and spend' means. Nor did Chapter 2 address one key question about the boundaries or limits of charity law that comes into view once it is accepted that the justification and desirability of the state's promotion of charitable purposes turns, at least in part, on the extent to which charitable purposes promote the conditions of autonomy: why does the state promote only some autonomy-promoting purposes via charity law and not others? Finally, Chapter 2 had nothing to say about the 'public' component of the public benefit test, perhaps the most litigated and controversial part of charity law; nor did it have anything to say about the disqualifying rules of charity law. Why does the state promote as charitable only purposes that in some sense are 'public' purposes, and what can be said about the conception of 'public' that figures in charity law? Why must charitable purposes pass the tests set out in disqualifying rules like the 'not for profit' rule or the rule against governmental purposes?

These questions about the choice and the boundaries of charity law are our focus in this chapter. First, the chapter will consider why the state might choose to promote charitable purposes via the facilitative, incentive and expressive strategies of charity law and not directly via 'tax and spend' means. We will see that, from the perspective of autonomy-based liberalism, the reasons underpinning the choice of charity law have to do with the conditions of autonomy for those who wish to pursue charitable purposes. We will also see that these reasons might help to explain the desirability of one of the disqualifying rules of charity law, the rule against governmental purposes, and might inform an evaluative framework with which to approach the state's dealings with charities, especially through funding agreements. Second, the chapter will address the question of why, via charity law, the state promotes only some autonomy-promoting purposes and not others. Here, we will see that the boundaries of charity law, as between different autonomy-promoting purposes, reveal the state taking an interest in altruism; this interest is manifested both in the 'public' component of the public benefit test and in another of the disqualifying rules of charity law, the 'not for profit' rule. Finally, the chapter will examine why the state might take an interest in altruism in the charity law setting, and will explore the idea that the state's interest in altruism in that setting is more precisely described as an interest in promoting a culture in which citizens are both able and encouraged to act altruistically. The chapter will argue that promoting altruism in this way serves the autonomy of citizens and to that extent is justified in light of autonomy-based liberalism, all else being equal.

2. The choice of charity law

The state could choose to promote charitable purposes in several ways.[1] Extending to those with charitable purposes the legal privileges of charity described in Chapter 1 is one such way, but it is not the only one. In other words, the particular blend of facilitative, incentive and expressive strategies that characterises modern charity law is not the only option available to the state in promoting charitable purposes. One could imagine a

---

[1] The state could also choose not to promote charitable purposes, leaving citizens to pursue such purposes in the absence of the facilities, incentives and endorsement that charity law offers. Indeed it may be that the state has no duty to promote charitable purposes. However, as it is hoped that this book shows, the state has reasons to promote charitable purposes even if it does not have a duty to do so. For related thoughts, see Jeremy Waldron, 'Autonomy and Perfectionism in Raz's *Morality of Freedom*' (1989) 62 *Southern California Law Review* 1097, 1138; Will Kymlicka, 'Liberal Individualism and Liberal Neutrality' (1989) 99 *Ethics* 883, 894.

charity law in which only an expressive strategy was pursued, or in which charitable purposes were facilitated but not incentivised,[2] or in which different incentives were offered in respect of different types of charitable purpose,[3] and so forth. The extent to which the various strategies of charity law are suited to promoting charitable purposes is a large and important question, but – except for assuming the efficacy of the incentive strategy and considering, as we did in Chapter 2, the extent to which that strategy might be consistent with the harm principle – it is not an appropriate question for this book. It takes us too far beyond the philosophical questions about state action and public discourse that are our central focus, and too far into questions of institutional design. That said, one question about the options available to the state in promoting charitable purposes is worth pursuing further. Why might the state choose to promote charitable purposes indirectly via the facilitative, incentive and expressive strategies of charity law, and not directly by raising taxes and then spending them in financing the pursuit of charitable purposes by state organs?

In considering this question, the first point to note is that of course the state does promote directly, by 'tax and spend' means, purposes of the type that it recognises as charitable in law. Many of the purposes entailed in the state's direct provision of private and public goods to citizens – in the form of pensions, unemployment benefits, health care, education, museums, libraries, parks and roads, to name just a few at random – are charitable according to the criteria of charity law. Of course, such purposes might offend the rule against governmental purposes, but even if they do, they still satisfy the criteria of charity law and in that limited sense may be called charitable purposes. Moreover, as we saw in Chapter 1, cases may be found in which purposes carried out by government have been found to be charitable in law, and in the United States there may not

---

[2] This is effectively what is proposed by those who would apply the criteria of charity law in ascertaining the validity of trusts for purposes, but not in ascertaining eligibility for tax privileges: see, e.g., Susan Bright, 'Charity and Trusts for the Public Benefit – Time for a Rethink?' [1989] *Conveyancer* 28; Michael Chesterman, 'Foundations of Charity Law in the New Welfare State' (1999) 62 *Modern Law Review* 333.

[3] In Australia, income tax exemptions are available to all charities, but deductions for donors are available only in respect of gifts to organisations that are 'deductible gift recipients' (DGRs) under the law. Around 40% of charities are DGRs: see Productivity Commission, *Contribution of the Not-for-Profit Sector* (Research Report, 11 February 2010), 177.

even be a rule against governmental purposes in the trusts law setting. In addition to directly providing private and public goods to citizens in ways that entail the pursuit of charitable purposes, in all jurisdictions the state funds a range of organisations that pursue charitable purposes, whether by making grants to such organisations or by entering into contracts with them under which state funding is made available in exchange for the achievement of certain outcomes or goals. Often, these funding agreements implicate organisations in governmental aims, forms and practices, and render the organisations in question subject to a measure of government control. As we saw in Chapter 1, there is uncertainty in charity law as to the circumstances in which such government control of an organisation will cause the purposes of the organisation to infringe the rule against governmental purposes. But whether or not such purposes do infringe the rule against governmental purposes, to the extent that government funds their pursuit by grant or pursuant to a funding agreement, government promotes those purposes directly by 'tax and spend' means.

The question that we framed for analysis was: why might the state choose to promote charitable purposes indirectly via the facilitative, incentive and expressive strategies of charity law, and not directly by raising taxes and then spending them in financing the pursuit of charitable purposes by state organs? We are now in a position to see that this framing of the question is not quite right. It implies that the state may promote charitable purposes indirectly or directly but not indirectly and directly. This is not the case: as we have just seen, the state promotes charitable purposes both indirectly via charity law and directly by 'tax and spend' means. The real question is whether or not there are reasons for the state to promote charitable purposes indirectly via charity law, regardless of whether or not it also promotes such purposes directly.

It cannot be doubted that there may be costs to autonomy associated with the state's choice of indirect rather than direct strategies when promoting charitable purposes. In some instances, those indirect strategies may generate and exacerbate inequalities in the distribution of wealth in society in ways that ultimately diminish the autonomy of citizens:[4] we will return to this thought in Chapter 4, in our discussion of charity law and distributive justice. At the same time, in some cases, the state's indirect promotion of charitable purposes may enable citizens

---

[4] See Michael Chesterman, *Charities, Trusts and Social Welfare* (Weidenfeld and Nicholson, London, 1979), 408–409.

to act towards others in ways that demean them, thus potentially diminishing their autonomy. This may occur where the pursuit of purposes for the 'relief of poverty' contributes to a public sense that the poor are inferior or lack agency, deserving of charity rather than entitled to justice; it may also occur where citizens discriminate against others via the pursuit of charitable purposes, a topic that we will examine in detail in Chapter 6. And in some cases the state may be able to promote charitable purposes more efficiently and in a more coordinated way if it does so directly than if it does so indirectly.[5]

On the other hand, as we saw in Chapter 2, the facilitative, incentive and expressive strategies of charity law are non-coercive strategies. As such, they may be contrasted with the coercive strategies entailed in direct 'tax and spend' means. From a liberal perspective centred on the ideal of autonomy, any such dividend in terms of freedom from coercion is significant and grounds a reason for the state to choose to promote charitable purposes via indirect means, all else being equal. Moreover, with the ideal of autonomy in view, we can point to a further reason for the state to promote charitable purposes indirectly via charity law. The facilitative, incentive and expressive strategies of charity law both enable and encourage citizens to pursue charitable purposes by means that would not otherwise be available to them. In other words, through charity law, the state gives to those of its citizens who wish to pursue charitable purposes certain options to choose from in pursuing those purposes. Nowhere is this clearer than in the part of charity law that overlaps with the law of trusts, a part of charity law that is largely made up of what H.L.A. Hart called 'power-conferring' rules, facilitating the creation by citizens of legal rights, powers and duties both in themselves

---

[5] Along different lines, Rob Atkinson has argued, from a republican perspective, that the pursuit of many charitable purposes should be taken away from the charitable sector and given to the state: 'Keeping Republics Republican' (2011) 88 *Texas Law Review* 235. We need not dwell on Atkinson's provocative account of 'republican philanthropy' here, except to note two points. First, it is not clear that there is any inconsistency between the ideal of autonomy and republicanism: see Philip Pettit, *Republicanism: A Theory of Freedom and Government* (Oxford University Press, 1997), 81–82. Second, to the extent that the state promotes charitable purposes via charity law, it already exercises a measure of *dirigisme* over those purposes. Putting these two points together, can it be argued that charity law itself is a means by which the state can achieve republican philanthropy in a way acceptable to an autonomy-valuing liberal? If so, then there may be little between Atkinson's account of republican philanthropy and the understanding of charity law presented in this book.

and in others.[6] For example, the recognition of charitable trusts as valid gives citizens the option, within certain limits, of crafting bespoke legal arrangements under which wealth is managed over a period of time or in perpetuity for public purposes.[7] Moreover, where regulatory law entails the creation of a legal status of 'charity', accorded to organisations whose purposes satisfy the criteria and disqualifying rules of charity law, that status makes available options to those organisations and others, for example by enabling donors to put in place funding arrangements triggered by possession of the status.

From the perspective of autonomy-based liberalism, the options that charity law makes available to those with charitable purposes amount to a contribution, all else being equal, to the conditions of autonomy. The qualification 'all else being equal' alludes to the possibility – a possibility that was raised in Chapter 2 and to which we will return in more detail in Chapters 5 and 7 – that some purposes regarded as charitable in law are indefensible in light of the value of autonomy, and that options associated with the pursuit of those purposes make no contribution to the conditions of autonomy to that extent. For now, though, let us assume that charitable purposes are defensible in light of the value of autonomy, and note that options that enable citizens to pursue such purposes by means that would not otherwise be available to them make a contribution to the conditions of self-determination in those citizens' lives. This is not to say that citizens with charitable purposes would necessarily lack an adequate range of options to choose from if charity law did not exist; whether or not such citizens would lack an adequate range of options in those circumstances would depend on the identity and character of other options that remained available to them. But it is to point to a reason for the state to provide options to such citizens via the indirect strategies of charity law; this reason also supports the proposition that if the state were to withdraw such options from citizens and instead were to seek to promote charitable purposes only via direct strategies, there would be a cost in terms of autonomy, and it is at least possible that this cost might turn out to be unacceptable.

---

[6] H.L.A. Hart, *The Concept of Law* (3rd edn, Clarendon Press, Oxford, 2012), 27–28, 32–33.

[7] Indeed, it is strongly arguable that prior to the decision of the House of Lords in *McPhail* v. *Doulton* [1971] AC 424 (House of Lords), it was only via charitable trusts that settlors could provide for wealth management to benefit a class of people who were not clearly and immediately ascertainable by the trustees. (Although note also *Re Denley's Trust Deed* [1969] 1 Ch 373 (Goff J).)

Reasons relating to the autonomy of those with charitable purposes not only illuminate why the state might choose to promote charitable purposes indirectly via charity law as well as directly via 'tax and spend' means; they may also help to explain the desirability of one of the disqualifying rules of charity law. This is the rule against governmental purposes. We saw in Chapter 1 that the rule rests on no clear distinction between governmental and non-governmental purposes. Sometimes government control over the pursuit of a purpose causes the purpose to fall foul of the rule, but sometimes this is not the case; in many cases the fact that government carries out a purpose is not an impediment to that purpose being regarded as charitable in law, and indeed in the United States 'governmental and municipal' purposes appear to be recognised as charitable in the trusts law setting. Nonetheless, as we saw in Chapter 1, a distinction might be drawn, when thinking about the rule against governmental purposes, between purposes that realise collective decisions of the political community acting through its institutions on the one hand, and purposes that realise individual autonomous choice on the other. While this distinction is not adhered to consistently in the case law, it seems more promising than other possible distinctions when trying to make sense of the rule against governmental purposes. This relatively promising distinction might be thought of as a distinction between administrative purposes on the one hand, and autonomous purposes on the other. In light of it, we are now in a position to see why a rule against governmental purposes might be desirable. If the liberal case for the indirect strategies of charity law points to the options those strategies give to those who would pursue charitable purposes autonomously then, in light of that case, there would seem no reason to extend the strategies to those who properly do not exercise autonomy in pursuing charitable purposes. Among those who may not exercise autonomy in pursuing charitable purposes are those who pursue, by administrative means, purposes of government that satisfy the criteria of charity law. It makes no sense to extend the indirect strategies of charity law to such cases of non-autonomous pursuit of charitable purposes. So understood, the rule against governmental purposes is not to be appraised in light of its success in maintaining a convincing conceptual distinction between government and charity; on such a score, the rule seems less than successful. Rather, the rule is to be evaluated according to its sensitivity to normative considerations bearing on the facilitative, incentive and expressive strategies of charity law. Assessed in this way, the rule seems desirable.

To repeat: the reasons why the state might choose the indirect strategies of charity law also appear to illuminate the choice of a rule against governmental purposes, at least to the extent that such a rule excludes from charity law purposes that are to be characterised as administrative rather than autonomous for the reasons we have just explored. That said, the fact that purposes are governmental in this way is not in itself a matter for liberal concern; after all, even hardcore libertarians can tolerate the governmental purposes that are entailed in a 'night watchman' state.[8] In other words, while the choice of a rule against governmental purposes might seem desirable in light of a liberal theory of charity law, it does not appear to be required by such a theory. What is of greater concern to the liberal looking at charity law is the situation in which government, via charity law, creates options for those with charitable purposes and then interferes with those options. Earlier, we encountered the state practice of entering into contracts with charities under which state funding is tied to the achievement of certain outcomes or goals. This practice, which has generated what is referred to in scholarly literature as a 'contract culture', has been criticised as representing a threat to the independence of charities.[9] The outcomes and goals to which funding is routinely tied are usually determined more by the state than by the charity in question; sometimes the state also uses funding agreements to exercise a measure of control over the management of charities, raising the possibility that in some cases the rule against governmental purposes might apply. But, once we put to one side the rule against governmental purposes, the reasons helping to explain why the state might promote charitable purposes indirectly via charity law inform an evaluative framework for approaching the 'contract culture' and the broader question of the state's dealings with those who pursue charitable purposes.

Recall that the reasons pointing to why the state might promote charitable purposes indirectly via charity law are reasons relating to the

---

[8] See, e.g., Robert Nozick, *Anarchy, State, and Utopia* (Basic Books, New York, 1974).

[9] See, e.g., Jean Warburton and Debra Morris, 'Charities and the Contract Culture' [1991] *The Conveyancer* 419; Jane Lewis, 'Reviewing the Relationship between the Voluntary Sector and the State in Britain in the 1990s' (1999) 10 *Voluntas* 255; Jonathan Garton, 'Charities and the State' (2000) 14 *Trust Law International* 93; Neil Brooks, 'The Role of the Voluntary Sector in a Modern Welfare State' in Bruce Chapman and David Stewart (eds), *Between State and Market: Essays on Charities Law and Policy in Canada* (McGill-Queens' University Press, Montreal and Kingston, 2001) 166–216; Alison Dunn, 'Demanding Service or Servicing Demand? Charities, Regulation and the Policy Process' (2008) 71 *Modern Law Review* 247.

autonomy of those with charitable purposes. Thus, in circumstances where the state creates conditions under which citizens may choose autonomously to pursue charitable purposes, but then interferes with that pursuit, the state's actions might shift from being acceptable in light of liberal commitments to being of concern from a liberal perspective. How are we to analyse any such shift? On one view, the 'contract culture' entails the deployment of incentive strategies by the state, although any incentives bound up with the 'contract culture' are likely to be much stronger than the incentives of charity law, which largely take the form of tax exemptions and subsidies. On this view, the question whether or not the 'contract culture' is objectionable would seem to turn on the extent to which incentives are apt to manipulate those to whom they are offered. In Chapter 2 we considered the extent to which the incentives of charity law, most notably the tax privileges of charity law, constitute interference with the autonomous pursuit of charitable purposes. We saw that there are reasons to doubt that those incentives manipulate citizens in a way that violates the harm principle, at least as that principle is understood in light of the demands of autonomy. When a person is incentivised to do something that she has independent reasons to do, it does not necessarily follow that she has not acted for those independent reasons. Moreover, incentives tend to encourage people to act such that they come to be in positions from which they are better able to understand and engage with independent reasons that apply to them. If these propositions are accepted, and if the 'contract culture' entails nothing more than the offering of incentives to charities, there may not be much to object to from a liberal point of view.

However, another view of the 'contract culture' might be available; according to this alternative view, the 'contract culture' entails the state abandoning indirect strategies for direct ones, seeking not to add to the mix of reasons that apply to the autonomous pursuit of charitable purposes so much as to override that pursuit by command and control. To the extent that this view of the 'contract culture' is accurate, from a liberal perspective that is sensitive to the autonomy-related reasons for the state to promote charitable purposes indirectly via charity law we are likely to join the critics of the 'contract culture', arguing that the state practices entailed in it at best distort and at worst narrow the range of options available to those with charitable purposes, such that their autonomy is diminished as a result. Most likely, we should respond to the 'contract culture' by acknowledging that sometimes it entails the state offering incentives to those who autonomously pursue charitable purposes, and that some of those incentives do not interfere with autonomy while others do; at the same time, we should be prepared to see that at times the state interferes with autonomy by substituting *dirigiste* methods for the indirect strategies of charity law and that, in light of the political ideal of autonomy, this is a matter for regret. Such a response should discern, for example, between funding arrangements that are experienced by charities as opportunities and those that are experienced as unwelcome necessities for survival.[10]

3. The boundaries of charity law

Chapter 2 gave us a sense of how we might think about the state promotion of charitable purposes that is at the core of charity law, and so far this chapter has hopefully given us a sense of how we might think about the facilitative, incentive and expressive strategies of charity law. But the boundaries of charity law remain only dimly illuminated. With the liberal ideal of autonomy in view, something can be said about the boundaries of charity law with reference to the extent to which purposes of one type or another promote the conditions of autonomy. Indeed, in Chapter 2 we saw that some purposes within the description 'promotion of . . . equality and diversity' in section 3(1) of the English Charities Act of 2011 might, on closer reflection, turn out not to generate autonomy-promoting goods, giving us a reason to think that the state should not promote those purposes via charity law. But we are not yet in a position to say anything about why the state might promote, via charity law, only some purposes that are undoubtedly autonomy-promoting and not others. Take, for example, a trust for the purpose of educating the children of the employees of a particular multinational company, and assume that the children number in the hundreds of thousands.[11] The purpose of this trust is not charitable according to charity law, and yet can anyone deny that the purpose is likely to generate substantial autonomy-promoting goods for many people? Or consider an entrepreneur who sets up an organisation for the relief of poverty, an organisation that is funded by donations; rather than drawing a fixed salary, the

---

[10] There may be reasons to think that the latter experience is the more common one: see Nick Seddon, *Who Cares? How State Funding and Political Activism Change Charity* (Civitas, Institute for the Study of Civil Society, 2007).

[11] This example is based on the facts of *Oppenheim* v. *Tobacco Securities Trust Co Ltd* [1951] AC 297 (House of Lords).

entrepreneur distributes to himself a share of the donations received, and then distributes what remains to poor relief.[12] Again, assuming that purposes within the description 'relief of poverty' typically, if not invariably, contribute in significant ways to the conditions of autonomy, why should the state refrain – as it almost certainly will – from promoting this entrepreneur's purpose via charity law? Why are the boundaries of charity law drawn where they are drawn as between different autonomy-promoting purposes?

A. Rule of law considerations

To begin with, it is worth pointing out that, in at least some cases, considerations relating to the political ideal of the rule of law may play a role in explaining how the boundaries of charity law are drawn. In Chapter 1, we saw that the criteria of charity law include a requirement that, in order to be regarded as charitable in law, a purpose must fall within one of a set of legally prescribed general descriptions of charitable purpose; this set is invariably open-ended so as to facilitate the recognition of new types of purpose as charitable, but it also invariably incorporates a constraint demanding that, before a new type of purpose is recognised as charitable, an analogy be drawn between it and some extant charitable purpose. In some jurisdictions, the necessary analogy must be to a purpose listed in the preamble to the Statute of Elizabeth; in others, a link to the preamble is not required. Thus, in a case where a decision-maker is required to reason by analogy when faced with a new type of purpose, there is a possibility that even though the purpose satisfies the public benefit test it will not be recognised as charitable because the decision-maker can discern no analogy between it and any extant charitable purpose.[13] And to the extent that decision-makers refuse to draw analogies between purposes before them and extant charitable purposes, there is a possibility that the state will refrain from promoting purposes via charity law, notwithstanding that those purposes are autonomy-promoting.

---

[12] See Anup Malani and Eric A. Posner, 'The Case for For-Profit Charities' (2007) 93 *Virginia Law Review* 2017, 2018–2019.

[13] See *Vancouver Society of Immigrant and Visible Minority Women* v. *Minister of National Revenue* [1999] 1 SCR 10 (Supreme Court of Canada), [44]–[49] (Gonthier J in dissent) and [151] (Iacobucci J).

From the perspective of autonomy-based liberalism, any state failure to promote autonomy-promoting purposes, whether via charity law or in some other way, seems to demand some sort of justification. It might be argued that decision-makers are not justified in refusing to recognise autonomy-promoting purposes as charitable simply because they are insufficiently analogous to extant charitable purposes; from this perspective, all else being equal, autonomy-promoting purposes ought to be recognised as charitable no matter what their type, and reasoning by analogy in charity law should cease. However, to argue in this way is to pay insufficient attention to rule of law considerations that bear on the development of charity law by decision-makers. Predictability in the development of the law over the course of time serves the ideal of the rule of law in important ways,[14] and the value of this predictability helps to justify decision-makers adopting a cautious posture towards the recognition of new types of purpose as charitable. Moreover, it is possible that reasoning by analogy is a defensible expression of this cautious posture towards new types of charitable purpose and, if it is, there may be a case for at least some autonomy-promoting purposes to be denied recognition as charitable because they are insufficiently analogous to extant charitable purposes.

That said, and with the indisputably important ideal of the rule of law in view, the soundness of reasoning by analogy in the charity law setting turns on the sorts of analogies that decision-makers draw when developing charity law. As Larry Alexander and Emily Sherwin argue in their important book on legal reasoning, a decision-maker might discern an analogy between the facts of a case before her and the facts of a precedent case either intuitively or by deduction in light of some principle of similarity. Alexander and Sherwin point out that only the latter sort of analogy, the analogy that is supported by a principle of similarity, is suited to generating the predictability in the development of the law that is necessary to the ideal of the rule of law.[15] In light of this theoretical point, reasoning by analogy in the charity law setting may be regarded as sound only to the extent that that reasoning appeals to a principle of similarity. In the well-known case of *Scottish Burial Reform and Cremation Society Ltd* v. *Glasgow Corporation*, members of the House of Lords

---

[14] See further Lon L. Fuller, *The Morality of Law* (rev. edn, Yale University Press, New Haven, 1969) ch 2.

[15] Larry Alexander and Emily Sherwin, *Demystifying Legal Reasoning* (Cambridge University Press, New York, 2008) ch 3.

found the purpose of promoting cremation of the dead to be charitable on the basis that the purpose was analogous to the purpose of maintaining a cemetery, which in earlier cases had been found to be analogous to the purpose of maintaining a burial yard attached to a church,[16] which in an even earlier case had been found to be analogous to the 'repair of churches',[17] a purpose listed in the preamble to the Statute of Elizabeth.[18] This string of analogies going back to the preamble arguably reflects an intuitive approach to reasoning by analogy that is not consistent with legal predictability. However, in his judgment in the *Scottish Burial Reform* case, Lord Wilberforce also stated that the 'repair of churches', along with several other purposes listed in the preamble, was a purpose of 'general public utility' and that, as promoting cremation of the dead was also a purpose of general public utility, it was analogous to the 'repair of churches' and charitable on that basis.[19] Whether or not 'general public utility' named an appropriate principle of similarity in the setting of the *Scottish Burial Reform* case, the fact that Lord Wilberforce appealed to a principle of similarity shows that he tried to find the sort of analogy that is apt to generate predictability in the development of the law. To that extent, his reasoning was consistent with the ideal of the rule of law.

B.   Altruism, the 'public' component of the public benefit test and the 'not for profit' rule

For present purposes, we need not dwell further on the rule of law considerations that go towards justifying reasoning by analogy in charity law cases. Instead, let us turn to two parts of charity law that promise, more than most, to explain why the boundaries of charity law might be drawn where they are drawn as between different types of autonomy-promoting purpose: the 'public' component of the public benefit test, and the 'not for profit' rule. In Chapter 1 we saw that purposes may be regarded as public in the charity law setting where they entail the provision of excludable private goods to a public class, or where they stand to realise non-excludable public goods. We also saw that, in the

---

[16] *In re Manser* [1905] 1 Ch 68 (Warrington J); *In re Eighmie* [1935] Ch 524 (Eve J).

[17] *In re Vaughan* (1886) 33 ChD 187 (North J).

[18] [1968] AC 138 (House of Lords), 152–153 (Lord Upjohn) and 155 (Lord Wilberforce). See also 148 (Lord Reid).

[19] Ibid, 156. See also *Royal National Agricultural and Industrial Association* v. *Chester* (1974) 48 ALJR 304 (High Court of Australia).

charity law setting, excludable private goods are not considered to be provided to a public class where they take the form of gifts to a class composed of members of a family, employees of a company or members of an association or club (except in the case of purposes within the description 'relief of poverty' or in cases where statute provides otherwise), where they are entailed in 'self-help' arrangements (except in Australia) or where they are entailed in 'member benefit' arrangements. Moreover, we saw that in at least some jurisdictions purposes which exclude the poor are not regarded as public purposes in charity law, and we also saw that in all jurisdictions purposes that aim at the generation of private profit are disqualified from being charitable, even if they incidentally realise private goods for a public class, or indeed non-excludable public goods. The remainder of this part of the chapter will argue that, with one possible exception, all of these elements of charity law reveal the state taking an interest in altruism. The exception, to which we will return below, is the principle endorsed in many parts of the British Isles to the effect that purposes that exclude the poor are not public purposes and therefore not charitable purposes. But before coming to that exception we should gain a sense of what altruism is, before considering how the 'public' component of the public benefit test and the 'not for profit' rule reveal the state taking an interest in it.

1. Altruism

Altruism is best brought into relief by comparing it with two other types of motivation animating actions that benefit other people. First, altruism may be distinguished from self-interest; the altruist is motivated to act by regard for the needs or welfare of other people and not by a sense of what she herself might gain from acting in ways that benefit others.[20] In this way, where altruism is present as a motivation for action, the action that it motivates is typically the sort of unconditional transaction that is commonly described as the giving of a gift; altruism stands in contrast to the motivations that usually underpin what we might call bargains, being transactions in which a transfer is 'expressly conditioned on a reciprocal exchange'.[21] We must acknowledge upfront that some have argued that altruism in this sense is not possible: economists whose

---

[20] See Richard A. Epstein, *Principles for a Free Society: Reconciling Individual Liberty with the Common Good* (Perseus Books, Reading, MA, 1998) ch 5, esp 135–138.

[21] Melvin Aron Eisenberg, 'The World of Contract and the World of Gift' (1997) 85 *California Law Review* 821, 823.

theoretical assumptions include self-interest as a motivation for all human action have argued that those who give gifts must be assumed always to seek a welfare gain in exchange, even if that welfare gain is something as intangible as a 'warm glow'.[22] However, while we cannot ignore the economists' challenge to the notion of altruism as distinct from self-interest, we are also free to reject that challenge on the basis that there is simply no reason to accept the theoretical assumption that underpins it; this is because there is no reason, in order to understand human action, to assume that self-interest is the only motivation for such action.[23] Indeed, when the action in question is the giving of a gift, there seem to be reasons not to commence analysis by assuming self-interest as a motivation for action. Most people do not usually experience gift-giving as self-interested, just as most people do not usually experience bargains as altruistic.[24] When analysing gifts and bargains, we should be looking for theoretical assumptions that reflect that experience, which is in many instances the experience of two distinct and basic types of action.[25] The reductive assumptions of economic theory which ascribe to all action self-interested motivations are not suited to that task.

Second, altruism may be distinguished from duty and attachment; the altruist is motivated to act by regard for other people as such, not by any sense of duty or obligation towards others, nor by special ties to or affection for others. Insofar as it entails regard for others as such, altruism is often combined with detached virtues such as justice and charity (understood in the non-legal sense), and is inconsistent with virtues, such as loyalty and trustworthiness, that presuppose attachments of one kind or another.[26] As with the distinction between altruism and

---

[22] James Andreoni, 'Giving with Impure Altruism: Applications to Charity and Ricardian Equivalence' (1989) 97 *Journal of Political Economy* 1447.

[23] See further Amartya K. Sen, 'Rational Fools: A Critique of the Behavioural Foundations of Economic Theory' (1977) 6 *Philosophy and Public Affairs* 317.

[24] See Adam Smith, *An Inquiry into the Nature and Causes of Wealth of Nations* (R.H. Campbell and A.S. Skinner eds, Clarendon Press, Oxford, 1976) bk I, ch II.

[25] Jacques T. Godbout and Alain Caillé, *The World of the Gift* (trans Donald Winkler, McGill-Queen's University Press, Montreal and Kingston, 1998), 130.

[26] For more on these virtues, see John Gardner, 'The Virtue of Charity and Its Foils' in Charles Mitchell and Susan R. Moody (eds), *Foundations of Charity* (Hart Publishing, Oxford, 2000) 1–27; Matthew Harding, 'Responding to Trust' (2011) 24 *Ratio Juris* 75; John Gardner, 'The Virtue of Justice and the Character of Law' in his *Law as a Leap of Faith* (Oxford University Press, 2012) ch 10. Note, though, that Gardner's account of the virtue of charity is of a secular virtue; in the Christian tradition, the virtue of charity may be a virtue of self-perfection and inconsistent with altruism: Will Kymlicka, 'Altruism in Philosophical and Ethical Traditions: Two Views' in Jim Phillips, Bruce Chapman and

self-interest, this distinction between altruism on the one hand and duty and attachment on the other is not uncontroversial. It has been argued that the practice of gift-giving, far from being divorced from notions of duty and attachment, actually expresses and fulfils duties and attachments deriving from religion, morality, kinship and other communities.[27] This thought is sometimes expressed by describing the gift economy as an economy of exchange or reciprocity, where 'exchange' and 'reciprocity' are understood to refer not to the bargains that characterise market transactions but rather to more diffuse, intangible and indirect transactions.[28] This account of gift-giving suggests that while it is possible to be motivated by self-interest, or by duty or attachment, it is not possible, given the cultural conditions in which we live, to be motivated by the sort of genuine unmediated regard for other people as such that is characteristic of altruism; if this is the case then altruism, at least in the conception outlined here, is of theoretical interest only.

That altruism might be of theoretical interest only is not as far-fetched as it might seem. There can be no doubt that much gift-giving carries cultural meaning associated with exchange and reciprocity; reflection on the customs surrounding the giving of gifts on birthdays and other special occasions testifies to this. Equally, it can scarcely be denied that at least some gifts are motivated by self-interest, as the economists would have us believe. Most likely, the motivations underlying a complex and diverse practice like gift-giving are multiple: some other-regarding, some self-interested, some bound up with duties and attachments and some reflecting a detached posture towards others. Nor should it be forgotten that the concept of altruism was unknown in intellectual history until the mid-nineteenth century, and that it was at that time resisted as a contender for a plausible and morally acceptable type of motivation for

---

David Stevens (eds), *Between State and Market: Essays on Charities Law and Policy in Canada* (McGill-Queen's University Press, Montreal and Kingston, 2001) 87–126, 106.

[27] See, e.g., Margaret Jane Radin, 'Market-Inalienability' (1987) 100 *Harvard Law Review* 1849, 1907; Eisenberg, above n 21.

[28] See, e.g., Marcel Mauss, *The Gift: The Form and Reason for Exchange in Archaic Societies* (trans W.D. Halls, foreword by Mary Douglas, W.W. Norton, New York, 1990, first published in French in 1950); Richard M. Titmuss, *The Gift Relationship: From Human Blood to Social Policy* (Allen and Unwin, London, 1970); Jane B. Baron, 'Gifts, Bargains and Form' (1989) 64 *Indiana Law Journal* 155; Carol M. Rose, 'Giving, Trading, Thieving and Trusting: How and Why Gifts Become Exchanges and (More Importantly) Vice Versa' (1992) 44 *Florida Law Review* 295; Paulette Kidder, 'Gift Exchange and Justice in Families' (2001) 32 *Journal of Social Philosophy* 157.

human action.[29] All of this notwithstanding, there are reasons to think that altruism – understood in contrast to self-interest and to duty and attachment – is possible as a motivation for human action. Altruism reflects a certain type of moral disposition: the disposition, in one's practical reasoning, to abstract from one's interests on the one hand, and from one's duties and attachments on the other. Thomas Nagel describes the product of this disposition as 'the conception of oneself as merely one person among others'.[30] There are reasons to think that this disposition, on which altruism depends, is one that people have the capacity to – and actually do – form. The institutional arrangements of modern political communities, along with much modern moral and political thought, have helped to generate a culture in which it is conceivable and feasible to abstract from one's interests, duties and attachments when regarding others, at least in respect of certain dealings.[31] This creates room, in the contemporary moral landscape, for altruism. And it creates room for the archetypal altruistic act: the selfless and unsolicited gift to a stranger.[32]

2.   The 'public' component of the public benefit test and the 'not for profit' rule

With a conception of altruism now in mind, we may turn to the 'public' component of the public benefit test and the 'not for profit' rule, and ask how they might reflect a state interest in altruism. The notion that, via these elements of charity law, the state takes an interest in altruism is not novel; decision-makers have said or implied this in a number of cases.[33] But we must be careful to isolate exactly how the state is

---

[29] Thomas Dixon, *The Invention of Altruism: Making Moral Meanings in Victorian Britain* (Oxford University Press, 2008).

[30] Thomas Nagel, *The Possibility of Altruism* (paperback edn., Princeton University Press, 1978), 19.

[31] Note that in order to agree with this statement it is not necessary to embrace the more radical proposition that it is possible for a person to abstract from all of her interests, duties and attachments at once. For criticism of the more radical proposition: Michael J. Sandel, *Liberalism and the Limits of Justice* (2nd edn., Cambridge University Press, 1998).

[32] Godbout and Caillé, above n 25, 78: '[a]n unknown gift made to the unknown, where religious motivation is not essential and which encompasses all social strata: this is the world of the modern gift between strangers, whose importance continues to grow.' See also Michael Walzer, *Spheres of Justice* (Basic Books, New York, 1983), 128.

[33] See, e.g., *Re Cranston, Webb* v. *Oldfield* [1898] 1 IR 431 (Court of Appeal), 446 (Fitzgibbon LJ); *Baptist Union of Ireland (Northern) Corporation* v. *Commissioner of Inland Revenue* (1945) 26 TC 335 (Macdermott J), 356–357; *In re Scarisbrick* [1951] 1 Ch 622 (Court of Appeal), 639 (Evershed MR); *R* v. *Assessors of the Town of Sunny Brae* [1952]

interested in altruism in the setting of charity law, lest we fall into the trap of thinking that decision-makers use the 'public' component of the public benefit test and the 'not for profit' rule to categorise actions according to whether or not they are motivated by altruism and then to exclude non-altruistic actions from charity law. It is a fundamental principle of charity law that in ascertaining whether or not a purpose is charitable, a decision-maker must not have regard to the motivations of the person or people whose purpose it is.[34] This of course rules out any inquiry into whether or not those who claim that their purposes are charitable pursue those purposes altruistically, since the only way in which it can be known whether or not an action is altruistic is by undertaking an inquiry into the motivations for that action. As altruism is a type of motivation, and as motivations are irrelevant to ascertaining whether or not a purpose is charitable in law, we cannot conclude from the mere fact that a purpose is charitable in law that the purpose is pursued altruistically. However, this conclusion is not inconsistent with the proposition that the state takes an interest in altruism in the charity law setting, because – as we will see – that interest is primarily in the public meaning of actions, and only secondarily in the motivations that animate them.

Rather than trying to establish a distinction between actions based on their motivations, the 'public' component of the public benefit test and the 'not for profit' rule reveal the state taking an interest in altruism in a more subtle way. To see this better, let us recall from Chapters 1 and 2 that charity law has an expressive dimension. In those earlier chapters, we emphasised the ways in which charity law entails the state expressing endorsement of charitable purposes and those who carry them out, and we also emphasised how this expression of endorsement functions as an indirect means by which the state promotes charitable purposes. But of

---

2SCR 76 (Supreme Court of Canada), 88 (Rand J); *National Deposit Friendly Society Trustees* v. *Skegness Urban District Council* [1959] AC 293 (House of Lords), 315 (Lord MacDermott); *Vancouver Society of Immigrant and Visible Minority Women* v. *Minister of National Revenue* [1999] 1 SCR 10 (Supreme Court of Canada), [37] (Gonthier J in dissent); [147] (Iacobucci J). See also Ontario Law Reform Commission, *Report on the Law of Charities* (1996) ch 6 and Ian Sheppard, Robert Fitzgerald and David Gonski, *Report of the Inquiry into the Definition of Charities and Related Organisations* (2001) ch 13.

[34] See generally Hubert Picarda, *The Law and Practice Relating to Charities* (4th edn, Bloomsbury Professional, Haywards Heath, West Sussex, 2010), 24; Gino Dal Pont, *Law of Charity* (Chatswood, LexisNexis Butterworths, 2010), [2.8]–[2.11].

course there is much more to say about the expressive dimension of charity law than that it functions as a strategy in the state's promotion of charitable purposes. The range of rules and criteria by which the state both identifies and isolates certain purposes as charitable and then extends to those who carry out charitable purposes legal consequences of one type or another all operate to create and sustain a complex of public meaning for charitable purposes and the actions entailed in their pursuit. Call this public meaning, which goes well beyond a simple association of charitable purposes and state endorsement, the public meaning of 'legal charity'.

The 'public' component of the public benefit test and the 'not for profit' rule contribute to giving public meaning to legal charity by associating legal charity with altruism, insofar as altruism is opposed to self-interest on the one hand and to duties and attachments on the other. Take the exclusion from charity law of purposes entailing 'member benefit' arrangements and the pursuit of private profit. Given that 'member benefit' arrangements and the pursuit of private profit are typically motivated, and are widely understood to be typically motivated, by self-interest, the exclusion of such purposes from charity law signals strongly that self-interest has no place in legal charity. Similarly, by rejecting the proposition that 'self-help' arrangements can be charitable in law, decision-makers in most jurisdictions reinforce a public meaning for legal charity that is inconsistent with motivations for action stemming from duties and attachments; this is because 'self-help' arrangements are typically motivated, and are widely understood to be typically motivated, by attachments of loyalty and trustworthiness.[35] In this regard, it is noteworthy that the exclusion of 'self-help' arrangements from charity law opposes the public meaning of legal charity to the sorts of attachments typically found in the associational sphere known as 'civil society', and that to this extent the project of charity law differs importantly from the project of promoting civil society.[36] In Australia, where 'self-help' arrangements are regarded as charitable in law, this distinction between the project of charity law and the project of promoting civil society is not so clearly discernable.

Gifts to a private class throw up more difficult questions. Recall once again that purposes that entail the provision of private goods to members

---

[35] A point made in Gardner, 'The Virtue of Charity and its Foils', above n 26, 22.

[36] This is a reason to be cautious in respect of efforts to collapse analysis of charity law into analysis of the legal framework for civil society activity: see, e.g., Jonathan Garton, *The Regulation of Organised Civil Society* (Hart Publishing, Oxford, 2009).

of a family, employees of a company or members of an association or club are usually not regarded as sufficiently public to satisfy the 'public' component of the public benefit test. And yet, according to Lord Wrenbury in the leading case of *Verge* v. *Somerville*, '[t]he inhabitants of a parish or town' are a sufficiently public class in the setting of that test.[37] So while, as we saw earlier, a gift for the purpose of educating the children of the employees of a multinational company is regarded as a gift to a private class and thus is not charitable in law,[38] a gift for the purpose of educating the children of inhabitants of a particular town is regarded as a gift to a public class and thus is charitable[39]. How, by excluding the first purpose from charity law while regarding the second as charitable, do decision-makers help to create a public meaning for legal charity that aligns it with altruism? Part of the answer to this question might be that when A provides private goods to a private class, A is relatively likely to share some personal connection with the private class in question, and thus is relatively likely to be motivated by a sense of duty or attachment. After all, people do not usually confer benefits on members of families, employees of companies or members of associations or clubs except where they themselves have some relationship with the family, company, association or club in question. However, even if we accept that A is relatively likely to be motivated non-altruistically when providing private goods to a private class, we are still left with the problem of working out why B, who provides private goods to the inhabitants of a parish or town, a class that is regarded as public in charity law, is any more likely than A to be motivated altruistically. After all, assuming that B is not self-interested, why should B choose to benefit the inhabitants of a parish or town unless B has a sense of duty or attachment to that parish or town? In the end, if we accept that the state takes an interest in altruism in the setting of the 'public' component of the public benefit test, we may be driven to conclude that that component of the test is not as well calibrated as it might be to serving the state's interest in altruism in the charity law setting.[40]

---

[37] [1924] AC 496 (Privy Council), 499 (Lord Wrenbury).

[38] *Oppenheim* v. *Tobacco Securities Trust Co Ltd* [1951] AC 297 (House of Lords).

[39] For even more perplexing distinctions: Ibid, 307 (Lord Simonds).

[40] See, e.g., Mark Freedland, 'Charity Law and the Public/Private Distinction' in Charles Mitchell and Susan R. Moody (eds), *Foundations of Charity* (Hart Publishing, Oxford, 2000) 111–123, 121, describing the test as 'loose' and 'indirect'.

That the 'public' component of the public benefit test may not be perfectly attuned to serving the state's interest in altruism in the charity law setting is even more apparent once we turn to a distinct sub-group of cases entailing gifts to a private class: those in which the gift is for the 'relief of poverty' of such a class. As we saw earlier in this chapter, a person is relatively unlikely to be motivated altruistically when providing the sorts of private goods entailed in poor relief to a private class; the more likely motivation of such a person – assuming that she is not motivated by self-interest – is one grounded in duty or attachment and formed because the person herself has some relationship with that class. Indeed, this seems to be reflected in charity law itself; cases in which gifts for purposes of relieving the poverty of a private class have been under scrutiny are customarily described as 'poor relations' and 'poor employees' cases, indicating that in them the motivation for the gift has stemmed from the donor's sense of duty or attachment either to his family members or to his employees.[41] As we saw in Chapter 1, the 'poor relations' and 'poor employees' cases show that purposes within the description 'relief of poverty' may be charitable in law notwithstanding that they stand to benefit only a private class. To this extent it would seem that the public meaning of legal charity diverges from a conception of altruism that contrasts it with motivations grounded in duty or attachment.

It is possible that the 'poor relations' and 'poor employees' cases constitute an anomaly in charity law, but some have also sought to reconcile those cases with the 'public' component of the public benefit test by suggesting that relieving the poverty of even a private class generates incidental public goods that benefit the community as a whole.[42] Adopting this latter perspective enables us to reconcile the 'poor relations' and 'poor employees' cases with the demands of the public benefit test – as we saw in Chapter 1, in some cases decision-makers have been prepared to find the public benefit test satisfied where purposes aim at the generation of private goods to a private class but also generate incidental public goods – but it does not establish that, by

---

[41] For descriptions of these cases as 'poor relations' and 'poor employees' cases: Picarda, above n 34, 47; Dal Pont, above n 34, [8.23]–[8.26].

[42] See *In re Compton* [1945] 1 Ch 123 (Court of Appeal), 139–140 (Greene MR); *Gibson v. South American Stores Ltd* [1950] Ch 177 (Court of Appeal), 197 (Evershed MR), discussed in *Attorney-General* v. *Charity Commission for England and Wales* [2011] UKUT 420 (Upper Tribunal), [40]–[49].

recognising purposes of relieving the poverty of a private class as charitable, the state aligns the public meaning of legal charity with altruism. Given that altruism is a matter of motivations, the public meaning of legal charity is likely to be consistent with altruism only to the extent that legal charity is plausibly interpreted as motivated by altruism. It is strongly arguable that most plausible interpretations of purposive actions will ascribe to those actions motivations that seek to bring about the direct rather than the indirect consequences of the actions in question. Thus, even if a purpose of relieving the poverty of a private class is likely to generate incidental public goods, an interpretation of the action entailed in pursuing that purpose is unlikely to be plausible if it ascribes to that action a motivation that seeks to bring about indirect benefit to the whole community. The more plausible interpretation of that action is that the motivation for it seeks to bring about the relief of poverty of the private class in question. In other words, donors in 'poor relations' and 'poor employees' cases are most plausibly understood as being motivated by regard for their poor relations or poor employees – motivations that are unlikely to be altruistic.

Similar points may be made in respect of statutory amendments to the 'public' component of the public benefit test in light of which gifts to a private class might be regarded as charitable in law in circumstances where otherwise they might not have been. As we saw in Chapter 1, in the Australian Charities Act of 2013, several types of purpose, based on the first three 'heads' of the *Pemsel* set, are presumed in the absence of evidence to the contrary to be 'public', and exemptions from the 'public' component of the public benefit test are available in respect of certain other types of purpose.[43] And in the charity law of New Zealand, in no case does a purpose fail the 'public' component of the public benefit test simply because it stands to benefit only a class of persons who are related by blood.[44] Arguably, these statutory interventions have decoupled the public meaning of legal charity on the one hand and altruism on the other in Australia and New Zealand. This would seem to be true especially in Australia, given the breadth of the presumption of the 'public' character of purposes established by section 7 of the Charities Act. In both jurisdictions, relaxation of the 'public' component of the public benefit test has been motivated in part by a desire to ensure that the purposes of Indigenous communities are recognised as charitable

[43] Charities Act 2013 (Australia) ss 7–10.
[44] Charities Act 2005 (New Zealand) s 5(2)(a).

notwithstanding that those communities have kinship ties; to this extent, the legislative interventions may reflect a sense that aligning the public meaning of legal charity with altruism is not appropriate to the extent that legal charity is carried out in a historical and cultural setting in which altruism does not figure.[45] However, in Australia at least, relaxation of the 'public' component of the public benefit test goes much further than is necessary to ensure the charitable character of the purposes of Indigenous communities; in that jurisdiction, the public meaning of legal charity and altruism would seem to have diverged significantly.

Along with cases of gifts to a private class, it might be thought that the state's interest in altruism is least evident in the charity law setting in cases where a purpose entailing the provision of private goods in exchange for the payment of fees or some other contract price is recognised as charitable in law.[46] As we saw in Chapter 1, in some jurisdictions such fee-charging is considered incompatible with the pursuit of charitable purposes to the extent that it excludes the poor from accessing the private goods being provided; we will return shortly to this approach to fee-charging. But, putting to one side the question whether or not the poor are excluded by fee-charging, it is well established in charity law that the fact that an organisation charges fees or some other contract price in exchange for the provision of private goods is no impediment to its purposes being regarded as charitable in law, so long as those purposes meet the criteria of charity law and satisfy pertinent disqualifying rules in all other respects.[47] We saw earlier that altruism, as a motivation for action, typically accompanies the unconditional giving of gifts and is usually inconsistent with the expressly conditional exchanges that constitute bargains. If altruism is usually inconsistent with bargains, and if organisations strike bargains to the extent that they charge fees or

---

[45] See further Fiona Martin, 'Convergence and Divergence with the Common Law: The Public Benefit Test and Charities for Indigenous Peoples' in Matthew Harding, Ann O'Connell and Miranda Stewart (eds), *Not-for-Profit Law: Theoretical and Comparative Perspectives* (Cambridge University Press, 2014) 159–178.

[46] For convenience, this practice will be referred to in the text as 'fee-charging', but the arguments of the text are intended to apply to any case where, in the pursuit of a charitable purpose, private goods are exchanged for a contract price.

[47] *Re Resch's Will Trusts, Le Cras v. Perpetual Trustee Co Ltd* [1968] 1 AC 514 (Privy Council); *Joseph Rowntree Memorial Trust Housing Association Ltd v. Attorney-General* [1983] 1 All ER 288 (Peter Gibson J); *Centrepoint Community Growth Trust v. Commissioner of Inland Revenue* [1985] 1 NZLR 673 (Tompkins J); *Liberty Trust v. Charities Commission* [2011] NZHC 577 (Mallon J).

another contract price in exchange for the provision of private goods, then how is the state's acceptance of fee-charging in the charity law setting consistent with its interest in altruism? Surely the recognition as charitable of purposes entailing fee-charging generates public meaning for legal charity that associates it more with self-interested motivations than with altruistic ones?[48]

In addressing these questions, let us start with the 'not for profit' rule, according to which purposes that aim at the generation of private profit are disqualified from being charitable purposes. As we saw earlier, this rule reveals the state aligning the public meaning of legal charity with a conception of altruism that contrasts altruism with self-interest as a motivation for action; after all, the pursuit of private profit is typically motivated, and typically understood to be motivated, by self-interest. Where fee-charging is deployed as a means to achieve the purpose of generating private profit, it is, just like the purpose of generating private profit itself, almost certainly inconsistent with altruism; this is hardly surprising given that the means of achieving a purpose typically share the motivations that underpin the purpose itself. However, where fee-charging is deployed as a means to achieve a purpose that does not aim at the generation of private profit, say in circumstances where a 'not for profit' purpose entails the provision of private goods and the cost of providing those goods cannot be met except by charging fees for them, fee-charging might be consistent with altruism. In part, whether or not fee-charging is consistent with altruism in such circumstances depends on factors other than that the purpose is 'not for profit'; for example, if the purpose is one that discloses a 'member benefit' arrangement it is likely to be inconsistent with altruism, notwithstanding that it is 'not for profit'. The fact that the purpose is 'not for profit' is in part a relevant factor, however;[49] if all else is equal, then the fact that the purpose is 'not for profit' may indicate the contrast with self-interest that is characteristic of altruism, making it possible that any fee-charging deployed as a means to the achievement of the 'not for profit' purpose is itself altruistic, notwithstanding that fee-charging entails the sorts of bargains that are more usually associated with self-interested motivations.

In order to say that the public meaning of legal charity in cases of fee-charging is aligned with altruism, it must not only be possible for

---

[48] See Chesterman, *Charities, Trusts and Social Welfare*, above n 4, ch 14.
[49] See Rob Atkinson, 'Altruism in Nonprofit Organizations' (1990) 31 *Boston College Law Review* 501, esp 551–553.

fee-charging to be motivated by altruism; it must also be likely that such fee-charging will be interpreted as motivated by altruism. For as long as the 'not for profit' rule demands that fee-charging be nothing more than a means to the end of achieving a 'not for profit' purpose, interpretations of fee-charging in the charity law setting as motivated in some degree by altruism seem not only possible but also likely. That said, pressure is exerted on charity law in certain cases of fee-charging such that any consistency that charity law has achieved between the public meaning of legal charity and altruism in such cases cannot be taken for granted. First, charity law is sometimes required to respond to cases in which private goods are exchanged for a contract price and the income represented by that contract price is then applied to a charitable purpose unrelated to the provision of the private goods in question. This occurred in an Australian case we encountered in Chapter 1, *Federal Commissioner of Taxation* v. *Word Investments Ltd*, in which funeral services were sold and the resulting income applied to the advancement of religion;[50] a contrast might be drawn between this case and the older Australian case of *Re Resch's Will Trusts*, in which a private hospital provided health care services in exchange for fees, the provision of those health care services itself being the charitable purpose of the hospital in question.[51] Second, charity law is sometimes required to respond to cases in which fee-charging is deployed as a means to achieve both 'for profit' and 'not for profit' purposes, in circumstances where neither the 'for profit' nor the 'not for profit' purpose is dominant. Such hybrid models for the delivery of private goods to the public have, to date, been excluded from the project of charity law, but some have argued that they should not be.[52] The pressure exerted in these types of case urges the state to permit legal charity to carry public meaning that is associated more than ever before with the self-interested motivations that underpin bargains. We will take up the question of how the state should respond to such pressure in the next part of this chapter.

In summary, then, although in some respects the association of legal charity and altruism in cases of fee-charging might be under pressure, as

---

[50] (2008) 236 CLR 204 (High Court of Australia).   [51] [1968] 1 AC 514 (Privy Council).
[52] For the argument that hybrid models should be regarded as charitable: Malani and Posner, above n 12. But see also Brian Galle, 'Social Enterprise: Who Needs It?' (2013) 54 *Boston College Law Review* 2025, arguing that there is no economic case for hybrid models; if Galle is right, then – all else being equal – hybrid models might be expected not to survive the test of time.

matters stand there are reasons to think that the public meaning of legal charity in those cases remains broadly consistent with altruism. In contrast, the public meaning of legal charity in cases entailing gifts to a private class seems, in certain respects, to diverge from altruism, especially in Australia in light of statutory innovations. But even if the public meaning of legal charity in cases of gifts to a private class is less than perfectly calibrated to serving the state's interest in altruism in the charity law setting, it is still open to us to maintain that the public meaning of legal charity, generally speaking, is associated closely with altruism. In order to subscribe to that proposition, we need not be convinced that a plausible interpretation is available that ascribes altruistic motivations to every instance of legal charity. All that is necessary is that such an interpretation be available in respect of most instances of legal charity. As we have seen in this part of the chapter, there are reasons to think that, in light of the strictures imposed by the 'public' component of the public benefit test and the 'not for profit' rule – strictures that bear upon gifts to a private class, 'self-help' arrangements, 'member benefit' arrangements and the pursuit of private profit – it is both possible and plausible to interpret most instances of legal charity as motivated by the sort of unmediated regard for others that is characteristic of altruism, and not by self-interest on the one hand or by a sense of duty or attachment on the other.

Before leaving the topic of altruism, the 'public' component of the public benefit test and the 'not for profit' rule, we should consider the principle that appears to prevail in the British Isles to the effect that purposes that exclude the poor are not public purposes and therefore not charitable purposes. Is the pursuit of a purpose that excludes the poor, say because it entails charging fees for the provision of private goods that the poor cannot afford, likely to be motivated non-altruistically? If so, then the exclusion of such purposes from the project of charity law via the 'public' component of the public benefit test seems once again to reflect the state's interest in altruism in the setting of charity law. In considering this question, one point may be dispensed with quickly: there would appear to be no reason to think that the pursuit of a purpose that excludes the poor is any more likely to be motivated by self-interest than the pursuit of a purpose that does not exclude the poor. Insofar as no distinction can be drawn between purposes that exclude the poor and purposes that do not exclude the poor based on the likelihood of the two classes of purpose to reflect self-interested motivations, the state's interest in altruism in the charity law setting is not obviously served by adopting different approaches to each class.

Whether or not purposes that exclude the poor are likely to be motivated by a sense of duty or attachment is a more interesting question. Writing in 1979, Michael Chesterman suggested that fee-charging schools whose fees exclude the poor have traditionally perpetuated the social and economic dominance of the upper and upper-middle classes who largely populate and fund them;[53] this suggestion implies that such schools might lack altruism because they are animated by notions of class loyalty and solidarity, rendering them analogous to 'self-help' arrangements. The likelihood that the motivations of those who establish and run schools whose fees exclude the poor are non-altruistic in this way depends on a range of factors, including the extent to which 'class' figures in contemporary understandings of identity and society, the extent to which links are perceived between attendance at one or another school and social and economic privilege in later life and the extent to which the upper and upper-middle classes really do populate fee-charging schools to the exclusion of others in society. These factors are likely to vary from society to society and from generation to generation, so much so that the proposition that the motivations of those who establish and run schools whose fees exclude the poor are unlikely to be altruistic cannot be accepted with confidence. These observations about fee-charging schools point to reasons to think that the principle that seems to prevail in the British Isles, that purposes that exclude the poor are insufficiently public to be charitable, may constitute a dimension of the 'public' component of the public benefit test that does not reflect the state's interest in altruism in the charity law setting. Indeed, as we will see in Chapter 4, it is arguable that this element of the public benefit test has less to do with altruism than with the state's interest in an entirely different type of consideration bearing on charity law: the demands of distributive justice.[54]

4. Charity law and altruism from a liberal perspective

To the extent that the 'public' component of the public benefit test and the 'not for profit' rule align the public meaning of legal charity with altruism, two consequences might be expected to follow. First, we might

---

[53] Chesterman, *Charities, Trusts and Social Welfare*, above n 4, 348.

[54] Indeed, Chesterman's anxiety about the charitable status of fee-charging schools seems to be more about the distributive implications of those schools than the extent to which they are characterised by altruism: ibid, 336; Chesterman, 'Foundations of Charity Law in the New Welfare State', above n 2.

expect that those who are motivated altruistically are encouraged to express their altruism by pursuing purposes that are recognised as charitable in law. To the extent that the public meaning of legal charity is aligned with altruism, the actions entailed in legal charity are likely to be interpreted as motivated by altruism; thus, charity law gives the altruistic some degree of assurance that, should they choose to express their altruism by pursuing charitable purposes, their expression of altruism will be successful in the sense that their altruistic actions will be correctly interpreted. Second, we might expect that those who pursue charitable purposes are encouraged to do so altruistically, in the sense that they are encouraged to think that altruism is a fitting motivation to have when pursuing such purposes and to adjust their motivations for pursuing charitable purposes accordingly. The state's interest in altruism in the charity law setting – an interest that, as we have seen, is revealed by the 'public' component of the public benefit test as well as the 'not for profit' rule – might thus be described more precisely as an interest in promoting a culture in which citizens are both able and encouraged successfully to act altruistically by pursuing charitable purposes. Put more simply, the state's interest in the charity law setting seems to be in promoting altruism.

At this point in the analysis, we once again face a difficulty that we considered in Chapter 2 when discussing charity law and the harm principle, as well as earlier in this chapter in our discussion of the power-conferring character of some of the rules of charity law. The difficulty is in reconciling the liberal justification of charity law with its incentive strategy, manifested largely in the tax privileges extended by the state to those with charitable purposes. In earlier discussions, the particular difficulty was in reconciling charity law's incentive strategy with the demands of autonomy. Now the difficulty is in reconciling that strategy with the state's interest in promoting altruism. This is because the incentive strategy of charity law appears to depend for its efficacy on an appeal to precisely the self-interest that is inconsistent with altruism; as Emad Atiq argues in a searching examination of the effect of legal incentives on human motivations, such appeals to self-interest risk 'crowding out' altruism both in the sense that there is a risk that the addressees of incentives will be self-interested and in the sense that the actions of the addressees of incentives will be interpreted by others as self-interested.[55]

---

[55] Emad H Atiq, 'Why Motives Matter: Reframing the Crowding Out Effect of Legal Incentives' (2014) 123 *Yale Law Journal* 1070. See also Malani and Posner, above n 12, 2066–2067.

Any such 'crowding-out' effect would render the state's project of promoting altruism via charity law self-defeating.

There can be no doubt that any appeal to self-interest that is embedded in the incentive strategy of charity law is inconsistent with altruism, to the extent that the incentive strategy leads to citizens pursuing and being understood to pursue charitable purposes in a largely self-interested way. And perhaps the incentive strategy, where it is successful, generates this outcome in respect of the motivations of some citizens who pursue charitable purposes.[56] However, it is worth reiterating two points that were made in Chapter 2 and earlier in this chapter – points that cast doubt on the thought that charity law's incentive strategy yields this result even much of the time. First, when a person is incentivised to do something that she has independent reasons to do, she may have acted both for reasons generated by the incentive and for independent reasons. To the extent that the incentive strategy of charity law figures in this non-exhaustive way in the practical reasoning of those who pursue charitable purposes, it is entirely plausible to assert that charitable purposes might be accompanied by motivations that, although self-interested to a degree, are also altruistic to a degree.[57] Second, incentives tend to encourage people to act such that they come to be in positions from which they are better able to understand and engage with independent reasons that apply to them. Thus, the incentive strategy of charity law may cause citizens to pursue charitable purposes self-interestedly at first, but may also set in train processes by which those citizens come to appreciate that altruism is a fitting motivation for the pursuit of charitable purposes and adjust their motivations accordingly. In this regard it is worth remembering that the public meaning of legal charity is aligned with altruism, and that charity law has operated by an incentive strategy for a long time;[58] this suggests that, to some degree, an incentive strategy has in fact been consistent with the state's promotion of altruism via charity law.[59]

---

[56] And, to the extent that tax subsidies are extended to charitable donors, in respect of the motivations of such donors as well.

[57] See Jane J. Mansbridge, 'On the Relation of Altruism and Self-Interest' in Jane J. Mansbridge (ed), *Beyond Self-Interest* (University of Chicago Press, 1990) 133–143.

[58] For example, charities have enjoyed exemptions from income tax for as long as income tax has been raised: see generally Ann O'Connell, 'Charitable Treatment? – A Short History of the Taxation of Charities in Australia' in John Tiley (ed), *Studies in the History of Tax Law: Volume 5* (Hart Publishing, Oxford, 2012) 91–124.

[59] For further reflections on the idea that the law may promote altruism successfully: Hanoch Dagan, *The Law and Ethics of Restitution* (Cambridge University Press, 2004), 103–106.

However, any such consistency cannot be taken as given, and we must hold open the possibility that the uneasy alliance of charity law's incentive strategy and the state's promotion of altruism via charity law might at some point come apart.[60]

In this last part of the chapter, let us assume that the state promotes altruism via charity law and that charity law – including its incentive strategy – is a plausible means by which the state may promote altruism; making that assumption, let us ask, from a liberal perspective, why the state might promote altruism via charity law. Once again, our starting point in considering this question is the liberal ideal of autonomy in the sense of self-determination. Recall from Chapter 2 that autonomy, thus understood, is possible only where certain conditions obtain; among these conditions is the existence of what Joseph Raz calls an 'adequate range' of options to choose from in forging a self-determining path in life.[61] Recall also that the existence of an adequate range of options depends to a significant degree on the existence of non-excludable public goods relating to cultural institutions, practices, understandings and arrangements: goods that, according to Raz, go towards shaping the 'general character of ... society'.[62] We are now in a position to see that the culture generated by the state's promotion of altruism via charity law – a culture in which citizens are both able and encouraged to act altruistically by pursuing charitable purposes – may be viewed as such an autonomy-promoting public good. Such a culture makes available, both to those who are altruistic and to those who are not altruistic but who might, through the pursuit of charitable purposes, come to be motivated by altruism, options to combine altruism and the pursuit of charitable purposes in ways that are likely to be successful. To the extent that the state's promotion of altruism in the charity law setting has these consequences, charity law generates a whole distinct mode of social interaction – the altruistic pursuit of charitable purposes – not only via the power-conferring and analogous rules that make it possible and attractive to pursue such purposes, but also by giving form and content to the public meaning of that pursuit. In a society where altruism is possible and where citizens choose to pursue purposes that are

---

[60] Atiq, above n 55, 1097–1098 suggests that misuse of the charitable deduction in the United States may bring about such a state of affairs.
[61] Joseph Raz, *The Morality of Freedom* (Clarendon Press, Oxford, 1986), 372.
[62] Ibid, 199, 206.

recognised as charitable in law, this is a significant contribution to the conditions of autonomy.

Of course, none of this is to say that citizens cannot act altruistically except by pursuing charitable purposes. It is possible to imagine a world in which citizens successfully express altruism in their dealings with one another even though there is no law of charity. That such a world can be imagined points to an argument against the proposition that the state has an unconditional duty to promote altruism via charity law, or indeed in any other way, but leaves intact the weaker proposition that, in the world as we find it, the state has reasons to promote altruism via charity law. For one thing, any project of promoting altruism, in the absence of charity law, via extant social institutions and arrangements such as the family, civil society and the market is likely to be frustrated by the fact that those institutions and arrangements are typically characterised by self-interest, or duties and attachments, or both. Moreover, in societies that have charity law, the close connection between altruism and the public meaning of legal charity may be such that if the state were to cease promoting altruism via charity law, say by abandoning the 'public' component of the public benefit test or by permitting 'for profit' purposes to be charitable in law, it would frustrate citizens' settled expectations about the ways in which altruism may successfully be expressed in their society. Where the state withdraws options or makes new options available, it ought, in light of the value of autonomy, to do so conservatively, paying due regard to the settled expectations of citizens.[63] This does not amount to an argument that the liberal state must always make it possible for citizens altruistically to pursue charitable purposes, but it does suggest that – in light of the ideal of autonomy – the liberal state may have good reasons, once it has enabled and encouraged citizens to express altruism by pursuing charitable purposes, to continue to do so.

Another argument, also pointing to cultural considerations, might reveal reasons for the liberal state to promote altruism via charity law. This argument begins with the proposition that in many societies the norms of the market, being the norms surrounding the expressly conditional exchanges that constitute bargains, have in recent history enjoyed considerable expansion in their range of operation; according to the argument, modes of social interaction that once entailed non-market norms – for example, modes of social interaction bound up with

---

[63] Ibid, 411.

government or civil society – have increasingly come to be characterised by market norms, leading, among other things, to the inexorable displacement of altruistic gift-giving by self-interested bargaining.[64] From the perspective of autonomy-based liberalism, this trend ought to be of concern. As we saw in Chapter 2, the exercise of autonomy in the sense of genuine choice among an adequate range of options depends on the existence of many sorts of value to choose from; it depends on value pluralism. All else being equal, then, autonomy demands that there be some diversity in the modes of social interaction; more specifically, it demands that it be possible for citizens to interact with each other according to norms other than the norms of the market.[65] On this view, there is a liberal argument for the state to maintain a bulwark against the encroachment of market norms into all spheres of social interaction, and to the extent that charity law assists in this task because of the close alignment of the public meaning of legal charity and altruism, there is a liberal argument for the state's promotion of altruism via charity law.

This last argument might be invoked against those who would argue for a watering down of the 'not for profit' rule of charity law. We saw earlier that in two types of case pressure is brought to bear on that rule: first, where private goods are exchanged for a contract price and the income represented by that contract price is then applied to an unrelated charitable purpose; and second, where fee-charging is deployed as a means to achieve both 'for profit' and 'not for profit' purposes, in circumstances where neither the 'for profit' nor the 'not for profit' purpose is dominant. To the extent that the 'not for profit' rule is relaxed in response to the pressure exerted by these types of case, decision-makers risk facilitating the encroachment of market norms into the sphere of social interaction that is constituted by legal charity, and any such development is – in light of the argument from diversity in the modes of social interaction just outlined – to be viewed with caution and possibly resisted.[66] Moreover, the argument from diversity in the modes

---

[64] See, e.g., Titmuss, above n 28; Peter Singer, 'Altruism and Commerce: A Defence of Titmuss against Arrow' (1973) 2 *Philosophy and Public Affairs* 312; Michael J. Sandel, *What Money Can't Buy: The Moral Limits of Markets* (Allen Lane, London, 2012).

[65] Note Hanoch Dagan, 'Pluralism and Perfectionism in Private Law' (2012) 112 *Columbia Law Review* 1409, 1424: 'law should facilitate (within limits) the coexistence of various social spheres embodying different modes of valuation.'

[66] In some jurisdictions, the state taxes business income that is applied in the pursuit of a charitable purpose where the business is unrelated to the purpose, thus withdrawing one of the incentives of charity law from charities to the extent that they carry on unrelated

of social interaction equips us in significant ways to see why the boundaries of charity law might be drawn where they are drawn as between different autonomy-promoting purposes. In light of the argument from diversity in modes of social interaction, we can see that drawing the boundaries of charity law so as to exclude some autonomy-promoting purposes from the project underpinning charity law might be justified to the extent that circumscribing charity law in this way generates a gain in the autonomy of those who carry out charitable purposes.

5. Conclusion

In order to illuminate the choice and the boundaries of charity law, this chapter has largely considered the implications of charity law for those who pursue charitable purposes, rather than those who stand to be affected by the pursuit of such purposes. Thus, the perspective of this chapter has been on what some have called the 'supply' rather than the 'demand' side of the pursuit of charitable purposes.[67] From this 'supply'-side perspective, reasons supporting the choice of charity law emerge from reflection on the ways in which the facilities and incentives of charity help to constitute options for those with charitable purposes; equally, the boundaries of charity law appear to be justified insofar as they reflect a state project of promoting a distinctive and potentially endangered mode of social interaction: altruism. If the chapter has shown anything, it is that the 'supply'-side perspective is an important one in

---

businesses. The reasons for and against such a tax are various, and the subject of much dispute; for present purposes, we need note only that an unrelated business income tax may, among other things, express state caution towards the encroachment of market norms into the traditionally donative sphere of legal charity. For further discussion, see Joyce Chia and Miranda Stewart, 'Doing Business to Do Good: Should We Tax the Business Profits of Not-for-Profits?' (2012) 33 *Adelaide Law Review* 335, esp 367–370.

[67] A focus on the 'supply' side has been urged elsewhere, usually in the course of critiquing the various demand-focused 'failure theories' that economists have put forward to explain (and sometimes justify) the existence of a not-for-profit (including a charitable) sector: for the critique see, e.g., Rob Atkinson, 'Altruism in Nonprofit Organizations', above n 49; Rob Atkinson, 'Theories of the Federal Income Tax Exemption for Charities: Thesis, Antithesis, and Synthesis' (1997) 27 *Stetson Law Review* 395; Matthew Turnour, *Beyond Charity: Outlines of a Jurisprudence for Civil Society* (PhD thesis, Queensland University of Technology, 2009); Rob Reich, 'Towards a Political Theory of Philanthropy' in Patricia Illingworth, Thomas Pogge and Leif Wenar (eds), *Giving Well: The Ethics of Philanthropy* (Oxford University Press, 2011) 177–195; Matthew Turnour and Myles McGregor-Lowndes, 'Wrong Way Go Back! Rediscovering the Path for Charity Law Reform' (2012) 35 *University of New South Wales Law Journal* 810.

developing a liberal theory of charity law grounded in the value and demands of autonomy.

That said, this chapter concludes by sounding two notes of caution about the 'supply'-side perspective. First, to argue that the boundaries of charity law may be illuminated by focusing on the 'supply' side of the pursuit of charitable purposes is not to say that the 'supply' side is somehow prior to or more important than the 'demand' side. In theory, if, by recognising a wider range of autonomy-promoting purposes as charitable in law, the state would generate a substantial enough dividend in terms of the conditions of autonomy for its citizens, then this might necessitate a watering down of the public benefit test or charity law's disqualifying rules and even the loss of options successfully to combine altruism and the pursuit of charitable purposes that such a watering down might entail. In assessing the justification of charity law from the perspective of autonomy-based liberalism, we must keep in view both the 'demand' side and the 'supply' side, and aim to grasp how charity law promotes the autonomy both of those who pursue charitable purposes and the autonomy of those who stand to benefit from charitable purposes being carried out. And a second note of caution is warranted too: even if promoting altruism justifies the state in refusing to promote some autonomy-promoting purposes via charity law, it does not necessarily mean that the state is justified in refusing altogether to promote those purposes; it is simply to say that there are reasons for the state to preserve the vehicle of charity law for the promotion of only some autonomy-promoting purposes. Indeed, in this connection it is worth noting that, even though 'for profit' purposes are not charitable in law, the state nonetheless promotes many such purposes in circumstances where they stand to generate beneficial consequences for the community, and this promotion is achieved via facilitative, incentive and expressive strategies entailed in bodies of law other than charity law.[68]

---

[68] See Malani and Posner, above n 12, 2031: 'We frequently observe government giving tax subsidies to for-profit firms that engage in community-minded activities. Consider the massive subsidies, for example, to alternative energy producers, including automobile manufacturers that develop hybrids and farmers who develop ethanol-based fuel.'

Charity law and distributive justice

1. Introduction

In Chapter 2, in thinking about a choice of perspective from which to develop a liberal theory of charity law, we saw that John Rawls's theory of social justice failed to engage the aspects of charity law – not least the state's promotion of charitable purposes – that do not fall to be analysed and evaluated first and foremost as questions of justice. We rejected Rawls's theory of social justice as a candidate in which to ground a liberal theory of charity law for that reason. But of course charity law does raise questions of justice, even if those questions are not the only questions, or the first or most important questions, we might ask about it, and the questions of justice that charity law raises demand consideration within a liberal theory of charity law, even if they do not exhaust such a theory. In this chapter, we will take up such questions about charity law and justice from a liberal perspective. More specifically, we will consider one question about justice that arises in the setting of a broader examination of charity law: in what ways, and to what extent, does distributive justice constitute a constraint on charity law? In keeping with the larger project of this book, we will explore the question of charity law and distributive justice in ways that are consistent with the autonomy-based liberalism that we first encountered in Chapter 2. But at the outset, it must be acknowledged that in a sense it is odd, from the perspective of autonomy-based liberalism, to talk about the possibility that distributive justice might constitute a constraint on charity law. For one thing, in the liberal tradition the claim that distributive justice is a constraint on state action is often thought to be a deontological claim, animated by some interpretation of the notion that the right is prior to the good and that the moral basis of distributive justice, like the moral basis of justice generally, is somehow fundamental and distinct from other moral considerations.[1] This sort of deontological claim finds no place in autonomy-based liberalism.[2] Moreover, distributive justice, at least as it figures in liberal political philosophy, is typically thought to be a matter of the demands of social and economic equality,[3] and yet egalitarian demands are downplayed in autonomy-based liberalism in favour of demands stemming from other political concerns, most obviously the demands of autonomy.[4] In short, with the demands of autonomy in view, to ask about the extent to which distributive justice might constitute a constraint on charity law is to risk asking the wrong sort of question.

Nonetheless, from the perspective of autonomy-based liberalism, it is plausible to speak of the possibility of distributive justice as a constraint on charity law; moreover, we can do so in ways that promise to illuminate the topic of charity law and distributive justice not only for those who are committed to autonomy-based liberalism, but also for liberals whose conception of distributive justice is either deontological or egalitarian or both, and indeed for at least some non-liberals who have a conception of distributive justice as a constraint on state action as well. Consider first how we might conceive of distributive justice as a constraint on charity law within a framework that does not admit of deontological grounds for the limits of state action and that instead appeals to the value of autonomy in working out such limits. The key to such a conception is in the proposition that distributive justice, rather than being a prior, fundamental and distinct sort of moral concern, is in fact an outworking of the demands of the political ideal of autonomy, especially the demands placed on the state to ensure that the conditions of autonomy are brought about and

---

[1] See, e.g., John Rawls, *A Theory of Justice* (rev. paperback edn, Oxford University Press, 1999). See also, from a libertarian perspective, Robert Nozick, *Anarchy, State, and Utopia* (Basic Books, New York, 1974) ch 3. For a discussion of the notion that the right is prior to the good: Michael J. Sandel, *Liberalism and the Limits of Justice* (2nd edn., Cambridge University Press, 1998) ch 1.

[2] Joseph Raz, *The Morality of Freedom* (Clarendon Press, Oxford, 1986), 214–216. See also Stephen Macedo, *Liberal Virtues: Citizenship, Virtue, and Community in Liberal Constitutionalism* (Clarendon Press, Oxford, 1990), 203–210.

[3] See, e.g., Rawls, *A Theory of Justice*, above n 1; Ronald Dworkin, *Sovereign Virtue: The Theory and Practice of Equality* (Harvard University Press, Cambridge, MA, 2000).

[4] Raz, *The Morality of Freedom*, above n 2, ch 9. See also Derek Parfit, 'Equality and Priority' (1997) 10 *Ratio* 202, esp 214. Note, however, that it is possible to conceive of equality in ways that are broadly consistent with autonomy-based liberalism: see, e.g., Samuel Scheffler, 'What is Egalitarianism?' (2003) 31 *Philosophy and Public Affairs* 5.

maintained.[5] In this view, distributive justice mediates between the ideal of autonomy and principles of state action. In this regard, an analogy might be drawn between the role of distributive justice and the role that Joseph Raz – the leading exponent of autonomy-based liberalism – ascribes to rights in his account of political morality; for Raz, rights are not objects of ultimate moral concern but instead are conventionally valuable because, and to the extent that, they serve objects of ultimate moral concern.[6] Insofar as distributive justice serves this sort of mediating role in political morality, it is, on what we might call the Razian view, a constraint on state action to the extent that the conditions of autonomy will be promoted better by the state adhering to the demands of distributive justice than by pursuing some goal that is inconsistent with those demands, even if the achievement of that goal would promote autonomy to some degree. However – and importantly – because on the Razian view distributive justice is an outworking of the demands of autonomy, it is a constraint on state action only to the extent that such a constraint is necessary to serve the demands of autonomy.[7] The critical question, then, taking the Razian view, is the question of when autonomy will be best promoted by adhering to the demands of distributive justice and when it will be best promoted by the pursuit of some autonomy-promoting goal, even though the demands of distributive justice will not be met by this pursuit.[8] On the Razian view, the scope of distributive justice as a constraint on state action turns on the answer to this question.

What does distributive justice demand within an account of political morality grounded in the value of autonomy? A complete answer to this question can be formulated only on the basis of detailed analysis of what autonomy demands, given various ways in which the citizens of a

---

[5] See Joseph Raz, 'Facing Up: A Reply' (1989) 62 *Southern California Law Review* 1153, 1233.

[6] Raz, *The Morality of Freedom*, above n 2, chs 7 and 8; Joseph Raz, 'Rights and Individual Well-Being' in his *Ethics in the Public Domain: Essays in the Morality of Law and Politics* (Oxford University Press, 1994) 44–59, 52–55.

[7] Thus a holder of the Razian view cannot agree with the proposition that justice is the primary virtue in the sense of being 'the [virtue] that must be met before others can make their claims': Sandel, above n 1, 2. For a defence of that proposition: Jeremy Waldron, 'The Primacy of Justice' (2003) 9 *Legal Theory* 269.

[8] In this way, in autonomy-based liberalism, distributive justice is a softer constraint than the harm principle that we first encountered in Chapter 2. The state is never justified in pursuing an autonomy-promoting goal if this will violate the harm principle, but the state may be justified in pursuing an autonomy-promoting goal at a cost to distributive justice.

political community might be differently situated. Such analysis would be extraordinarily complex and difficult. Fortunately, for present purposes, we can be much more tentative and modest; it will suffice to notice that, whatever else distributive justice might entail within autonomy-based liberalism, it will almost certainly demand some redistribution of goods from those members of society who are not poor to those members of society who are poor, so as to ensure that those members of society who are poor enjoy the conditions of autonomy to some sufficient degree. Recall from Chapter 2 that the conditions of autonomy include the development and maintenance of what Raz calls 'inner capacities' that are necessary to living a self-determining life, as well as freedom from coercion and manipulation, and of course an adequate range of options to choose from in living autonomously. In varying degrees and for different reasons, people who live in poverty are likely not to enjoy the conditions of autonomy in their lives in ways that ought to be of concern within autonomy-based liberalism, and in some cases in severe ways that demand urgent attention from that perspective. For example, poor people may not have the chance to develop through education certain capacities necessary to being autonomous; their lack of personal security may render them susceptible to intolerable coercion and interference in their lives;[9] or they may be unable, simply by virtue of expending all their energies on the daily grind, to access the adequate range of options that is so important to an autonomous life. The position of poor people, then, ought to be a matter of special concern within autonomy-based liberalism.[10]

---

[9] See Jeremy Waldron, 'Homelessness and the Issue of Freedom' in his *Liberal Rights: Collected Papers 1981–1991* (Cambridge University Press, 1993) 309–338; G.A. Cohen, 'Freedom and Money' in his *On the Currency of Egalitarian Justice and Other Essays in Political Philosophy* (Princeton University Press, Princeton, 2011) 166–192.

[10] Indeed, the position of people who lack welfare in other ways that compromise their enjoyment of the conditions of autonomy – because they suffer from ill health or have disabilities, for example – also ought to be of special concern within autonomy-based liberalism, and a conception of distributive justice based on the demands of autonomy almost certainly requires redistributions to such people. For the purposes of this chapter, however, it will be sufficient to focus on redistributions to the poor. Moreover, such a focus assists in presenting arguments about distributive justice and charity law that may be accepted by the holders of a variety of views about distributive justice; although philosophers debate what counts as a lack of welfare for the purposes of distributive justice, they typically agree that being poor counts as such a lack of welfare. For an overview of the debate: Will Kymlicka, *Contemporary Political Philosophy: An Introduction* (2nd edn., Oxford University Press, 2002) ch 3.

Autonomy, understood as a political ideal, demands that the state take steps to improve the position of poor people so that they may enjoy the conditions of autonomy to some sufficient degree, first through the provision of the public goods on which an adequate range of options depends, but also through ensuring that the poor are provided with private goods such as education and health care that contribute to the conditions of autonomy in various ways. This, in itself, does not amount to a demand of distributive justice. As we saw in Chapter 2, and will consider in further detail shortly, justice is a matter of rights or distribution. And it is possible for the state to take steps to improve the position of poor people without necessarily adopting a mindset attuned to questions of rights or distribution in the way that is characteristic of justice. In particular, it is possible for the state to improve the position of the poor without comparing the positions of potential or actual claimants for distribution in the way that is distinctive of distributive justice.[11] For example, the state might try to improve the position of the poor by acting in a community-minded way, or humanely, or charitably (in the non-legal sense), or mercifully.[12] However, to the extent that, in order to improve the position of the poor so as to serve their autonomy, the state must redistribute goods from those who are not poor to those who are poor, the state must adopt the distributive and comparative mindset that is characteristic of distributive justice, and to that extent the state is within the purview of an autonomy-based conception of distributive justice.

Of course, it is possible to imagine societies in which the state makes improvements to the position of the poor so as to serve their autonomy without at the same time redistributing goods from those who are not poor, say by financing the provision of public goods by selling some state-owned asset or exploiting some new-found natural resource; this reveals that the demands of an autonomy-based conception of distributive justice are contingent on the existence of social and economic

---

[11] On the comparative aspect of distributive justice, see further John Gardner, 'Part 1: The Virtue of Justice and the Character of Law' in his *Law as a Leap of Faith* (Oxford University Press, 2012) 238–269, 242–246.

[12] Incidentally, we are now in a position to see why, from the perspective of autonomy-based liberalism, social and economic equality are downplayed as important dimensions of political morality. What often seems to matter most once the demands of autonomy are in view is not the position of the poor relative to other potential recipients of distributable goods but rather that the poor are poor, irrespective of how others are situated, and that improving the position of the poor will enhance their autonomy. See further Raz, *The Morality of Freedom*, above n 2, 233–244.

conditions that compel the state to redistribute goods among citizens. However, it is undoubtedly the case that in modern capitalist societies, the social and economic conditions under which state-organised improvements to the position of the poor necessarily require redistribution from those who are not poor invariably do prevail. Those conditions include the institutions of private property and the free market. Thus, the contingency of the demands of an autonomy-based conception of distributive justice is of academic interest only; for us, from the perspective of autonomy-based liberalism, the demands of distributive justice are real demands.

This account of an autonomy-based conception of distributive justice is broad and general and does not tell us much of what we might wish to know were we to set about systematically working out the implications of distributive justice for a particular political community. In a sense it might be described best as setting out some general contours of the demands of distributive justice understood in light of autonomy as a political ideal. That said, those contours will suffice for present purposes because, in order to understand the arguments about charity law and distributive justice that we will encounter in this chapter, we need only have a general sense of a conception of distributive justice that demands some redistribution of goods to the poor. Moreover, insofar as it requires those who are not poor to shoulder a burden of some sort in order to improve the position of the poor, the autonomy-based conception of distributive justice with which we will work in this chapter is likely to have broad philosophical appeal. It is not implausible to assert that if one cares about distributive justice at all, unless one is the sort of libertarian for whom questions of historical entitlement are the only legitimate concern of distributive justice,[13] one's conception of distributive justice will in some way endorse or mandate some redistribution to the poor. And, indeed, the idea that distributive justice demands some such redistribution to the poor is consistent with a range of principles of distributive justice at large in mainstream political philosophy, from John Rawls's well-known 'difference principle',[14] to the Maximin principle,[15] to

---

[13] See, e.g., Nozick, above n 1.

[14] See Rawls, above n 1, 266: 'Social and economic inequalities are to be arranged so that they are ... to the greatest benefit of the least advantaged.'

[15] According to the Maximin principle, the best outcome is the one in which the worst-off people are best off. This is often thought to be the same as Rawls's difference principle, and Rawls himself appears to have thought of the two as closely connected: John Rawls, 'Some Reasons for the Maximin Criterion' (1974) 64 The American Economic Review 141.

Ronald Dworkin's principles of equality of resources,[16] to the principle of priority for the worst off (a principle that has affinities with an autonomy-based conception of distributive justice),[17] to capability approaches to questions of distribution.[18] We are now in a position to see why an examination of charity law and an autonomy-based conception of distributive justice, broadly understood, promises to be illuminating for liberals with deontological commitments and certain other philosophers who take an interest in questions of distribution but do not identify as liberals: to the extent that such an examination takes an autonomy-based conception of distributive justice to demand nothing more specific than redistribution to the poor, it is consistent with any conception of distributive justice that, in general terms, can be said to make the same demand.

A short summary is in order. In this chapter we will consider the ways in which, and the extent to which, distributive justice constitutes a constraint on charity law. In viewing distributive justice as a 'constraint', the chapter will depart from deontological understandings and instead take the Razian view that in some circumstances the demands of autonomy are such that distributive justice must be achieved even though this might interfere with or limit the state in its pursuit of other goals, including autonomy-promoting goals. The conception of 'distributive justice' that will figure in the chapter is a conception according to which some redistribution of goods to the poor is required. This conception is consistent not only with autonomy-based liberalism but also with other liberal and non-liberal theories of distributive justice; moreover, it is a conception that describes only general contours, rather than detailed outworkings, of autonomy-based distributive justice. The remainder of the chapter will explore two ways in which it might be thought that distributive justice, thus understood, operates as a constraint on charity law. First, we will consider the possibility that distributive justice might constrain the state in its recognition of one or another purpose as charitable in law; this possibility raises the question of the extent to which, because of the demands of distributive justice, the state should refuse altogether to promote a particular purpose via the facilitative,

However, there are differences: Derek Parfit, *Reasons and Persons* (Oxford University Press, 1984), 490–491.

[16] Dworkin, above n 3, ch 2.

[17] See Parfit, 'Equality and Priority', above n 4, for a description.

[18] See Amartya Sen, *Inequality Reexamined* (Clarendon Press, Oxford, 1992).

incentive and expressive strategies of charity law. This first inquiry is of particular interest given that, in some jurisdictions, charity law incorporates a requirement that a purpose, in order to be charitable, must not exclude the poor. Second, we will consider the possibility that distributive justice constrains the state in the means by which it promotes those purposes that it recognises as charitable in law; this possibility raises the question of the extent to which, because of the demands of distributive justice, the state should refrain from pursuing particular facilitative, incentive or expressive strategies of charity law. This second inquiry most obviously demands consideration of the requirements of distributive justice in relation to one of the most controversial and complex dimensions of charity law: the tax privileges that the state extends to those with charitable purposes. The focus in the last part of this chapter will be on those tax privileges.

2.   Distributive justice and the recognition of charitable purposes

In Chapter 1, we saw that in many parts of the British Isles, a purpose that excludes the poor is not regarded as charitable in law. This phenomenon seems of interest in light of a conception of distributive justice according to which some redistribution to the poor is required; can it be said that, in jurisdictions where a purpose that excludes the poor is not charitable, the criteria of charity law incorporate or reflect the demands of distributive justice, requiring at least some of those who carry out charitable purposes to achieve some redistribution to the poor? On one view, a requirement that charitable purposes include the poor is not animated by considerations of distributive justice at all; on this view, such a requirement is instead best understood as trying to ensure that the purposes that are regarded as charitable in law keep faith in some way with the non-legal understanding of charity.[19] However, if the aim of a requirement to include the poor is to align the public meanings of legal charity and non-legal charity in this way, then arguably the requirement serves its aim less than well. As John Gardner has argued, the virtue of charity, understood in its non-legal sense, does not concern itself with questions of inclusion and exclusion; for Gardner, the charitable person is interested in helping the poor not because they are unable to access goods that are enjoyed by others, but

---

[19] Arguably, this view is consistent with the reasoning in *In re Macduff* [1896] 2 Ch 451 (Court of Appeal).

simply because they are poor.[20] To a degree, the criteria of charity law enable the expression of the virtue of charity in the non-legal sense; the criteria do this most obviously in respect of purposes within the general description 'relief of poverty' (although, as we saw in Chapter 3, in the 'poor relations' and 'poor employees' cases the public meaning of legal charity departs from altruistic virtues such as charity in the non-legal sense). However, and importantly for present purposes, this enabling of the virtue of charity in the non-legal sense has nothing to do with any requirement to include the poor, because in 'relief of poverty' cases, a requirement to include the poor is otiose. If a requirement to include the poor somehow ensures that the virtue of charity in the non-legal sense can be expressed through the pursuit of charitable purposes, it must be in respect of purposes other than those meeting the description 'relief of poverty'.

Indeed, we may narrow further the class of cases in which a requirement to include the poor might do any meaningful work as an enabler of charity in the non-legal sense: as in cases of purposes within the description 'relief of poverty', a requirement to include the poor is otiose in cases where charitable purposes stand to realise public goods. The very nature of public goods is such that questions of inclusion and exclusion are meaningless when asked with respect to them.[21] This leaves charitable purposes that entail the provision of private goods and do not fall within the description 'relief of poverty'; purposes within the description 'advancement of education' constitute one clear sub-class, but there are many others, including purposes relating to health care, housing and disability support. It is in cases of purposes such as these that a requirement to include the poor makes particular demands on those who

---

[20] John Gardner, 'The Virtue of Charity and Its Foils' in Charles Mitchell and Susan R. Moody, *Foundations of Charity* (Hart Publishing, Oxford, 2000) 1–27, 11–12, although note also Will Kymlicka, 'Altruism in Philosophical and Ethical Traditions: Two Views' in Jim Phillips, Bruce Chapman and David Stevens (eds), *Between State and Market: Essays on Charities Law and Policy in Canada* (McGill-Queen's University Press, Montreal and Kingston, 2001) 87–126, 106.

[21] Of course the poor may benefit more or less than other citizens from the provision of some public good: for example, an immunisation programme may protect citizens against a disease that historically has afflicted the poor and thus generate relatively great benefits for the poor, or a botanical garden may be enjoyed most by those citizens with leisure time, which the poor lack because they must work long hours to make ends meet. Questions about who benefits most from the provision of public goods are different from questions of inclusion and exclusion and may be asked only once it is accepted that the goods in question are non-excludable.

formulate and carry out the purposes in question. In having regard to the requirement, such persons must gain some sense of who, among those who might enjoy the private goods that are on offer, is poor and who is not, and then form a view as to how those private goods are to be distributed so as to ensure that the poor are able to enjoy them in some way. This is a comparative exercise, demanding that the poor be taken into account relative to others who are not poor. We are now in a position to see why a requirement to include the poor is ill suited to enabling the expression of the virtue of charity in the non-legal sense. As we saw earlier, the virtue of charity in the non-legal sense entails a direct, unequivocal regard for the poor because they are poor; that virtue is inconsistent with the sort of comparative exercise that a requirement to include the poor demands in cases where purposes entail the provision of private goods and do not fall within the description 'relief of poverty'. Once one starts thinking in a comparative way, one is no longer acting from charity in the non-legal sense. In the only type of case in which a requirement to include the poor could plausibly make a difference to the mindset of those who formulate and carry out charitable purposes, then, such a requirement tends to influence the practical reasoning of such persons in a way that is inconsistent with the expression of the virtue of charity in the non-legal sense.

For the moment, let us leave to one side the question of the likely effect of a requirement to include the poor on the practical reasoning of those who formulate and carry out charitable purposes; we will return to that important question shortly. For now, on the basis that a requirement to include the poor is not best understood as an effort to align the public meanings of legal and non-legal charity, let us turn to a different sort of question. Is the principle of distributive justice that appears to animate a requirement to include the poor a genuine constraint on state action in the cases in which the requirement is of relevance?[22] Michael Chesterman has argued vigorously that the recognition of purposes as charitable should depend on whether or not those purposes redistribute goods to the poor in some

---

[22] It may seem odd to assert that a principle can be a principle of distributive justice and yet not be a constraint on state action. However, a principle can be a principle of distributive justice based on its formal qualities – i.e., it has to do with the distribution of goods, demands a comparative mindset, and is not a principle of justice of some special type, viz, corrective, procedural, etc – and yet lack normative force because it is morally unsound. For the distinction between sound and unsound principles of justice: John Gardner, 'What is Tort Law For?', above n 11, 13–14.

way.[23] For Chesterman, '[v]irtually every review of wealth distribution in this age of economic rationalism identifies a widening gap between rich and poor. If the institutions that we call charities are not consistently engaged in seeking to narrow this gap, it is difficult to think of a reason why they should deserve to be called "charities"'.[24] Chesterman's argument is that the state should refuse to promote, via the facilitative, incentive and expressive strategies of charity law, those purposes that do not include the poor. If the requirement to include the poor embodies a conception of distributive justice that itself constitutes a genuine constraint on the state's project of promoting charitable purposes, then Chesterman's argument is a sound one. And indeed, insofar as it demands some redistribution to the poor, the requirement to include the poor looks as if it embodies a principle of distributive justice that, from the perspective of autonomy-based liberalism, is a genuine constraint on state action in at least some circumstances. In cases where it is not otiose, the requirement demands that, to some extent, private goods realised by the pursuit of charitable purposes be allocated to the poor, and this invariably requires some redistribution from those who stand to enjoy the private goods in question and are not poor. For a private hospital, this might mean reserving a certain number of beds, which would otherwise have been available to fee-paying patients, for impecunious patients; for a private school, it might mean raising fees so as to offer scholarships based on need. Thus, in cases where it plays a meaningful role, a requirement to include the poor demands a redistribution of goods from those who are not poor to those who are poor, and this demand is consistent with the autonomy-based conception of distributive justice that we encountered earlier.

However, from the perspective of autonomy-based liberalism, because distributive justice is nothing more than an outworking of the political ideal of autonomy, whether or not distributive justice is a genuine constraint on state action in cases raising the requirement to include the poor depends on the answers to at least three questions. First, to what extent is the autonomy of the poor likely to be served by a requirement

---

[23] See Michael Chesterman, *Charities, Trusts and Social Welfare* (Weidenfeld and Nicholson, London, 1979), 349–350, 403–404; Michael Chesterman, 'Foundations of Charity Law in the New Welfare State' (1999) 62 *Modern Law Review* 333, 334.

[24] Chesterman, 'Foundations of Charity Law in the New Welfare State', above n 23, 334.

that charitable purposes include the poor? Second, what sort of cost to autonomy is likely to be occasioned by such a requirement? And finally, assuming that the autonomy of the poor is likely to be served in some non-trivial way by a requirement to include the poor, but that this gain to the autonomy of the poor comes at some cost to the autonomy of another group, how is the gain to be weighed against the cost so as to reach a judgment as to whether or not there is an overall gain to autonomy? In the remainder of this part of the chapter, we will consider these three questions together.

Gauging the extent to which one or another state of affairs is likely to generate gains or costs to autonomy can be a difficult matter. In part, this is because there is no baseline against or metric with which to measure such gains and losses; whether or not some state of affairs is likely to be autonomy-promoting, or autonomy-hindering, or make no or only a negligible difference to the conditions of autonomy is invariably to some degree a matter of moral argument and cannot be precisely calculated. In part, assessing gains and costs to autonomy is impeded by what might be called an empirical deficit, viz, the fact that our knowledge of the world as we find it and as it could be is insufficiently broad and detailed to make reasonable assessments of the likely effects on the conditions of autonomy of one or another state of affairs. That said, it seems possible, in the sorts of cases in which a requirement to include the poor might be relevant in the charity law setting, to make at least some assertions about the likely gains and costs to autonomy entailed in meeting the requirement.

To illustrate, take a private school that must meet the requirement to include the poor in order to enjoy charitable status. The school might meet the requirement by raising fees by 5 per cent so as to offer scholarships based on need. It seems plausible that there is likely to be some resulting gain to the autonomy of the poor pupils who take up the scholarships. It does not seem unreasonable to assert that the life options available to a person educated at an elite private school are, all else being equal, greater than those available to someone who has attended an inadequately resourced state school of the type that the poor are often compelled to attend, even if we might wish to see empirical evidence about the extent to which school education determines life options before making such a claim in an unqualified way. Assuming that the scholarships will lead to a gain for the autonomy of poor pupils, it also seems plausible to assert that such a gain is likely to come at no substantial cost to the autonomy of the other pupils attending the school;[25] the modest increase in fees that their parents will have to absorb is unlikely to make anything but a trivial difference to their lives, and even in the event that the increase in fees makes the school unaffordable to some parents, those parents will most likely be able to place their children in other private schools whose fees are slightly more affordable, thus ensuring that those children continue to access the various autonomy-promoting goods associated with an education at a private school. In the case of the private school that raises fees by 5 per cent to fund scholarships for poor pupils, it is plausible to suggest that, once the positions of the poor pupils and those pupils who are not poor are taken into account, the requirement to include the poor generates a greater gain to autonomy than it does any cost to autonomy. And from this case, we can generalise to suggest that where the redistribution demanded by the requirement to include the poor is a modest redistribution, it is likely to yield such an overall dividend in terms of the autonomy of the group composed of those from whom goods are taken and those to whom they are given. To the extent that the requirement to include the poor, where it forms part of the criteria of charity law, does demand nothing more than such modest redistributions, we may conclude provisionally that the requirement seems to embody a conception of distributive justice that may be reconciled with the demands of autonomy.

In the law of England and Wales, where a requirement to include the poor exists and has received some attention in recent years, it is uncertain whether or not the requirement demands only modest redistributions in all of the cases in which it might apply. In R (Independent Schools Council) v. Charity Commission for England and Wales, the case in which the requirement to include the poor was affirmed for English charity law, the Upper Tribunal (Tax and Chancery Chamber) considered at length the question of precisely what sorts of redistribution might be required, depending on the facts of different sorts of cases, in order to ensure the inclusion of the poor in the pursuit of purposes within the general description 'advancement of education'.[26] Although the discussion was extensive, it was also inconclusive, the Tribunal insisting that the

---

[25] Indeed, it seems arguable that the autonomy of those pupils may be enhanced by the increased diversity in their school that the scholarships will yield: see generally Harry Brighouse, On Education (Routledge, New York, 2006).

[26] R (Independent Schools Council) v. Charity Commission of England and Wales [2012] 2 WLR 100 (Upper Tribunal), [196]–[223] and [237]–[258].

question of what measure of redistribution might be required is a matter to be determined on a case-by-case basis.[27] At some points the Tribunal made remarks consistent with the proposition that in certain cases a requirement to include the poor might require private schools to effect non-modest redistributions to poor pupils; for example, the Tribunal at one point suggested that a school that supported poor pupils through offering means-tested bursaries to 10 per cent of its total number of pupils would only 'probably' be doing enough to ensure inclusion of the poor.[28] Elsewhere, though, the Tribunal suggested that in certain cases a non-modest redistribution in order to include poor pupils might entail an unacceptable cost to pupils who are not poor; the example given was of a specialist music school that may, if it directs too many resources to ensuring access to poor pupils, compromise the quality of the specialist education on offer.[29] The Tribunal's treatment of the case of the specialist music school was consistent with the proposition that, in certain circumstances, achieving distributive justice in the sense of redistributing goods to the poor might come at too great a cost to the autonomy of those from whom the goods in question are redistributed. Talented musicians who require specialist training and miss out on receiving it have their life options compromised in ways that should be of concern from the perspective of autonomy-based liberalism.

Arguably, then, to the extent that a requirement to include the poor demands non-modest redistributions of goods from those who are not poor to those who are poor in the pursuit of charitable purposes, it may, depending on the circumstances, be inconsistent with the demands of autonomy, and to the extent that this is so, any conception of distributive justice that it embodies may not be a genuine constraint on the state promoting the purposes in question via charity law. In contrast, modest redistributions to improve the position of the poor are unlikely to generate an overall cost to autonomy, taking into account the positions of those people – poor and not poor – who stand to benefit from charitable purposes being carried out. As we saw earlier, we may conclude provisionally that, to the extent that it demands such modest redistributions, an autonomy-based conception of distributive justice is a genuine constraint on the state promoting charitable purposes – but only provisionally. The discussion so far has concentrated on the consequences of a requirement to include the poor for the autonomy of those

[27] Ibid, [242]–[243].   [28] Ibid, [253].   [29] Ibid, [258].

who will be affected directly by that requirement. In order to assess all of the consequences for autonomy that might be generated by such a requirement, however, it is necessary to look beyond the class of persons who will be affected directly by the requirement and to consider the position of persons who will be affected indirectly as well. For example, in the case of a private school that offers scholarships to poor pupils, the overall consequences for autonomy might be complicated in circum- stances where those scholarships are both means- and merit-tested and there is a broader social pattern of academically able poor pupils leaving under-resourced state schools to take up scholarship places at well- resourced private schools. For the less academically able pupils who remain in the state school system, this 'bright flight' might have effects on the culture and programmes of their schools that compound their disadvantage and impair their autonomy.[30] These sorts of complications, which come into view once those who will be indirectly affected by the requirement to include the poor are taken into account, are exacerbated by the empirical deficit alluded to earlier; after a point it becomes difficult to make any sort of assertion about indirect social consequences with confidence, given the multitude of causes that social phenomena and patterns tend to have.

The discussion so far has concentrated on what, in Chapter 3, was referred to as the 'demand' side of the pursuit of charitable purposes; in other words, it has taken into account the position of those who stand to be affected in one way or another – beneficially or otherwise – by charitable purposes being carried out. But of course, as we saw in Chapter 3, in order to understand the full implications for the autonomy of citizens of the state action entailed in charity law we must also consider the 'supply' side of the pursuit of charitable purposes, asking questions about the consequences of charity law for the autonomy of those with such purposes. And when we turn to the 'supply' side in the setting of an inquiry into the likely consequences of a requirement to include the poor, we find that another possible cost to autonomy comes into view. In Chapter 3 we saw that, via the 'public' component of the public benefit test and the 'not for profit' rule, the state promotes altruism in the pursuit of charitable purposes. We saw in that chapter that altruism, as a type of motivation for action that may be contrasted with self-interest on the one

---

[30] For a wide-ranging discussion of these and other problems associated with selective school practices: Melissa Benn, *School Wars: The Battle for Britain's Education* (Verso, London, 2011).

hand and duty or attachment on the other, is inconsistent with certain virtues and consistent with others. In particular, we saw that altruism is inconsistent with virtues – such as loyalty and trustworthiness – that presuppose attachments of one sort or another. It is also inconsistent with virtues that reflect a sense of moral duty.[31] Now it is time to notice the range of virtues – virtues that are selfless but do not reflect a sense of duty or attachment – that are consistent with altruism. The critical point for present purposes is that while this range of altruistic virtues includes justice, it is not limited to justice. No doubt the virtue of justice is consistent with the selfless regard for others as such that is the hallmark of altruism, but so are many other virtues as well, from charity in the non-legal sense, to public-spiritedness, to humanity, to benevolence, to mercy.[32] In other words, the richness of our understanding of the moral dimensions of human action is such that there are many ways to be altruistic, and being just is simply one such way.

Earlier, we considered the likely effect of a requirement to include the poor on the practical reasoning of those who formulate and carry out charitable purposes. We saw that because it demands of those who formulate and carry out charitable purposes comparative thinking about the distribution of goods, it is inconsistent with the successful exhibition of the virtue of charity in the non-legal sense. We also saw that to think comparatively about the distribution of goods is to think about distributive justice. Thus, in its focus on questions of inclusion and exclusion and questions of access, and in the comparative thinking about the poor and those who are not poor that it demands, a requirement to include the poor asks that those who formulate and carry out charitable purposes adopt a mindset that is characteristic of the virtue of justice.[33] In doing

---

[31] Such as the virtue of conscientiousness: see W.D. Ross, *The Right and the Good* (Clarendon Press, Oxford, 1930), 157–158.

[32] For discussions of these and other altruistic virtues, see generally T.D. Campbell, 'Humanity before Justice' (1974) 4 *British Journal of Political Science* 1; Allan Buchanan, 'Justice and Charity' (1987) 97 *Ethics* 558; William K. Frankena, 'Beneficence/Benevolence' (1987) 4 *Social Philosophy and Policy* 1; Gardner, 'The Virtue of Charity and Its Foils', above n 20; John Tasioulas, 'Mercy' (2003) 103 *Proceedings of the Aristotelian Society* 101; Yuval Livnat, 'Benevolence and Justice' (2003) 37 *Journal of Value Inquiry* 507; Thomas Nagel, 'The Problem of Global Justice' (2005) 33 *Philosophy and Public Affairs* 113; John Gardner, 'The Virtue of Justice and the Character of Law', above n 11.

[33] It is worth noting that a focus on questions of access, and a mindset interested in questions of justice, need not be accompanied by a special concern for the poor: see John D. Colombo, 'The Role of Access in Charitable Tax Exemption' (2004) 82

so, it makes it difficult for those who formulate and carry out charitable purposes to express any virtue other than justice in responding to its demands; to this extent, it tends to bring about conditions under which it is possible to be altruistic in the pursuit of charitable purposes only by being just, and not by being charitable (in the non-legal sense), or public-spirited, or virtuous in some other altruistic way.[34]

To illustrate, consider the trustees of a private school who must satisfy a requirement to include the poor. When thinking about what charity law requires of them if they are to maintain their charitable status, it is not open to such trustees, if they are to take seriously the requirement to include the poor, to act solely from a sense that there are substantial public goods associated with school education and that their school, as much as any, contributes to the production of such public goods irre-spective of the fact that none of the pupils in it are poor. If they are to take seriously a requirement to include the poor, the trustees must act, at least to some degree, from a sense that there are distributive problems to be solved in the pursuit of the purposes of their school. To this extent, a requirement to include the poor is likely to lead the trustees to exhibit the virtue of justice rather than the virtue of public-spiritedness in their deliberations and their subsequent actions. And to the extent that the trustees do exhibit the virtue of public-spiritedness in those deliberations and actions, it is likely to be because they have not tried to make their thinking and actions responsive to a requirement to include the poor, or perhaps because they wish to act in spite of such a requirement.

From the perspective of autonomy-based liberalism, any contraction of the ways in which people can pursue charitable purposes altruistically, including a contraction of the ways in which people can express virtues by that pursuit, is bound to occasion some concern. Recall from Chapter 2 that among the conditions of autonomy is an adequate range of options from which to choose in living a self-determining life. As we saw in Chapter 3, an adequate range of options is constituted not only by options relating to the goals or projects that we pursue, but also in part by options relating to the modes of social interaction by which we pursue

---

Washington University Law Quarterly 343; John D. Colombo, 'The Failure of Community Benefit' (2005) 15 *Health Matrix* 29 for an argument that charity law should require access, but not necessarily with an emphasis on the poor.

[34] In this regard, note the following observation of Sandel, above n 1, 34: 'acting out of a sense of justice can be contagious; it reinforces the assumptions it presupposes and enhances its own stability by encouraging and affirming like motivations in others.'

those goals or projects; in Chapter 3, that fundamental point was reiterated in the course of an argument that options to express altruism are options that the state has reasons to promote given the encroachment of the norms of the market into a wide sphere of human activity. Now we may draw out of the fundamental point a further implication: a range of options is adequate only where it includes options to express a variety of virtues in social interaction, i.e., options successfully to be just, or charitable, or humane, and so on. To the extent that a requirement to include the poor limits or thwarts such options for those with certain charitable purposes, by bringing about conditions under which such persons are led to conceive of their task in formulating or carrying out their charitable purposes in terms of justice, this ought to trouble anyone who views autonomy as the core political ideal; it amounts to a cost to autonomy on the 'supply' side that must be taken into account in any evaluation of the overall gains and costs to autonomy associated with a requirement to include the poor.[35]

But, it might be objected, surely in cases where charitable purposes entail the provision of private goods, and there are some people who might not be able to access those private goods because they are poor, even if it is possible to respond to the situation by expressing virtues other than justice, the most appropriate virtue to express in responding to that situation is that of justice? Michael Sandel has warned against the tendency, pronounced in much recent political philosophy, to think that just because a problem *can* be conceived as a problem of justice, it *should* be so conceived. Sandel argues that the encroachment of the virtue of justice onto the terrain traditionally occupied by other altruistic virtues is a matter of regret; justice is a desideratum only when compared to injustice and not when compared to other altruistic virtues whose expression in human action render justice unnecessary.[36] On Sandel's view, in certain cases it might be desirable to refuse to conceive of political concerns as distributive problems, even though it is possible – indeed, even though it might seem natural, given the tendency to frame political concerns in terms of justice – to conceive

---

[35] Note Gardner, 'The Virtue of Justice and the Character of Law', above n 11, 268, arguing that the law should be 'charitable enough to understand and accommodate (in their own terms) the actions of charitable people'.

[36] Sandel, above n 1, 31–35. Rawls, on the other hand, regards a process by which a 'sense of justice' comes to characterise the thinking of citizens about a wider and wider range of political concerns, as a desideratum: *A Theory of Justice*, above n 1, 413–416.

them so.[37] Thus, for example, in the charity law setting, in a case where a purpose entails the provision of private goods but also stands to realise incidental public goods, it might be desirable not to think about the purpose by formulating questions about the distribution of the private goods, but instead to articulate non-distributive questions about the public goods. Such choices stand to be made in many cases where charitable purposes entail the provision of private goods; for example, as was alluded to earlier, it is possible to conceive of the purposes of a private school in terms of incidental public goods relating to education that the school contributes to producing.[38]

Exactly how any 'supply'-side cost to autonomy is to be factored into an evaluation of the overall gains and costs to autonomy associated with a requirement to include the poor depends on several variables. To begin with, we must not forget that a requirement to include the poor is otiose in cases falling within the description 'relief of poverty', as well as in cases in which charitable purposes stand to realise public goods. To that extent, the tendency of such a requirement to diminish the range of options for those with charitable purposes is limited. And, perhaps more importantly, any cost to autonomy on the 'supply' side occasioned by a requirement to include the poor must be weighed against any gain to autonomy on the 'demand' side that is yielded by adherence to that requirement. As we saw earlier in the discussion of the example of the private school that raises fees by 5 per cent to fund scholarships for poor pupils, where a requirement to include the poor demands only modest redistributions from those who are not poor to those who are poor, there may be an overall gain to autonomy on the 'demand' side, although any such gain must be weighed against possible wider costs to autonomy occasioned by the indirect effects of satisfying the requirement. It is not inconceivable that such 'demand'-side gains, taken in aggregate, might outweigh not

---

[37] See Michael J. Sandel, *Democracy's Discontent: America in Search of a Public Philosophy* (Belknap Press, Cambridge, MA, 1996), 333, arguing that even the gap between the rich and the poor in a society is not necessarily best conceived as a problem of justice. Sandel argues that a more creative way of thinking about this problem is as a problem demanding the provision of more or different public goods that all can enjoy irrespective of their wealth. See also Michael Walzer, *Spheres of Justice: A Defense of Pluralism and Equality* (Basic Books, New York, 1983).

[38] Recall from Chapter 1 that in some cases (e.g., R *(Independent Schools Council)* v. *Charity Commission for England and Wales* [2012] 2 WLR 100 (Upper Tribunal)) decision-makers have been sceptical of arguments pointing to incidental public goods, while in other cases (e.g. Re *Resch's Will Trusts, Le Cras* v. *Perpetual Trustee Co Ltd* [1968] 1 AC 514 (Privy Council)) they have accepted such arguments.

only wider costs to autonomy but also any aggregate costs on the 'supply' side occasioned by the loss of options to express different virtues in the pursuit of charitable purposes. But it is also unclear how we might know whether or not 'demand'-side gains outweigh 'supply'-side costs in these circumstances, and vice versa; for example, such knowledge seems to depend on whether variety in the modes of social interaction is more important to autonomy than variety in the goals and projects that might be achieved by one or another of such modes, a question to which there is no obvious answer. In the end, once we take both 'demand'-side and 'supply'-side considerations into account, there seems to be no strong argument either for the proposition that autonomy will be promoted overall in circumstances where the criteria of charity law incorporate a requirement to include the poor, or for the proposition that autonomy will be diminished overall in such circumstances. It is therefore an open question whether or not an autonomy-based conception of distributive justice is a genuine constraint on state action in cases where a require-ment to include the poor operates; it follows that we should hold open the question of the soundness of the conception of distributive justice that the requirement seems to embody.

Once again, a short summary seems appropriate at this point. The requirement to include the poor that characterises the criteria of charity law in many parts of the British Isles both raises and purports to resolve problems of distributive justice for those who formulate and carry out charitable purposes that entail the provision of private goods and do not fall within the description 'relief of poverty'. The requirement purports to resolve problems of distributive justice by specifying redistribution, among those who stand to benefit from the purposes in question being carried out, from those who are not poor to those who are poor. To this extent, the requirement aims to resolve the problems of distributive justice that it creates by specifying a conception of distributive justice that seems consistent with what is required in order to enhance the autonomy of the poor. However, from the perspective of autonomy-based liberalism, whether or not an autonomy-based conception of distributive justice is a genuine constraint on state action in the cases to which the requirement to include the poor applies depends on the overall gains and costs to auton-omy occasioned by the requirement. Where the requirement can be satisfied by modest redistributions, an overall gain to autonomy on the 'demand' side is likely. However, any such gain must be weighed against possible wider costs to autonomy occasioned by the consequences of the requirement on the 'demand' side and also weighed against possible costs to autonomy on the 'supply' side, most notably costs associated with a contraction of the ways in which citizens may express altruistic virtues other than of the virtue of justice by pursuing charitable purposes in cases where the requirement is not otiose. It is not clear how these weighing exercises should be undertaken, and to that extent it cannot be said either that an autonomy-based conception of distributive justice is a constraint on state action in cases where a requirement to include the poor operates or that it is not such a constraint. Should the state refuse to promote charitable purposes that entail the provision of private goods, do not fall within the description 'relief of poverty' and do not include the poor? The demands of distributive justice, understood as outworkings of the demands of autonomy, yield no clear answer to this question.

3.   Distributive justice and the tax privileges of charity law

We have seen that the question whether or not distributive justice – understood as requiring some redistribution of goods to the poor so as to serve their autonomy – constrains the state in its recognition of purposes as charitable in law, and to that extent constrains the state in its project of promoting charitable purposes, is not susceptible of any clear answer. In this part of the chapter, we will consider a different question: does distributive justice, again understood as demanding some redistribution to the poor so as to serve their autonomy, constrain the state in the means by which it promotes charitable purposes? In other words, to what extent does distributive justice require that the state refrain from pursuing one or another of the facilitative, incentive or expressive strategies of charity law, whether with respect to an individual charitable purpose, a type of charitable purpose or charitable purposes generally? This question clearly demands consideration of those strategies of charity law that most obviously have implications for the distribution of goods across society: the incentive strategies embodied in the tax privileges that the state extends to those with charitable purposes.[39] Recall from Chapter 1 that these tax privileges are both direct, in the case of exemptions from income tax and other taxes for those with charitable purposes, and indirect, in the case of state support via deductions, credits and other means for those who make gifts to organisations with charitable

---

[39] The questions may also demand consideration of other dimensions of charity law, for example the rules conferring validity on trusts for charitable purposes. We will not pursue such further questions here.

purposes. As we will see, ascertaining the distributive implications of these tax privileges is no easy matter, but at a minimum we can say that, all else being equal, the tax privileges extended to taxpayers with charitable purposes represent an additional tax burden for other taxpayers; this modest but undeniable claim suffices to ground the further claim that the tax privileges of charity law raise questions of distributive justice of some sort. From our perspective, the question of most interest, and the one we will take up in what follows, might be formulated in these terms: to what extent, if at all, are the tax privileges of charity law justified in light of the demands of distributive justice, those demands being understood to require some redistribution of goods to the poor so as to serve their autonomy?

We should begin by clarifying exactly when and how distributive justice is an appropriate evaluative tool for thinking about the tax privileges of charity law. In part, working out whether or not distributive justice is an appropriate evaluative tool for this purpose depends on the broader inquiry within which the tax privileges of charity law are considered. If those tax privileges are considered pursuant to a broader inquiry into why the state should promote charitable purposes, or into how the state might most effectively promote charitable purposes, then distributive justice has no obvious evaluative role to play. Indeed, in the discussion in Chapter 2, from the perspective of autonomy-based liberalism, of the reasons for the state to promote charitable purposes, we touched on the tax privileges of charity law but not in a way that raised questions of distributive justice. On the other hand, if the tax privileges of charity law are considered within a broader inquiry into the distributive function of the tax system, then in an obvious sense distributive justice is the appropriate evaluative tool; it is this latter perspective that we will adopt in this part of the chapter. That said, it is important to notice that an inquiry into the distributive function of the tax system is just one of several sorts of evaluative inquiry that one might make into the tax system. As Liam Murphy and Thomas Nagel have pointed out in their seminal book on justice and the tax system, the distribution of goods is just one of two key functions of the tax system; the other is to determine the extent to which goods are to be under the control of government and the extent to which they are to be under the private control of citizens.[40]

---

[40] Liam Murphy and Thomas Nagel, *The Myth of Ownership: Taxes and Justice* (Oxford University Press, 2002) ch 4. See also Liam Murphy and Thomas Nagel, 'Taxes, Redistribution, and Public Provision' (2001) 30 *Philosophy and Public Affairs* 53.

This latter function is plausibly evaluated by asking questions about it that do not implicate distributive justice – questions about how to maximise efficiency in the financing of public goods, for example,[41] or indeed about whether autonomy is better served by the state promoting the private provision of public goods or by the state providing public goods directly by 'tax and spend' means, a topic that we explored in Chapter 3.[42] Distributive justice is an appropriate evaluative tool for thinking about the tax privileges of charity law, then, in the setting of an inquiry into the distributive function of the tax system rather than into: (a) the state's promotion of charitable purposes; or (b) the tax system's function of determining the extent to which goods will come under the control of the state.

In passing, we should note that such an inquiry is viable however the tax privileges of charity law are conceptualised. There is a large body of literature debating whether income tax exemptions for those with charitable purposes and deductions for those who give to charity are better conceptualised as state subsidies or as reflections of a correct definition of 'income' for tax purposes.[43] There is also a strand of scholarship arguing

---

[41] Questions about how most efficiently to finance public goods intersect with questions about how most efficiently to provide public goods; these latter questions have been discussed in much economic literature on the nature and role of a not-for-profit, including a charitable, sector. See, e.g., Burton A. Weisbrod, 'Toward a Theory of the Voluntary Nonprofit Sector in a Three Sector Economy' in Susan Rose-Ackerman (ed), *The Economics of Nonprofit Institutions: Studies in Structure and Policy* (Oxford University Press, New York, 1986) 21–44; Burton A. Weisbrod, *The Voluntary Nonprofit Sector* (Lexington Books, New York, 1977); Henry B. Hansmann, 'The Role of Nonprofit Enterprise' (1980) 89 *Yale Law Journal* 835; Lester M. Salamon, 'Of Market Failure, Voluntary Failure, and Third-Party Government: Toward a Theory of Government-Nonprofit Relations in the Modern Welfare State' (1987) 16 *Nonprofit and Voluntary Sector Quarterly* 29; Avner Ben Ner and Theresa Van Hoomissen, 'Nonprofit Organizations in the Mixed Economy: A Demand and Supply Analysis' (1991) 62 *Annals of Public and Cooperative Economics* 519; John D. Colombo and Mark A. Hall, *The Charitable Tax Exemption* (Westview Press, Boulder, CL, 1995); Bruce R. Kingma, 'Public Good Theories of the Nonprofit Sector: Weisbrod Revisited' in Helmut Anheier and Avner Ben-Ner (eds), *The Study of the Nonprofit Enterprise: Theories and Approaches* (Kluwer, New York, 2003) 53–65.

[42] See also Murphy and Nagel, 'Taxes, Redistribution, and Public Provision', above n 40, 68 and John G. Simon, 'Charity and Dynasty under the Federal Tax System' (1978) 5 *The Probate Lawyer* 1.

[43] See, e.g., Edward H. Rabin, 'Charitable Trusts and Charitable Deductions' (1966) 41 *New York University Law Review* 912; William D. Andrews, 'Personal Deductions in an Ideal Income Tax' (1972) 86 *Harvard Law Review* 309; Boris Bittker, 'Charitable Contributions: Tax Deductions or Matching Grants' (1972) 28 *Tax Law Review* 37; Boris Bittker and G.K. Rahdert, 'The Exemption of Nonprofit Organizations from Federal Income

that the tax privileges of charity law are the product of a sense that those with charitable purposes are in some way 'sovereign' and therefore, for political reasons, fall beyond the tax base.[44] Whether the tax privileges of charity law are state subsidies or the product of principles defining 'income' or setting the scope of the tax base in other ways, they are susceptible to evaluation in light of distributive justice to the extent that they constitute part of a tax system with a distributive function. The correct conceptualisation of the tax privileges of charity law is an important matter, but in the setting of the present inquiry it is important only insofar as it enables us accurately to describe what stands to be evaluated according to the requirements of distributive justice – in other words, whether what is distributively just or unjust is the giving of state subsidies to charity, the definition of the tax base so as to exclude income applied for charitable purposes, or the refusal of the state to impose tax on charities on sovereignty grounds.

Our question was: to what extent, if at all, are the tax privileges of charity law justified in light of the demands of distributive justice? With a clearer sense of when and how distributive justice is an appropriate evaluative tool for thinking about the tax privileges of charity law, and armed with a conception of distributive justice as demanding some redistribution of goods to the poor so as to serve their autonomy, we are now ready to consider this question. The first point to note is that the question cannot be answered by concentrating on the tax privileges of charity law taken in isolation. This is because the extent to which the tax privileges of charity law are consistent with the demands of distributive justice can be known only once the distributive implications of those tax privileges are known, and those distributive implications can be known only in light of some assessment of the distributive implications of the tax

Taxation' (1976) 85 *Yale Law Journal* 299; Mark G. Kelman, 'Personal Deductions Revisited: Why They Fit Poorly in an "Ideal" Income Tax and Why They Fit Worse in a Far from Ideal World' (1979) 31 *Stanford Law Review* 831; Henry Hansmann, 'The Rationale for Exempting Nonprofit Organizations from Corporate Income Taxation' (1981) 91 *Yale Law Journal* 54; S.A. Koppelman, 'Personal Deductions Under an Ideal Income Tax' (1987) 43 *Tax Law Review* 679; Richard Krever, 'Tax Deductions for Charitable Donations: A Tax Expenditure Analysis' in Richard Krever and Gretchen Kewley (eds), *Charities and Philanthropic Institutions: Reforming the Tax Subsidy and Regulatory Regimes* (Comparative Public Policy Research Unit, Monash University, 1991) 1–28; Daniel Halperin, 'Is Income Tax Exemption for Charities a Subsidy?' (2011) 64 *Tax Law Review* 283.

[44] The seminal contribution is Evelyn Brody, 'Of Sovereignty and Subsidy: Conceptualizing the Charity Tax Exemption' (1998) 23 *Journal of Corporation Law* 585.

system as a whole, the ways in which the government spends revenue, and broader social and economic institutions, conditions and behaviours.[45] In other words, the distributive implications of the tax privileges of charity law depend on the distributive implications of the whole of what we might, following John Rawls, call the 'basic structure' of society.[46] The breadth of inquiry that is required in order to evaluate aspects of the tax system, including tax privileges, with reference to the demands of distributive justice has led at least one commentator to remark that 'there may be nothing to say about justice and taxation at all; perhaps we can only evaluate more comprehensive policies that consider all aspects of economic life'.[47] This scepticism about the possibility of meaningful evaluation of particular elements of the tax system taken in isolation – or even the whole tax system taken in isolation – in light of distributive justice suggests that the more fruitful inquiries about the justification of the tax privileges of charity law are those that avoid questions of distributive justice, instead focusing on questions such as those about efficiency in the provision of public goods and the demands of autonomy that we canvassed earlier.

That the question of distributive justice and the tax privileges of charity law quickly turns into a question about distributive justice and the basic structure of society as a whole may be usefully illustrated by working through a hypothetical example with reference to a conception of distributive justice according to which some redistribution of goods to the poor is required so as to serve their autonomy. Imagine a society in which charities carry out purposes that directly benefit the rich, purposes that entail the provision of elite education or that promote arts like opera and ballet that are typically patronised by the upper classes.[48] Now imagine that in this society, the tax law allows deductions from

---

[45] See John G. Head, 'Tax-Fairness Principles: A Conceptual, Historical and Practical Overview' in Allan M. Maslove (ed), *Fairness in Taxation: Exploring the Principles* (University of Toronto Press, 1993) 3–62; Murphy and Nagel, *The Myth of Ownership*, above n 40; Eric Rakowski, 'Can Wealth Taxes Be Justified?' (2000) 53 *Tax Law Review* 263; Linda Sugin, 'Theories of Distributive Justice and Limitations on Taxation: What Rawls Demands from Tax Systems' (2004) 72 *Fordham Law Review* 1991; Liam Murphy, 'Taxes, Property, Justice' (2005) 1 *New York University Journal of Law and Liberty* 983.

[46] Rawls, above n 1, 6 and passim.   [47] Sugin, above n 45, 1992.

[48] It should not be difficult to imagine such a society: see Paul Valentine, 'A Lay Word for a Legal Term: How the Popular Definition of Charity Has Muddied the Perception of the Charitable Donation' (2010) 89 *Nebraska Law Review* 997, 1016–1027 and 1042, citing figures suggesting that in the United States, only 8% of charitable donations (and only 4% of such donations from rich donors) go to purposes associated with poor relief.

assessable income in respect of any donations to charity. And imagine that most of these deductions are claimed by the rich because – perhaps unsurprisingly, given that charitable purposes in this society directly benefit the rich – the rich are especially highly motivated to make charitable donations. At first glance, these deductions might appear to be distributively unjust; after all, is it not the case that if the rich can reduce their tax burden by claiming deductions for charitable donations, this augments the tax burden for those who are not rich, a class of persons that includes the poor? And is it not the case that the availability of deductions in respect of donations to charitable purposes that benefit the rich reflects a state-organised distribution of goods, via charitable donors, to the rich beneficiaries of the pursuit of charitable purposes, goods that might otherwise have been distributed to the poor? Surely distributive justice demands that, in this society: (a) the rich should not be able to shift a tax burden onto those who are not rich; and (b) the state should (i) rein in the distribution of goods to the rich via deductible donations to charity by limiting or eliminating deductions in respect of such donations, and (ii) through government expenditure, redistribute those goods to the poor with a view to promoting the autonomy of the poor.[49]

Perhaps. But before we can draw these conclusions with any confidence, we must know the answers to a number of prior questions. One set of questions relates to the distribution of the tax burden across society. Contrary to much thinking on principles of fairness in taxation, Murphy and Nagel argue convincingly that the distribution of the tax burden is of no moral significance in and of itself; the fact that A pays more tax than B, or even that A pays a lot of tax and B pays no tax at all, is neither here nor there as far as distributive justice is concerned, except in conjunction with other facts about distribution that implicate the positions of A and B.[50] In order to know whether or not distributive justice demands that the distribution of the tax burden be adjusted or overhauled in some way, we need to know about the distributive implications not just of that tax burden, but also, at least, of the government

---

[49] This, to a degree, describes the position in Australia, where – as we saw in Chapter 1 – charitable donors may claim deductions only in respect of donations to 'public benevolent institutions' and other nominated organisations. The purposes of 'public benevolent institutions' have an element of poor relief. See further Chesterman, 'Foundations of Charity Law in the New Welfare State', above n 23, 340–343 for a description and a defence of the Australian position.

[50] Murphy and Nagel, *The Myth of Ownership*, above n 40, ch 2.

expenditure of the revenue that is collected through the imposition of the tax burden. So, in our hypothetical society, the fact that the rich are able to claim deductions for donations to charity, thus increasing the tax burden borne by everyone else, might be of no consequence in terms of distributive justice if such taxes as are collected are then spent in ways that substantially improve the position of the poor, thereby ensuring that the poor enjoy the conditions of autonomy to a sufficient degree. The only sort of scenario in which the shifting of the tax burden represented by the rich claiming deductions for charitable donations, taken on its own, would be bound to cause concern in light of our conception of distributive justice is a scenario in which the tax burden that is shifted is shifted onto the poor;[51] and if, in our hypothetical society, there is a progressive tax system under which the poor pay relatively little tax, or even a tax system made up largely of consumption taxes that spread the tax burden widely, this scenario is not likely to eventuate. All else being equal, if the middle classes pay more tax so that the rich can claim their deductions for donations to the opera or their alma mater while a sufficient redistribution of goods to the poor is maintained then, with an autonomy-based conception of distributive justice in hand as an evaluative tool, the response must be: so be it.[52]

Another set of questions focuses on the consequences of the pursuit of charitable purposes for the poor. Even if the charities in our hypothetical society pursue purposes that directly benefit the rich, do their purposes nonetheless generate goods that are enjoyed indirectly by the poor? Perhaps those purposes entail the provision of public goods that are enjoyed by everyone, including the poor. In our hypothetical society, charities pursue purposes to do with elite education and arts; as we saw in

---

[51] See Sugin, above n 45, 1999, arguing that Rawls's difference principle rules out only a tax system 'that burdens exclusively the poorest group'. The autonomy-based conception of distributive justice with which we are working in this chapter is likely to rule out a wider class of tax systems than that, but its interest in the distribution of the tax burden – as opposed to the distributive implications of the tax system and government expenditure taken as a whole – is similarly an interest in the extent to which that burden is borne by the poor.

[52] Of course, this argument assumes that the state's promotion of purposes to do with elite education and the arts is justified by the demands of autonomy, quite apart from distributive justice considerations. As discussed in Chapter 2 and further in the text below, there are reasons to think that this assumption is sound, but if it turns out not to be then, from the perspective of autonomy-based liberalism, there is no reason for the state to promote such purposes, and no question of distributive justice to answer with respect to such promotion.

Chapter 2, there are arguments in favour of the proposition that such purposes contribute to the production of cultural public goods, and to this extent the prospect that the charitable purposes pursued in the hypothetical society generate goods for the poor is not a remote one. A second question now arises: assuming that charitable purposes in our hypothetical society do yield public goods that are enjoyed by the poor, what effect will withdrawing deductions for donations to at least some such charitable purposes have on the provision of these public goods? Will the withdrawal of deductions cause charitable donors to stop donating to charity to such an extent that there is a significant impact on the provision of public goods via the pursuit of charitable purposes?[53] If so, then withdrawing deductions from charitable donors might have an adverse effect on the position of the poor, and another question presents itself: is this adverse effect outweighed by such improvement to the position of the poor as might result from the withdrawal of deductions? In order to answer this question, we must ask another set of questions, this time about the measures that are likely to accompany the withdrawal of deductions from charitable donors. Will equivalent tax benefits be allocated to other taxpayers, thus neutralising the effect on revenue of the withdrawal of the deductions? If not, how is the state likely to spend the additional revenue it generates through the withdrawal of the deductions? How much additional revenue will be generated thus? Will it be spent financing redistributions to the poor through the provision of private goods? Will it be spent on public goods in which the poor can share? Will these expenditures generate greater improvements to the position of the poor than might be generated by retaining the deductions, assuming that charitable purposes that directly benefit the rich can nonetheless entail indirect distributions to the poor via the generation of public goods?

Now let us imagine that, with respect to this hypothetical society, we conclude that, all else being equal, the poor will be better off if charitable donations are not tax deductible than if they are. Even now, we are not in a position to state confidently that distributive justice demands the restriction or elimination of deductions for charitable donors; all else is

---

[53] This question was recently the subject of public debate in the United Kingdom: see Debra Morris, 'Recent Developments in Charity Taxation in the UK: The Law Gives and the Law Takes Away' in Matthew Harding, Ann O'Connell and Miranda Stewart (eds), *Not-for-Profit Law: Theoretical and Comparative Perspectives* (Cambridge University Press, 2014) 254–275.

not equal. In order to be able to state with confidence that, in our hypothetical society, deductions for charitable donors are insupportable in light of the demands of distributive justice, we must know the answers to a further set of questions about the system of taxation and government expenditure and the social and economic setting in which the government raises taxes and spends revenue, as a whole.[54] Will any improvement to the position of the poor that is yielded by the withdrawal of deductions be sufficient given the demands of distributive justice – will it ensure that the poor enjoy the conditions of autonomy to a sufficient degree – or will more be required? Is it possible to improve the position of the poor to a sufficient degree without interfering with charitable deductions at all? For example, if, in our hypothetical society, a tiny elite possesses vast inherited wealth that is not being put to productive use, perhaps the position of the poor can be improved to a sufficient degree by imposing taxes or additional taxes on this elite and redistributing the revenue raised to the poor in some way, thus rendering unnecessary any interference with the tax privileges of charity law. As between improving the position of the poor by redistributing goods from the extremely wealthy but unproductive elite and improving the position of the poor by redistributing goods from the rich who donate to and benefit from the pursuit of charitable purposes, efficiency and especially autonomy arguments suggest that the first option is the better one. This last point reveals that a conception of distributive justice that demands some redistribution of goods to the poor does not pick out particular solutions among a range of combinations of taxation and government expenditure; rather, it establishes a baseline that any such combination must pass, but above which a multitude of combinations might be possible.[55]

We seem to have reached the same impasse we reached when considering whether or not the demands of distributive justice rule out the

---

[54] Some scholars lose sight of this point when they suggest that principles of liberal justice demand the restriction or elimination of one or another tax privilege of charity law without first considering whether the demands of such principles might be met in ways that do not implicate tax privileges. For examples, see Rob Reich, 'Philanthropy and its Uneasy Relation to Equality' in William Damon and Susan Verducci (eds), *Taking Philanthropy Seriously: Beyond Noble Intentions to Responsible Giving* (Indiana University Press, Bloomington, 2006) 27–49; Miranda Perry Fleischer, 'Theorizing the Charitable Tax Subsidies: The Role of Distributive Justice' (2010) 87 *Washington University Law Review* 505; Miranda Perry Fleischer, 'Equality of Opportunity and the Charitable Tax Subsidies' (2011) 91 *Boston University Law Review* 601.

[55] See Sugin, above n 45, 1998–2005, discussing Rawls's difference principle as articulating such a baseline.

state's promotion of charitable purposes that exclude the poor. It is conceivable that the tax privileges of charity law are not justified according to a conception of distributive justice that requires some redistribution to the poor. However, it is also clear that whether or not those tax privileges are so justified depends on the answers to an array of questions, and it is far from clear that we are in a position to answer them. Many of the questions we explored earlier in relation to our hypothetical society demand empirical data and knowledge about counterfactual worlds that is either difficult or impossible to obtain. Indeed, it is possible that we cannot reasonably hope to possess sufficient knowledge of the distributional implications of the basic structure of society, as well as the distributional implications of various alternatives within and to the basic structure, to confidently mount an argument either for or against the proposition that the tax privileges of charity law are distributively just in light of the demands of autonomy. It would seem equally difficult to inquire into whether or not the tax privileges of charity law satisfy the demands of distributive justice from the perspective of any theory of distributive justice whose demands entail the achievement of patterns of distribution. In the end, two conclusions suggest themselves. First, while an inquiry into the tax privileges of charity law and distributive justice is not necessarily futile, it may be impractical to such a degree that we would be better served concentrating our efforts on other inquiries, such as an inquiry into the extent to which the state's project of promoting charitable purposes is likely to promote the conditions of autonomy regardless of its distributive implications. Second, even if distributive justice is the best measure of the morality of the basic structure of society – a proposition that we should reject from a perspective that views distributive justice as the outworking of more fundamental moral concerns – it may not be a measure that we are equipped to use.[56]

Before concluding this chapter, let us consider one relatively specific sense in which we might inquire into the extent to which the tax privileges of charity law satisfy the demands of distributive justice. As we saw in Chapter 3, the state might promote charitable purposes in several ways; most significantly for present purposes, the state might on

---

[56] See generally Bo Rothstein, *Just Institutions Matter: The Moral and Political Logic of the Universal Welfare State* (Cambridge University Press, 1998) ch 1, criticising the lack of interest in questions of institutional design and public policy that characterises much political philosophy.

the one hand raise taxes and spend the revenue thus generated on directly pursuing charitable purposes, and on the other indirectly promote charitable purposes by facilitative, incentive and expressive means. On one view, to the extent that the state chooses the latter method of promoting charitable purposes – which is the method of modern charity law – the state spends revenue on subsidising the private pursuit of such purposes by citizens via the tax privileges of charity law, revenue that it might otherwise have used directly to pursue charitable purposes.[57] Conceived in this way, it is not implausible to argue that the tax privileges of charity law are accompanied by power in choosing the purposes on which revenue is to be spent. To the extent that it is exercised through the democratic and representative institutions of government, this power over the expenditure of revenue is – all else being equal – distributed equally among all citizens. However, when power over the expenditure of revenue is distributed to citizens via the tax privileges of charity law, it is distributed unequally; this is most notably because of the regressive effect of those tax privileges, a regressive effect that is especially pronounced in the case of deductions for charitable donations, but that also characterises other forms of state support for charitable giving, as well as exemptions from income and other taxes for those with charitable purposes.[58]

To illustrate, take two simple examples. In the first example, imagine charitable donor A, who must pay 40 cents in the dollar in income tax, and now imagine that A gives $1,000 to charity. If A claims a deduction in respect of this gift, it will reduce her assessable income by $1,000, thus saving her $400 in tax. A has been subsidised by the state in the amount of $400; she has determined the purpose to which that amount of revenue is to be put. Now imagine charitable donor B, who must pay

---

[57] See Krever, above n 43.

[58] See generally David G. Duff, 'Charitable Contributions and the Personal Income Tax: Evaluating the Canadian Credit' in Jim Phillips, Bruce Chapman and David Stevens (eds), *Between State and Market: Essays on Charities Law and Policy in Canada* (McGill-Queen's University Press, Montreal and Kingston, 2001) 407–456; Neil Brooks, 'The Tax Credit for Charitable Contributions: Giving Credit Where None is Due' in Jim Phillips, Bruce Chapman and David Stevens (eds), *Between State and Market: Essays on Charities Law and Policy in Canada* (McGill-Queen's University Press, Montreal and Kingston, 2001) 457–481; Sugin, above n 45, 2005; Perry Fleischer, 'Theorizing the Charitable Tax Subsidies', above n 54, 551; Perry Fleischer, 'Equality of Opportunity', above n 54, 655; David G. Duff, 'The Tax Treatment of Charitable Contributions in a Personal Income Tax: Lessons from Theory and Canadian Experience' in Matthew Harding, Ann O'Connell and Miranda Stewart (eds), *Not-for-Profit Law: Theoretical and Comparative Perspectives* (Cambridge University Press, 2014), 199–231.

only 20 cents in the dollar in income tax, and again imagine that B gives $1,000 to charity. B will be subsidised only in the amount of $200; her power over the expenditure of the revenue represented by that subsidy is half that of A. Given that in progressive tax systems, taxpayers with higher incomes pay higher rates of tax, inequalities in power over the expenditure of revenue such as that between A and B are, in such systems, likely systemically to benefit those with higher incomes, and to benefit most those with the highest incomes. In the second example, imagine that taxpayer C, had it not been a charity, would have been liable to pay $100,000 in land tax; it may exercise power over the expenditure of revenue to that extent. Now contrast the position of taxpayer C with that of taxpayer D which, had it not been a charity, would have been liable to pay $50,000 in land tax. Taxpayer D receives a state subsidy of $50,000 and has power over the expenditure of revenue to that extent. Again, the effect of land tax exemptions as between taxpayers situated as taxpayers C and D are in this example is to distribute more power over the expenditure of revenue to those charities that would, were they not charities, be liable to pay more tax. If, in this second example, land tax is levied at a flat rate, the power over the expenditure of revenue that taxpayer C enjoys is not disproportionate; in this way the position of taxpayer C might be thought to be of less concern than the position of taxpayer A in our first example. But taxpayer C still enjoys power over the expenditure of more revenue than taxpayer D, and this inequality seems to call for some investigation.

Is power over the expenditure of revenue the sort of good that should, on a sound understanding of the requirements of distributive justice, be distributed equally? From the perspective of autonomy-based liberalism, there would appear to be no reason why this must be so; the extent to which an equal distribution of power over the revenue is demanded by political morality turns on the extent to which such an arrangement contributes to the conditions of autonomy in ways that cannot be achieved otherwise. Once the problem is articulated in these terms, it seems implausible that a strictly equal distribution of power over the expenditure of revenue is required in autonomy-based liberalism. It is not unlikely that extreme concentrations of such power might impair those conditions in some way; take, for example, a society in which the rich claim charitable deductions of such a collective magnitude that the government cannot raise sufficient revenue to finance autonomy-serving public programmes. But it would be strange if it turned out that the conditions of autonomy for the citizens of a political community could not be achieved except in circumstances where no-one received subsidies in respect of their income for any purpose, which is effectively what the argument for equal distribution in the case of tax privileges amounts to. With the demands of autonomy in view, an evaluation of the justifiability of inequalities in the distribution of power over the expenditure of revenue, including those occasioned by the tax privileges of charity law, is likely to turn on a range of considerations related to the conditions of autonomy, including the sorts of public goods associated with political participation that help to foster autonomous lives; the corrosive influence on those public goods of a lack of trust or confidence in government, along with the contribution that inequalities in wealth and power make to such a lack of trust or confidence; and the extent to which such inequalities are nonetheless associated with augmentations of the conditions of autonomy in ways unrelated to political participation. This last point is important; we should not forget, when thinking about the regressive character of the tax privileges of charity law, that in the end – and all else being equal – those tax privileges, assuming their efficacy, enable more people to pursue more charitable purposes to a greater degree. To the extent that the pursuit of charitable purposes serves autonomy – and, as we saw in Chapters 2 and 3 and will see again in Chapters 5 and 6, there are good reasons to think that in important ways it does – any cost to autonomy occasioned by the unequal distribution of power over the expenditure of revenue that accompanies the tax privileges of charity law must be weighed against gains to autonomy occasioned by the pursuit of charitable purposes. The outcome of such a weighing exercise seems far from clear.

4. Conclusion

Readers who expected this chapter to deliver robust arguments prescribing the content of charity law in light of the demands of distributive justice may be disappointed. The conclusions of the chapter might be thought to be deflating and equivocal. The extent to which an autonomy-based conception of distributive justice justifies the requirement to include the poor that plays a role in charity law in much of the British Isles is unclear. An inquiry into the distributive implications of the tax privileges of charity law cannot be undertaken except in the setting of a much larger inquiry into the distributive implications of the whole basic structure of society; and it is all but impossible to predict distributive patterns likely to emerge from changes to elements of the basic structure and, to that extent, difficult to talk about the distributive justice of the basic structure except in the most general terms. Even the regressive elements of the tax privileges accorded to charity cannot be questioned in an unqualified way on the basis that they deliver to rich donors and well-resourced charities, as opposed to poorer donors and charities with fewer resources, a relatively greater share of power over the expenditure of revenue. Charity law undoubtedly raises questions of distributive justice, as is evidenced by the requirement to include the poor and the tax privileges extended to those with charitable purposes. But we have reasons to doubt that questions about charity law and distributive justice are likely to yield productive answers.

Problems raised by possession of insufficient empirical data about actual and counterfactual worlds, coupled with challenges for ideal theory in generating prescriptions for the design of social institutions, are not unique to inquiries into distributive justice. They attend even the core inquiries of autonomy-based liberalism. For example, as we saw earlier in this chapter, indeterminacies may arise in working out the implications of the ideal of autonomy in the charity law setting in circumstances where promoting the autonomy of those on the 'demand' side of the pursuit of charitable purposes is inconsistent with promoting the autonomy of those on the 'supply' side. Eschewing inquiries into charity law and distributive justice in favour of inquiries into the demands of autonomy does nothing to eradicate the need for weighing and balancing exercises, with all their uncertainties; it simply changes the parameters of such exercises in certain ways. Indeed, where weighing and balancing exercises are required, inquiring into the demands of autonomy invariably raises questions of distributive justice of a sort: questions about the distribution of autonomy itself. In many cases weighing and balancing exercises are not required, however, because the state may promote the autonomy of those on the 'demand' and the 'supply' sides by pursuing the one course of action. And even to the extent that inquiring into the demands of autonomy leads us to articulate questions about the distribution of autonomy itself, we may, up to a point, pursue such questions meaningfully in the charity law setting without at the same time saying everything that there is to say about the political morality of the basic structure of society. Once we seek a liberal theory of charity law, and not a liberal theory of the state which may or may not have implications for charity law, that seems to be an important theoretical advance.

5

Religious purposes

1. Introduction

From a perspective informed by liberal philosophical commitments, perhaps the most troubling aspect of charity law is its recognition of a variety of religious purposes as charitable. As we saw in Chapter 1, the recognition of religious purposes as charitable in law occurs in two ways: first, purposes within the general description 'advancement of religion' are considered to be charitable in law, subject to satisfaction of the public benefit test and pertinent disqualifying rules; and second, religious purposes are often, but not invariably, found by decision-makers to satisfy the public benefit test that stands at the heart of charity law, including in some cases – although no longer in several jurisdictions – by the application of a presumption of benefit. By recognising religious purposes as charitable in law, the state promotes such purposes by the facilitative, incentive and expressive strategies – including the provision of various tax privileges – to which we were introduced in Chapters 1 and 2. Little wonder, then, that the treatment of religious purposes in charity law is troubling from a liberal perspective, for the state promotion of religious purposes has been one of the greatest sources of anxiety to the liberal mind since the early days of liberalism.[1] In particular, liberal neutrality-based accounts of state action and public discourse, some of which we touched on in Chapter 2, tend to view the state promotion of religious purposes as a paradigm or core case to worry over.

In this chapter, we will consider the treatment of religious purposes in charity law in light of autonomy-based liberalism, which, as we have seen, stands for the proposition that the state is required to promote, and is justified in promoting, conditions under which citizens may realise the ideal of personal autonomy, in the sense of self-direction, in their lives. In

---

[1] John Locke, 'A Letter Concerning Toleration' in his *A Letter Concerning Toleration and Other Writings* (ed Mark Goldie, Liberty Fund, Indianapolis, 2010, first published 1689), 1.

the first part of the chapter, we will consider a key question when thinking, from the perspective of autonomy-based liberalism, about the political morality of charity law insofar as it recognises religious purposes as charitable: what effect, if any, is the state's promotion of religious purposes via charity law likely to have on the conditions of autonomy? Answering this question demands consideration of a more specific question: to what extent are religious purposes likely to make a contribution to the conditions of autonomy? In the second part of the chapter, we will consider the extent to which the reasoning of decision-makers who deliberate about religious purposes in the charity law setting lives up to aspirations for public discourse identified with reference to the liberal ideal of autonomy. We will see that in many, but not all, respects, the treatment of religious purposes in charity law appears to be consistent with the demands of political morality and the aspirations for public discourse that emerge from autonomy-based liberalism. Thus, from the perspective of autonomy-based liberalism, the recognition of religious purposes as charitable in law turns out on reflection to be less troubling than might first appear to be the case.

2. Religious purposes and the conditions of autonomy

In Chapter 2 we saw that, from the perspective of autonomy-based liberalism, state action that has the consequence of promoting the conditions of autonomy is both justified and desirable, all else being equal. Thus, in asking whether or not the promotion of religious purposes via charity law is justified from a liberal point of view, one key question is: to what extent does the state's promotion of religious purposes via charity law have the consequence of promoting the conditions of autonomy? The answer to this question, in turn, depends on the extent to which religious purposes are likely to make a contribution to the conditions of autonomy. In thinking about the ways in which religious purposes might be autonomy-promoting, we should begin by noticing that many autonomy-promoting purposes are motivated by religious beliefs and commitments but aim to produce outcomes that relate only indirectly if at all to matters of religious belief or practice: for example, consider the various programmes for poor relief, education, health care and support for the disabled that are established by religious groups. In a sense, these purposes are religious purposes – they may be viewed as such by the people whose purposes they are – but in the setting of the present inquiry, let us leave them to one side. In order to see the ways in which they are autonomy-promoting, it is not necessary to view these purposes as religious purposes; rather, the propensity of such purposes to enhance autonomy is best appreciated in light of what they are directed at: 'advancement of poverty', 'advancement of education', and so forth. In this chapter, let us focus instead on purposes that stand or fall as autonomy-promoting according to the contribution that religion itself makes to the conditions of autonomy: purposes that are directed at the maintenance and promotion of religious beliefs and practices.[2] It is the promotion of these purposes via charity law that seems to present the greatest challenge from a liberal point of view.

In this part of the chapter, we will consider in three ways the extent to which religious purposes, understood now to be purposes that are directed at the maintenance and promotion of religious beliefs and practices, are likely to contribute to the conditions of autonomy. First, we will consider to what extent it can be said in general terms that religious lives are autonomous lives. Second, we will consider the ways in which religious purposes might generate private and public goods that contribute to the conditions of autonomy, whether by helping to constitute options that may be the subject of autonomous choice or otherwise. Finally, we will consider cases in which the pursuit of religious purposes impairs autonomy. As we will see, there are reasons to think that religious purposes make a substantial contribution to the conditions of autonomy; to the extent that this is so, it helps to show how, from a liberal perspective, the state's promotion of many (but not all) religious purposes via charity law is both justified and desirable.

A.   Are religious lives autonomous lives?

An argument that religious purposes are likely to generate autonomy-promoting goods, and that in light of this the state's promotion of religious purposes via charity law is both justified and desirable, seems plausible only if we accept that people exercise autonomy in living religious lives. If religious lives are never, or even not generally, autonomous lives, then it would seem that any argument to the effect that

---

[2] Sometimes it is not clear whether or not a purpose is directed at the maintenance and promotion of religious beliefs or practices. In charity law, such cases turn on whether or not a purpose 'advances' religion: see, e.g., *Roman Catholic Archbishop of Melbourne v. Lawlor* (1934) 51 CLR 1 (High Court of Australia); *Liberty Trust v. Charity Commission* [2011] NZHC 577 (Mallon J).

religious purposes are likely to contribute to the conditions of autonomy faces considerable challenges. To the extent that religious lives are not autonomous lives, it is not obvious how such goods – whether private or public – as are likely to be realised by religious purposes might contribute to the conditions of autonomy, whether by helping to constitute options that may be the subject of autonomous choice or in other ways. In these circumstances, any state promotion of religious purposes via charity law must be justified – if indeed it can be justified – on the basis that religious purposes contribute to the conditions of autonomy of non-religious people (or of religious people but not *qua* religious), or on grounds that do not appeal to the value of autonomy at all.[3] Are religious lives autonomous lives? Arguments asserting that religious lives are not autonomous insofar as they are religious may be found in some of the voluminous literature dealing with questions of religion and the state. The writers who make these arguments tend to emphasise the ways in which religion is experienced as unchosen, a matter of duty rather than preference, largely informed by traditions, commitments, obedience to authority and revealed truth: in other words, it would seem, the very opposite of the path of self-direction that is an autonomous life.[4] In order to get a better sense of how to approach the treatment of religious purposes in charity law from the perspective of autonomy-based liberalism, we need to form a view on arguments that deny that religious lives are lived autonomously.

There are several reasons to be sceptical of arguments asserting that, in general terms, religious lives are non-autonomous. First, different religions, and different denominations within religions, accommodate autonomy in matters of belief and practice to different degrees. At one end of the scale are religious worldviews that emphasise tradition, submission to authority and the obedient discharge of duty, and in which very little (if any) value is placed on autonomy; at the other end of the scale are religious worldviews in which individual inquiry and engagement in matters of spirituality, as well as innovation and self-direction in

---

[3] Similarly, if religious lives are not lived autonomously, it is difficult to argue that, by promoting religious purposes, the state contributes to the conditions of autonomy of those with religious purposes in the ways described in Chapter 3.

[4] See, e.g., Michael J. Sandel, 'Religious Liberty – Freedom of Conscience or Freedom of Choice?' [1989] *Utah Law Review* 597; Michael J. Sandel, *Democracy's Discontent: America in Search of a Public Philosophy* (Belknap Press, Cambridge, MA, 1996), 65–71; Rex Ahdar and Ian Leigh, *Religious Freedom in the Liberal State* (Oxford University Press, 2005), 60–61; Sonu Bedi, 'Debate: What Is So Special About Religion?' (2007) 15 *The Journal of Political Philosophy* 235.

religious practice, are tolerated and even celebrated.[5] Given the diversity
of religious beliefs and practices, it seems difficult to locate with confidence any one religion, or even any one denomination, at a particular
point on this scale: for example, all fundamentalist Christian churches
emphasise submission to the revealed word of God in scripture, but
many encourage experimentation and self-expression in the forms of
worship; equally, the old association of the Roman Catholic Church with
unquestioning obedience to institutional authority is no longer sound, if
indeed it ever was.[6] In some respects, Islam presents as a set of duties –
consider the demands of the Five Pillars of Islam – and yet Abdullahi
Ahmed An-Na'im opens his important book on Islam and the secular
state by asserting that 'the only way one can be a Muslim' is 'by conviction and free choice'.[7] But even if it is difficult to place various religions
and denominations precisely on the scale, the very fact that it is plausible
to think of religion in terms of such a scale suggests strongly that to assert
that, in general terms, religious lives are not autonomous lives is to
underestimate the extent to which religion accommodates autonomy.
Moreover, even in cases where the demands of religion in matters of
belief and practice are not experienced as invitations to exercise autonomy, those demands may be such that autonomous choice is required in
realising them; for example, a Christian may consider it her religious
duty to give to the church, but also consider herself free to settle on the
amount of the gift as a matter of personal choice.[8]

---

[5] Note Kent Greenawalt, *Religious Conviction and Political Choice* (Oxford University Press, New York, 1988), 21, distinguishing between liberal and non-liberal religion, and Andrew Koppelman, *Defending American Religious Neutrality* (Harvard University Press, Cambridge, MA, 2013), 38–39, describing the trend towards individualism in matters of religion in the United States.

[6] See Martha C. Nussbaum, *Liberty of Conscience: In Defense of America's Tradition of Religious Equality* (Belknap Press, Cambridge, MA, 2008), 58, 215–216, 276, and the discussion of the Second Vatican Council's Declaration on Religious Liberty (1965) ('Dignitatis Humanae') in John Finnis, 'Religion and Public Life in Pluralist Society' in his *Religion and Public Reasons: Collected Essays: Volume V* (Oxford University Press, 2011) 42–55, 49, emphasising the importance 'for each human being to seek, find and live according to *the truth* about God and man' (Finnis's emphasis). 'Seeking' and 'finding' are not compatible with unquestioning obedience.

[7] Abdullahi Ahmed An-Na'im, *Islam and the Secular State: Negotiating the Future of Sharia* (Harvard University Press, Cambridge, MA, 2008), 1.

[8] Although this sense of freedom in choosing the amount to give to the church may be observed in many Christian churches today, it is not a necessary characteristic of Christian giving to the church; indeed, the payment of a traditional tithe reflects an understanding of such giving that regards the amount of the gift not to be a matter of free choice.

A second reason to be sceptical of arguments that assert in general terms that religious lives are non-autonomous emerges from closer reflection on the nature of autonomy. At times, scholars who doubt that religious lives are autonomous write as though autonomy entailed nothing more than individuals making unfettered choices in order to satisfy their personal preferences.[9] If autonomy is thus understood, then of course religious lives are likely to appear to be non-autonomous to the extent that religion is experienced in the forms of the claims of tradition, commitment, authority and duty; on the view of autonomy as unfettered preference-satisfaction, religious claims cannot but figure as autonomy-impeding fetters. However, as we saw in Chapter 2, autonomy need not – indeed, should not – be understood as unfettered preference-satisfaction. Recall from that chapter that autonomy should be understood as what Joseph Raz calls an 'enabling' value, the point of which is to enable engagement with other values; understood thus, autonomy entails self-directed engagement with values whose goodness is established independently of their being chosen. Given that autonomy entails self-directed engagement with independently established value, unfettered choices made in order to satisfy personal preferences and unresponsive to independently established value are not central cases of autonomy and in some respects are the opposite of what autonomy entails. In asking whether religious lives can be autonomous lives, then, we should not be looking to elucidate the ways in which the claims of religion fetter free choice; this fails to appreciate that, as Leslie Green puts it, 'the unchosen finds a natural place within a theory of freedom that emphasises choice'.[10] Rather, our aim should be to understand better the ways in which religious people engage with the values associated with religion, asking which of those ways are sufficiently voluntary to be autonomous.

Still, a person who doubted that religious lives are autonomous lives might insist that people do not typically respond to the claims of religion – understood as claims of tradition, commitment, authority and duty – in ways that are sufficiently voluntary to be autonomous. Undoubtedly, certain central experiences in the religious lives of at least

---

[9] Sandel, 'Religious Liberty', above n 4, 615; John Finnis, 'Religion and State' in his *Religion and Public Reasons: Collected Essays: Volume V* (Oxford University Press, 2011) 80–102, 86–87.

[10] Leslie Green, 'What is Freedom For?', available on SSRN, abstract id 2193674. For further reflections on how unchosen associations are necessary to the conditions of autonomy: Michael Walzer, 'On Involuntary Association' in Amy Gutmann (ed), *Freedom of Association* (Princeton University Press, Princeton, 1998) 64–74.

some people are not characterised by choices among options: a Damascene conversion, for example, can scarcely be described as an instance of self-determination. And the sorts of commitments and practices typically entailed in religion often lead religious people to renounce autonomy in favour of other values; consider the nuns who shut themselves away in a convent to live a life of spiritual rigour. These are reasons to think that religious lives are not likely to be central cases of autonomous lives. But they are not reasons to think that religious lives are non-autonomous. As we saw in Chapter 2, autonomy is not exhausted by choice, and to the extent that religious lives are characterised by voluntarism not amounting to choice, they are characterised in ways that manifest the value of autonomy. Thus, even the Damascene convert might – perhaps some time after her conversion – aim to reflect on her beliefs and practices, and might seek to engage with those beliefs and practices for the purposes of that exercise in ways that are self-determining. If we must express this thought using the language of choice, then let us say that the Damascene convert might choose to appraise for the first time beliefs and practices to which she previously adhered in an unquestioning fashion. Even if that appraisal results in a renewed commitment to the beliefs and practices in question, it has still in an important sense been an exercise in autonomy.

Against the backdrop of an autonomy-promoting culture, such as exists in many modern societies, it seems plausible to suggest that the religious lives of many and perhaps most religious people entail some combination of autonomous and non-autonomous responses to the claims of religion, and that among the autonomous responses a range of voluntary activity, including but not limited to choice, may be found. This is not to say that wherever an autonomy-promoting culture is to be found, religious lives are invariably characterised by this combination of autonomous and non-autonomous engagement with the claims of religion. Even within such a culture, there may be religious groups which insist on strict adherence to tradition and doctrine, or on submission to authority and the obedient discharge of duty in all aspects of life, and many of the individuals within those groups presumably live non-autonomously. And there are bound to be people who have grown up in one or another religious tradition and have been taught unquestioningly to accept the beliefs and practices of the tradition in question, but have ceased to identify with those beliefs and practices and have become alienated from their faith. To the extent that, because of their upbringing, such people lack the inner capacities to detach themselves from their beliefs and practices and subject them to the sort of scrutiny that might trigger a renewed commitment or a clean break, they are not autonomous in any meaningful way. Nonetheless, given the diversity of religious beliefs and practices and the range of voluntary activity that typically characterises autonomous lives, we have reasons to think that the religious lives of highly traditional groups and the helplessly alienated are not typical of religious lives played out against the backdrop of an autonomy-promoting culture.

B.   Religious purposes and autonomy-promoting goods

On the assumption that religious lives are at least sometimes and in some respects – and more likely often and in many respects – autonomous lives, let us now explore some of the ways in which goods associated with religious purposes might be autonomy-promoting. (Recall from earlier that 'religious purposes' refers to purposes directed at the maintenance and promotion of religious beliefs and practices.) Turning first to purposes directed at the maintenance and promotion of religious beliefs, the obvious point to make is that such purposes have a propensity to generate substantial private goods in the form of the spiritual, emotional and intellectual resources that religion offers to people who are searching for answers to questions about the origins and meaning of the universe, the relationship of the human and the divine, and ethics and morality. Not least among these resources is the phenomenon of faith: a phenomenon that plays a unique role in the epistemic lives of many people and that, it would seem, cannot be experienced except via religion.[11] The spiritual, emotional and intellectual resources of religion – centred on faith – help people to make sense of the world and their place in it, and are the source and form of fundamental lessons about how to live and to treat others. These substantial private goods might be autonomy-promoting in at least two ways: first, they might contribute to the development of inner capacities – such as an ability to form commitments, reflect on the direction and purpose of one's life and evaluate and respond to

---

[11] Timothy Macklem, 'Faith as a Secular Value' (2000) 45 McGill Law Journal 1. For present purposes, we need not make too much of Macklem's observation about the uniqueness of faith; our aim here is not to define religion but rather to point to some of the private goods that religion is likely to realise. We will return below at 170–171 to the question of the definition of religion.

one's options[12] – that are necessary to autonomy; and second, they might help to constitute options – especially where they take the form of religious creeds, worldviews or doctrines – that may be the subject of autonomous choice or other forms of voluntary engagement. The options of being a Jew, or a Buddhist, or a Druid, or an adherent of any other religious creed, worldview or doctrine depend on the private goods that are realised by the maintenance and promotion of religious beliefs, and in this way purposes that maintain and promote such beliefs make an important contribution to the conditions of autonomy.

Purposes directed at the maintenance and promotion of religious practices are also likely to generate substantial private goods; these are goods associated with belonging to religious communities, whether those communities are defined with reference to the maintenance of certain practices over the course of time or with reference to shared practices in the here and now.[13] Religious practices of one type or another make possible shared forms of worship, including the collective participation in religious rites that brings individual people into the experience of a larger spiritual unity; they also give form and substance to celebrations and rites that signify and interpret important events in life, such as birth, marriage and death. As is the case with the private goods associated with the maintenance and promotion of religious beliefs, the private goods relating to the maintenance and promotion of religious practices are autonomy-promoting in important ways: they substantially constitute a range of options relating to membership in one or another religious organisation or group or adherence to one or another religious tradition; they also make possible religious outlooks such as iconoclasm and radicalism. This special contribution that religious practices make to the constitution of options also informs the distinction between 'practising' a religion on the one hand, and affirming the beliefs of a religion but not participating in its communal life on the other.[14]

---

[12] Andrew Koppelman (following Charles Taylor) describes religion as a 'hypergood' that enables the weighing and assessing of other goods: 'Is It Fair to Give Religion Special Treatment?' [2006] *University of Illinois Law Review* 571, 593–594.

[13] Emile Durkheim, *The Elementary Forms of Religious Life* (trans and with an introduction by Karen E. Fields, Free Press, New York, 1995, first published 1912) emphasises the communal dimension of religion, going so far as to say (at 44) that 'religion must be an eminently collective thing'. We need not agree with Durkheim that the concept of religion depends on community in order to appreciate that the value of religion often inheres in community.

[14] Note that this latter option is likely to develop only in an autonomy-promoting culture.

At this point, it might be objected that we are making too much of the propensity of the private goods associated with religion to contribute to the conditions of autonomy. Even if we accept that those private goods are autonomy-promoting, must people engage with the private goods in question in order to be autonomous? Or might autonomy be achieved by people who never engage with the private goods associated with religious beliefs and practices? After all, surely atheists can be autonomous too? To this objection, two related points may be raised. First, while we cannot assert that the state is under a duty to promote religious purposes unless and until we are certain that religious purposes make a contribution to the conditions of autonomy that cannot be made via any other means, we need not make such a strong assertion in order to make the case for the state's promotion of religious purposes via charity law. All we must do in order to achieve that latter aim is to show that the demands of autonomy ground reasons for the state to promote religious purposes, and establishing that religious purposes generate autonomy-promoting goods is a way of showing just that. Second, if autonomy is to be a meaningful ideal in personal ethics and political morality, it cannot be abstracted from the epistemic lives of the people whose ideal it is.[15] For many people, given the architecture of their beliefs – including the conceptual categories that they utilise in giving form to and structuring such beliefs – autonomy in matters that traditionally have been the province of religion would be meaningless unless it enabled engagement with the private goods associated with religion via engagement with religious options. This is true of the atheist no less than the religious person; after all, the atheist cannot make sense of her beliefs *qua* atheist except in opposition to religion. Indeed, given the prominence of religion in world history and cultures, there are reasons to think that autonomy, in matters that have traditionally been the province of religion, invariably depends on the availability of religious options; a world in which people could autonomously respond to ultimate questions, or negotiate ethics and morality, or experience true community without having religious options available to them would be unrecognisable to us. We will return to this point below when we consider whether the state is justified in singling out 'advancement of religion' as a distinct type of charitable purpose.

As well as enabling engagement with private goods, purposes directed to the maintenance and promotion of religious beliefs and practices

---

[15] See also Green, above n 10, for similar points.

might, under certain conditions, make a contribution to the realisation of non-excludable public goods. It is possible to discern, in academic literature and case law on the topic of religion and the state, at least two types of argument drawing a link between religion and public goods. First, there is an argument that the ethical and moral teachings typically associated with religion contribute to social order and stability in a society populated to some sufficient degree by religious people who adhere to those teachings.[16] This argument is problematic for at least two reasons. First, although the connection between religion and adherence to moral teachings can scarcely be doubted, and although in many societies religious people do live in circumstances of social order, there are enough instances of sectarian division and conflict to call into question the proposition that there is in every society a strong connection between religion, adherence to moral teachings and social order.[17] Second, the argument assumes that social order is a public good – an assumption that, when applied to circumstances of religious diversity, must be qualified if it is to be reconciled with liberal commitments. Some degree of social order is undoubtedly a great good, in the absence of which autonomous living would not be possible; to this extent, social order is a liberal value. However, social order – whether generated by coincidence of adherence to moral teachings by religious people or in some other way – can be at odds with the conditions of autonomy and, to that extent, is not valuable from a liberal perspective. Thus, in a society in which most of the citizens are adherents of one religion and share common beliefs about ethics and morality, there might be a high degree of social order, but to the extent that this social order is achieved by sidelining or suppressing the unwelcome beliefs of a religious (or non-religious) minority, it is not a public good according to a liberal conception of the good.[18]

The first type of argument drawing a link between religion and public goods may thus run into trouble in circumstances of religious diversity. In contrast, a second type of argument seeking to connect religion and public goods identifies religious diversity, as part of a wider culture of

---

[16] See Patrick Devlin, *The Enforcement of Morals* (Oxford University Press, 1965); Murray Gleeson, 'The Relevance of Religion' (2001) 75 *Australian Law Journal* 93; Matthew Turnour, *Beyond Charity: Outlines of a Jurisprudence for Civil Society* (PhD thesis, Queensland University of Technology, 2009), 335–341.

[17] See the comments of Lord Scott in *Gallagher* v. *Church of Jesus Christ of Latter-Day Saints* [2008] 1 WLR 1852 (House of Lords), 1867.

[18] See H.L.A. Hart, *Law, Liberty and Morality* (Oxford University Press, 1963).

diversity in various beliefs, traditions and practices, itself as a public good. According to an argument along these lines, the pursuit of religious purposes by the adherents of a variety of religions helps to ensure that those religions are at least sustained and ideally flourish over the course of time, and a culture characterised by such religious diversity is a public good, enjoyed necessarily by everyone irrespective of whether or not they are religious.[19] In light of autonomy-based liberalism, the key question is whether and, if so, to what extent the public good of religious diversity contributes to the conditions of autonomy. And there appears to be an argument in support of the proposition that religious diversity makes a substantial contribution to those conditions. A culture of religious diversity gives people opportunities they would otherwise lack to become familiar with a range of religious beliefs and practices. Such opportunities enable people to compare their own religious or non-religious beliefs and practices with those of others and thereby to understand their options in matters relating to such beliefs and practices – remembering from earlier that these options are not exhausted by simple choices between beliefs and practices, but extend also to people's more or less voluntary engagement with their own beliefs and practices – more fully and deeply.

Moreover, it is through familiarity with religious difference that people are likely to acquire and cultivate attitudes of empathy, trust and even respect in thinking about and dealing with different religious – and, for that matter, non-religious – beliefs and practices. This is not to say that familiarity with religious difference is a necessary condition of the development of attitudes of empathy, trust and respect. Rather, it is to make the more subtle point that familiarity with religious difference helps to bring about conditions under which such attitudes may be developed and cultivated in dealings with those whose religious or non-religious beliefs and practices differ from one's own. In a society characterised by diversity of any sort, including of course religious diversity, the development and cultivation of empathy, trust and respect in such dealings is of obvious importance in light of the demands of autonomy. For one thing, these attitudes contribute to the development of autonomy-enhancing capacities, largely through disposing their holders to grasp and respond to the value in different options. Empathy, trust and respect, where widely held, also help to sustain social conditions that make diversity, and the range of options for autonomous choice that is entailed in

---

[19] For a judicial endorsement of the public good of religious diversity in a constitutional setting: *SL* v. *Commission scolaire des Chênes* [2012] SCC 7 (Supreme Court of Canada).

diversity, possible. In the case of religious diversity, those social conditions are often referred to as 'freedom of religion'. Religious diversity is thus a public good in part because it helps to bring about and sustain the conditions of its own existence.

C. Conflicts between religion and autonomy

We have now seen that religious lives can be, and perhaps in an autonomy-promoting culture often are, characterised by autonomy. Moreover, we have seen that religious purposes generate private and public goods that we have reasons to think make substantial contributions to the conditions of autonomy. That said, it is undoubtedly true that conflicts between religion and autonomy can arise, and that the pursuit of religious purposes sometimes impairs autonomy. Such conflicts might arise in a variety of ways. Devout people might commit themselves once and for all to living in highly non-autonomous ways.[20] A religious group might, in light of their religious beliefs or practices, refuse to allow their children to gain the sort of education that is necessary both to developing the inner capacities and to accessing the options on which autonomy depends.[21] A set of religious teachings might require that heretics be 'shunned' by the faithful, denying to those who receive this treatment the opportunity to enjoy continuing relationships with spouses and children and impairing autonomy in other severe ways.[22] Members of a religious sect or cult might be subjected to manipulation and even coercion by a charismatic or overbearing leader. A strident preacher might preach intolerance or hatred of those with

---

[20] Consider the closed religious orders under scrutiny in *Cocks* v. *Manners* (1871) 12 LR Eq 574 (Sir John Wickens VC); *Gleeson* v. *Phelan* (1914) 15 SR(NSW) 30 (Harvey J); *Gilmour* v. *Coats* [1949] AC 426 (House of Lords); *Leahy* v. *Attorney-General for New South Wales* [1959] AC 457 (Privy Council).

[21] Good examples, drawn from US constitutional law, are *Wisconsin* v. *Yoder* 406 US 205 (1972) (US Supreme Court) and *Mozert* v. *Hawkins County Board of Education* 827 F 2d 1058 (1987) (Sixth Circuit Court of Appeals). For a discussion of the latter case, emphasising the importance of education to the maintenance of cultural public goods in a liberal society: Nussbaum, above n 6, 327–334. Nussbaum is a well-known critic of autonomy-based liberalism – see Martha Nussbaum, 'Perfectionist Liberalism and Political Liberalism' (2011) 39 *Philosophy and Public Affairs* 3 – but here her thinking comes close to Raz's liberal conception of the good.

[22] See the discussion in Kent Greenawalt, 'Freedom of Association and Religious Association' in Amy Gutmann (ed), *Freedom of Association* (Princeton University Press, Princeton, 1998) 109–144, 127–129, 132–136.

different beliefs and practices, undermining the culture of religious diversity that, as we have seen, makes a contribution to the conditions of autonomy.

From the perspective of autonomy-based liberalism, these conflicts between religion and autonomy should be resolved in favour of autonomy, especially where what is under threat is the future autonomy of children whose lives are directed in accordance with the religious beliefs and practices of their parents.[23] In some circumstances, the resolution of such conflicts in favour of autonomy may be consistent with state toleration of religious beliefs and practices – for example, where a small religious group is organised according to beliefs that deny the value of autonomy, but keeps to itself and has no interaction with the wider society. In such circumstances, it might be heavy-handed and wasteful for the state to interfere with the group by exercising coercive power against it.[24] In other cases – extreme instances of 'shunning' and the preaching of intolerance or hatred might furnish good examples – the harm principle, interpreted along Razian lines in the way that we considered in Chapter 2, may give the state good reason to exercise coercive power against and even suppress religious practices that conflict with autonomy. But whether or not the state ought to refrain from exercising coercive power to interfere with the holders of religious beliefs and practices that conflict with autonomy is one thing; whether or not the state ought to promote such religious beliefs and practices is another. The case against promoting religious beliefs and practices that conflict with autonomy is more easily made than the case against coercively interfering with such beliefs and practices and, given that the state promotes charitable purposes via charity law, this has a bearing on how the state ought to respond to conflicts between religion and autonomy in the setting of charity law. From the perspective of autonomy-based liberalism, then, charity law should be generous in its acknowledgement of the extent to which private and public goods associated with religion contribute to the conditions of autonomy, but

---

[23] See Joel Feinberg, 'The Child's Right to an Open Future' in William Aiken and Hugh LaFollette (eds), *Whose Child? Children's Rights, Parental Authority and State Power* (Rowman and Littlefield, Totawa, NJ, 1980) 124–153.

[24] See generally Yossi Nehushtan, 'Secular and Religious Conscientious Exemptions: Between Tolerance and Equality' in Peter Cane, Carolyn Evans and Zoë Robinson (eds), *Law and Religion in Theoretical and Historical Context* (Cambridge University Press, 2008) 243–267.

it should also be willing to withdraw its privileges in cases where religious purposes harm people by diminishing their autonomy.

3. Religious purposes and public discourse in charity law

In Chapter 2, we noted that one way in which decision-makers may promote autonomy in the charity law setting is to express respect, and at the very least to refrain from expressing disrespect, for autonomy in their reasoning about whether or not to recognise some purpose or type of purpose as charitable in law. We also noted that decision-makers working with charity law might be said to express respect for autonomy where their reasoning reflects the general architecture of a liberal conception of the good grounded in the value of autonomy, or where their reasoning makes connections between charitable purposes and goods that, once examined philosophically, may be seen to make a contribution to the conditions of autonomy in some way. In this part of the chapter, we will consider the reasoning of decision-makers deliberating about religious purposes in the charity law setting, asking to what extent that reasoning lives up to liberal aspirations for public discourse based on the requirements of respect for autonomy. The analysis will proceed in four stages. First, we will consider the extent to which the reasoning of decision-makers, when considering religious purposes in the charity law setting, is characterised by the secularism that is entailed in a liberal conception of the good grounded in the value of autonomy. Second, we will consider the extent to which decision-makers, in charity law cases about religious purposes, recognise goods that turn out on philosophical reflection to be autonomy-promoting. Third, we will consider how conflicts between religion and autonomy are dealt with in charity law. Finally, we will consider whether the state is justified, in light of autonomy-based aspirations for public discourse, in singling out 'advancement of religion' as a distinct type of charitable purpose.

A.   Secularism

Autonomy-based liberalism is committed to what might be called 'secularism', not in the sense that it is hostile to religion or even neutral in some sense with respect to religion,[25] but rather in the sense that it seeks

---

[25] For the view that secularism is not synonymous with hostility to religion: Charles Taylor, 'What Does Secularism Mean?' in his *Dilemmas and Connections* (Belknap Press,

to appeal to non-religious values and principles – chiefly, autonomy – when thinking about the justification and desirability of state action. Of course, some sort of commitment to secularism is not peculiar to autonomy-based liberalism; indeed, a commitment to secularism may be described as a core commitment of liberals of all stripes, so that a person who rejected the notion of secularism altogether simply would not be a liberal.[26] Nonetheless, in autonomy-based liberalism the commitment to secularism is relatively strong, because autonomy-based liberalism goes beyond the proposition that the state should remain in some sense neutral as between differing religious and non-religious conceptions of the good; according to autonomy-based liberalism, the state should promote a non-religious conception of the good – a conception of the good centred on the value of autonomy – and this should occur even though it might demand state disapproval or even suppression of religious conceptions of the good.[27] This sounds harsh and indeed almost illiberal; however, as we have seen, promoting the conditions of autonomy is actually compatible with promoting many (although not all) religious purposes, and may be compatible with toleration of some others. Indeed, and perhaps ironically, the relatively strong secularism of autonomy-based liberalism is consistent with a greater degree of state accommodation of religion than is the relatively weak secularism of neutrality-based liberal accounts that rule out state recognition and promotion of religion altogether within certain spheres of action and reason.

Liberal aspirations for public discourse developed with reference to the ideal of autonomy entail the commitment to secularism that characterises the liberal conception of the good centred on the value of autonomy. Thus, respect for autonomy demands that decision-makers not endorse, or take as a reason for action, a proposition that may be embraced as true only in light of some religious belief; in other words, respect for autonomy rules out any state establishment of religion. From this perspective,

Cambridge, MA, 2011) 303–325; for a discussion, and rejection, of the notion of secularism as neutrality with respect to religion: Rex Ahdar, 'Is Secularism Neutral?' (2013) 26 *Ratio Juris* 404.

[26] See generally Russell Blackford, *Freedom of Religion and the Secular State* (Wiley-Blackwell, Chichester, 2012).

[27] See Joseph Raz, *The Morality of Freedom* (Clarendon Press, Oxford, 1986), 423–424; Joseph Raz, 'Multiculturalism: A Liberal Perspective' in his *Ethics in the Public Domain: Essays in the Morality of Law and Politics* (Clarendon Press, Oxford, 1994) 170–192, 182–183.

it is not permissible for decision-makers to support a particular religious organisation on the basis that the religious teachings of that organisation are true, and equally impermissible for decision-makers to deny support to or to disadvantage an organisation on the basis that its religious teachings are false. When looked at in light of autonomy-based aspirations for public discourse, in some respects the history of charity law yields disappointing results. Perhaps most notably, prior to the advent of religious toleration in England, trusts for religious purposes other than those associated with the Church of England were unenforceable in law;[28] moreover, in some cases judges ordered *cy-pres* application of funds intended for such purposes with the result that those funds ended up in the hands of the established church.[29] Arguably, it is unreasonable to evaluate such early cases in light of liberal ideals, given that in many ways the cases pre-date a recognisably modern liberalism. The same may not be said of the nineteenth-century case of *Mitford* v. *Reynolds*, in which Lord Lyndhurst expressed the view that an application of funds for 'idolatrous purposes' such as building a Hindu temple would not be of benefit to the people of Bengal.[30] This illiberal view almost certainly rested on the injunction of Exodus 20:4: 'Thou shalt not make unto thee any graven image'.[31] Nor need we be shy about applying liberal standards of public discourse to the 1996 *Report on the Law of Charities* of the Ontario Law Reform Commission, in which the Commission stated that '[t]he good of religion lies in the worship of God, and a life of relationship and obedience to Him'.[32] This statement may be accepted as true only by those whose religious commitments are both monotheistic and entail belief in the possibility of a personal relationship with God and, to that extent, it cannot be reconciled with autonomy-based aspirations for public discourse.[33]

---

[28] See generally Gareth Jones, *History of the Law of Charity 1532–1827* (Cambridge University Press, 1969).

[29] *Attorney-General* v. *Baxter* (1684) 1 Vern 248 (Sir Francis North); *Da Costa* v. *Da Paz* (1754) 1 Dick 259 (Lord Hardwicke LC); *Cary* v. *Abbot* (1802) 7 Ves Jun 490 (Sir William Grant MR).

[30] (1842) 1 Ph 185; [1835–42] All ER Rep 331 (Lord Lyndhurst LC), 336.

[31] For Jews and Protestants (but not Roman Catholics), this injunction forms part of the second of the Ten Commandments.

[32] Ontario Law Reform Commission, *Report on the Law of Charities: Volume 1* (1996), 200–201.

[33] The report relied heavily on the work of John Finnis, a Roman Catholic philosopher in the natural law tradition.

That said, from the secular perspective that characterises autonomy-based aspirations for public discourse, there is also much to celebrate in the history of charity law. That history reveals decision-makers repeatedly refraining from reaching for religious beliefs in making judgments about religion. As we have seen, during the seventeenth century the purposes of dissenting Protestant groups were not tolerated in English law and therefore trusts for such purposes were unenforceable; nonetheless, once the Act of Toleration of 1689 removed the legal impediment to toleration, English law was quick to enforce as charitable trusts for dissenting Protestant purposes, even though such trusts were motivated by beliefs at odds with the teachings of the established church.[34] The reasons for this acceptance of dissenting Protestant purposes as charitable are not spelt out in the scant law reports of the time, but we can fairly assume that they rested more on a perceived association between religion and charity than on any particular religious beliefs. A similar story may be told about trusts for the purpose of saying the Roman Catholic mass; in England such trusts were struck down as 'superstitious uses' until as late as the mid-nineteenth century,[35] but once the doctrine of superstitious uses was finally laid to rest in 1919[36] the enforcement of trusts for masses as charitable soon followed, based at first on deference to the beliefs of Roman Catholic citizens and later on an appreciation of secular goods associated with the performance of religious rites (but only to the extent that the secular goods in question were sufficiently public in orientation to satisfy the 'public' component of the public benefit test).[37] And consider also the well-known case of *Thornton v. Howe*, in which Sir John Romilly had to decide whether or not a trust for the purpose of disseminating literature written by the controversial religious leader Joanna Southcote was charitable.[38] Although he assessed the religious claims made in that literature as 'foolish' and 'ignorant', he refrained from making that assessment the basis of his decision;[39] instead, he invoked a principle of neutrality, stating that the court ought to make

---

[34] *Attorney-General* v. *Hughes* (1689) 2 Vern 105; *Attorney-General* v. *Hickman* (1732) 2 Eq Cas Abr 193 (Lord King).

[35] *West* v. *Shuttleworth* (1835) 2 My & K 684 (Pepys MR); *Heath* v. *Chapman* (1854) 2 Drew 416 (Kindersley VC).

[36] *Bourne* v. *Keane* [1919] AC 815 (House of Lords).

[37] *In re Caus, Lindeboom* v. *Camille* [1934] 1 Ch 162 (Luxmoore J) (deference); *In re Hetherington (deceased)* [1990] 1 Ch 1 (Sir Nicolas Browne-Wilkinson VC) (secular goods).

[38] (1862) 31 Beav 14; 52 ER 1042 (Sir John Romilly MR).   [39] Ibid, 18.

no distinction between religions or between denominations within a religion, and he upheld the trust as a result.[40]

Gilmour v. *Coats*, a case that we considered in earlier chapters, is often cited as the *locus classicus* of charity law's secularism when dealing with religious purposes.[41] Recall that the case was about a trust for the purposes of a Carmelite order of nuns who spent their lives in intercessory prayer and other spiritual exercises within their convent. Three arguments were put to the House of Lords on the question of the likely public benefit of the nuns' purposes. First, it was argued that, according to the teachings of the Roman Catholic Church, the nuns' intercessory prayers were heard and answered by God and caused divine blessings to be bestowed on the world. Second, it was argued that the example of the nuns' pious lives brought spiritual edification to the wider church. Finally, it was argued that the convent provided an opportunity for women of the Roman Catholic faith to practise their religion in the distinctive way that characterises the Carmelite order. The House of Lords accepted none of these arguments.[42] We will return below to the rejection of the second and third arguments. For now, let us note that, looking at *Gilmour* v. *Coats* in light of liberal aspirations for public discourse that entail a commitment to secularism, the House of Lords was surely right not to accept the first argument; to accept that argument would have meant accepting a proposition – that intercessory prayers are heard and answered by God – regarded as true only by Roman Catholics and other religious people whose beliefs coincide relevantly with Roman Catholic beliefs.[43] It would have been an illiberal establishment of religion.

Interestingly, in applying the public benefit test in *Gilmour* v. *Coats*, the House of Lords had available to it another strategy for dealing with the argument about the efficacy of intercessory prayer: it could have

---

[40] Ibid, 19–21. It is sometimes suggested that *Thornton* v. *Howe* provides no reason for liberal celebration after all, because the effect of finding the trust in that case charitable was to render it void under the Mortmain Act of 1736. However, there are reasons to doubt that this is an appropriate response to the decision: see Pauline Ridge, 'Legal Neutrality, Public Benefit and Religious Charitable Purposes: Making Sense of *Thornton v Howe*' (2010) 31 *Journal of Legal History* 177.

[41] [1949] AC 426 (House of Lords).

[42] Ibid, 446–447, 449 (Lord Simonds), 450–454 (Lord du Parcq), 454 (Lord Normand), 454 (Lord Morton of Henryton), 454–462 (Lord Reid).

[43] Importantly, the House of Lords did not reject the argument either; rather, their Lordships remained agnostic on the question of the efficacy of intercessory prayer. For a clear expression of this agnosticism: ibid, 446 (Lord Simonds).

deferred to Roman Catholic beliefs on the subject, as decision-makers in Ireland and Australia have done.[44] We saw in Chapter 1 that by refusing to defer to Roman Catholic beliefs about the efficacy of intercessory prayer, the House of Lords in *Gilmour v. Coats* reinforced the emphasis on objectivity when applying the 'benefit' component of the public benefit test that characterises charity law. This refusal to defer to Roman Catholic beliefs was of course consistent with secularist aspirations for public discourse; however, it is worth pointing out that the path of deference, had it been chosen, might also have been consistent with such aspirations. Deferring to religious beliefs is not the same as accepting the beliefs in question or taking them to be reasons for action, and it is possible to follow or endorse the practice of deference from a secular perspective, for instance by viewing it as a means by which the preferences of the citizens whose beliefs they are may be satisfied. That the strategy of deference is consistent with secularism may be seen in the reasoning of Irish judges who have adopted that strategy: perhaps the clearest statement of that reasoning is in the judgment of Fitzgibbon LJ of the Irish Court of Appeal in the leading case of *O'Hanlon v. Logue*:[45]

> [all religions and denominations] stand equal before the secular Courts in a country like Ireland, where no particular religion is established by law, and no particular faith has ever been declared superstitious by statute. In determining whether the performance of any particular rite promotes any particular religion, and benefits the members of the Church or denomination, or body, who profess it, the secular Court must act upon evidence of the belief of the members of the community concerned. It can have no other guide upon that subject.

In this passage, the link between deference and secularism is unmistakable.

B.   *Autonomy-promoting goods*

In ascertaining the extent to which the reasoning of decision-makers with respect to 'advancement of religion' has recognised connections between religious purposes and autonomy-promoting goods, we might as well

---

[44] *O'Hanlon v. Logue* [1906] 1 IR 247 (Irish Court of Appeal); *Attorney-General* v. *Becher* [1910] 2 IR 251 (King's Bench); Charities Act 2009 (Ireland), s 3(6); *Nelan* v. *Downes* (1917) 23 CLR 546 (High Court of Australia). See also *In re Caus, Lindeboom* v. *Camille* [1934] 1 Ch 162 (Luxmoore J), a pre-*Gilmour* v. *Coats* case from England.

[45] [1906] 1 IR 247 (Irish Court of Appeal), 279. The judgment of Palles CB is more often quoted, but its commitment to secularism is less clear.

start by considering the extent to which decision-makers point to goods associated with religion in the 'advancement of religion' setting, before considering the extent to which these goods are autonomy-promoting. That decision-makers do point to goods associated with religion in the 'advancement of religion' setting can scarcely be doubted. In general terms, the very fact that 'advancement of religion' is identified in charity law as a distinct type of charitable purpose indicates that decision-makers readily accept the possibility that religious purposes produce goods of various sorts, even if this is not spelt out explicitly.[46] Moreover, in many 'advancement of religion' cases, decision-makers do explicitly point to goods associated with religious beliefs and practices. For example, endorsement of the proposition that religion is a private good for religious people may be found in the case law, although it is typically accompanied by endorsement of the proposition that it is better to be a religious person than a non-religious person – a proposition that, for reasons we will explore below, is problematic from the perspective of autonomy-based liberalism.[47] In *Crowther* v. *Brophy*, an Australian case, Gobbo J of the Supreme Court of Victoria referred to the private goods in the form of the 'comfort and peace of mind' associated with intercessory prayer and the 'edification' entailed in the celebration of the Roman Catholic mass.[48] And it might be possible to infer from the espousal of a principle of neutrality in *Thornton* v. *Howe*, in which a purpose of disseminating religious literature was in view, an acceptance that there are private goods associated with reading, digesting and discussing such literature.[49]

In other cases, decision-makers point to what they take to be public goods associated with religion when reasoning in the charity law setting. This happens in cases where the immediate consequence of some religious purpose is the provision of private goods to a private class in a way that ordinarily would fail the public benefit test, but decision-makers perceive that those private goods are accompanied by incidental public goods that do support a finding of public benefit. In Chapter 1, we

---

[46] For a description, and defence, of state recognition of a general connection between religious purposes and goods of various sorts in the American constitutional setting, see Koppelman, *Defending American Religious Neutrality*, above n 5.

[47] *Attorney-General* v. *Becher* [1910] 2 IR 251 (King's Bench), 267–268 (Gibson J); *Neville Estates Ltd* v. *Madden* [1962] 1 Ch 832 (Cross J), 853.

[48] [1992] 2 VR 97 (Gobbo J), 100.

[49] (1862) 31 Beav 14; 52 ER 1042 (Sir John Romilly MR), 19–20. See also *Re Watson (deceased), Hobbs* v. *Smith* [1973] 3 All ER 678 (Plowman J).

considered two such cases that are worth revisiting for present purposes. The first was *Neville Estates Ltd v. Madden*, the case in which a trust for the purposes of a synagogue closed to the public was under consideration.[50] Recall that Cross J made a finding of public benefit on the basis that, notwithstanding that the synagogue was closed to the public, 'some benefit accrues to the public from the attendance at places of worship of persons who ... mix with their fellow citizens'.[51] The second was *Joyce v. Ashfield Municipal Council*, the case about whether a hall used for private worship was used for charitable purposes: for the New South Wales Court of Appeal, the worship services, although conducted in private, nonetheless had 'public value in improving the standards of the believer in the world'.[52] The views expressed in these two cases suggest the argument associating religion, adherence to moral teachings and social order, that we encountered earlier in this chapter. By contrast, in the Irish case of *Attorney-General v. Becher*, Gibson J of the King's Bench expressed the view that 'liberty and equality in religion, as well as in other fields of thought and action, are for the public good', a view more in keeping with the argument – also discussed earlier – that identifies a culture of religious diversity as a public good.[53]

To reiterate: there is evidence that, in the charity law setting, decision-makers appeal to what they take to be private and public goods associated with religion. However, the evidence does not all point one way. *Gilmour v. Coats* suggests that in some circumstances, decision-makers are reluctant to recognise goods associated with religion. As we have just seen, in that case three arguments were put to the House of Lords on the question of the likely public benefit of the nuns' purposes. We dealt with the first argument, appealing to the efficacy of intercessory prayer, earlier. The second argument was that the example of the nuns' pious lives brought spiritual edification to the wider church; in effect, this argument pointed to private goods in the form of encouragement and inspiration for the holders of religious beliefs. The House of Lords rejected the second argument on the basis that the private goods associated with edification were 'too vague and intangible' to support a

---

[50] [1962] 1 Ch 832 (Cross J).
[51] Ibid, 853. A general link between private religious purposes and public goods was also alluded to by Chitty J in the pre-*Pemsel* case of *Re Joy* (1889) 60 LTR 175, but the purpose in *Re Joy* – 'united prayer' – was found not to be charitable because it was not analogous to any purpose in the preamble to the Statute of Elizabeth.
[52] [1975] 1 NSWLR 744 (New South Wales Court of Appeal), 751–752 (Hutley JA).
[53] [1910] 2 IR 251 (King's Bench), 267–268 (Gibson J).

finding of public benefit.[54] The third argument was that, in carrying out their purposes, the nuns in *Gilmour* v. *Coats* made available to Roman Catholic women the opportunity to practise their religion in the distinctive way that characterises the Carmelite order. This opportunity surely entailed private goods for Roman Catholic women. However, the House of Lords made no reference to such goods. Instead, in rejecting the third argument, their Lordships reasoned that it could not benefit the public to make available to Roman Catholic women the opportunity to become Carmelite nuns except where this resulted in some wider public benefit, and that there was no wider public benefit in the case at hand.[55]

In many respects, the reasoning of decision-makers in the 'advancement of religion' setting reflects a recognition that there are substantial connections between religious purposes and the conditions of autonomy. Given the propensity of religious purposes to generate a range of private and public goods that contribute in meaningful ways to the conditions of autonomy, decision-makers' willingness to recognise such purposes as charitable would, taken on its own, appear to be consistent with autonomy-based aspirations for public discourse, at least up to a point. Moreover, in cases such as *Attorney-General* v. *Becher*, decision-makers making findings of public benefit point specifically to autonomy-promoting goods such as religious diversity. Even the application of a presumption of benefit to certain religious purposes – a practice that, as we saw in Chapter 1, continues in several jurisdictions even if it has ceased in others – might be consistent with aspirations for public discourse understood with reference to the liberal ideal of autonomy; in situations where the links between religious beliefs and practices and the private and public goods associated with the conditions of autonomy have been clearly demonstrated over the course of time, there might be a case for presuming the benefit of purposes relating to the maintenance and promotion of those beliefs and practices.[56] This is most clearly an argument for applying a presumption of benefit to religions that have

---

[54] Gilmour v. *Coats* [1949] AC 426 (House of Lords), 446 (Lord Simonds).

[55] Ibid, 448–449 (Lord Simonds), 462 (Lord Reid). Note that the reasoning of the House of Lords on this point appears to be inconsistent with the proposition, uncontroversial in other areas of charity law, that a purpose may be of public benefit where it entails the provision of private goods to a public class: see Patrick J. Ford, 'Public Benefit Versus Charity: A Scottish Perspective' in Charles Mitchell and Susan R. Moody (eds), *Foundations of Charity* (Hart Publishing, Oxford, 2000) 205–248, 240.

[56] For similar thoughts: Macklem, above n 11, 48–50.

enriched the lives of large numbers of adherents over long periods of time; implied in the argument is the suggestion that it might be appropriate, in the charity law of a liberal state, to require new religions to demonstrate via the public benefit test the connections between their beliefs and practices and the goods that serve the value of autonomy. This suggestion is arguably reflected in the remarks of the Charity Commissioners for England and Wales, in their 1999 decision about the Church of Scientology, that public benefit may be more difficult to establish in the case of a new religion than an old one.[57]

In other respects, the reasoning of decision-makers in the 'advancement of religion' setting may not be consistent with a sound assessment of the relation of religious purposes and autonomy-promoting goods. In some cases, decision-makers point to goods that appear to play no role in promoting the conditions of autonomy – the 'comfort and peace of mind' alluded to in *Crowther* v. *Brophy* is an example – and in others they point to states of affairs – the 'improved standards' referred to in *Joyce* v. *Ashfield Municipal Council*, for example – that are not obviously goods at all. However, in some cases in which decision-makers make findings as to whether or not religious purposes are charitable based on reasons that are not consistent with a conception of the good grounded in the value of autonomy, their decisions may be justified in light of the demands of autonomy, even if their reasoning is not. For example, the decision of the New South Wales Court of Appeal in *Joyce* v. *Ashfield Municipal Council* might have been justified on the basis that religious diversity is an autonomy-promoting public good, even though the Court did not have regard to that good in reaching its decision. Similarly, while it is possible that the House of Lords was overly hasty in rejecting the second and third arguments on the question of public benefit in *Gilmour* v. *Coats* because those arguments pointed to genuine goods associated with religion, nonetheless their Lordships' decision not to recognise the purposes of the nuns as charitable might have been justified because even if those purposes stood to generate goods associated with religion, those goods were not autonomy-promoting.[58]

---

[57] *Decision of the Charity Commissioners for England and Wales, Application for Registration as a Charity by the Church of Scientology (England and Wales)*, 17 November 1999, 41–42.

[58] It is not obvious how spiritual edification contributes to the conditions of autonomy, nor is it obvious how enabling women to become Carmelite nuns promotes autonomy, given that being a Carmelite nun entails living non-autonomously: see *Gilmour* v. *Coats* [1949] AC 426 (House of Lords), 428–429 for a description of Carmelite practices.

C. *Conflicts between religion and autonomy*

Earlier we saw that, from the perspective of autonomy-based liberalism, conflicts between religion and autonomy should be resolved in favour of autonomy. To what extent does the reasoning of decision-makers in the charity law setting reflect this proposition? The history of charity law shows some willingness on the part of decision-makers to refuse to recognise as charitable religious purposes that are likely to conflict with autonomy. In *Thornton* v. *Howe*, Sir John Romilly expressed the view that religious purposes 'adverse to the foundations of all religion' or 'subversive of all morality' ought not to be regarded as charitable in law;[59] as we saw in Chapter 1, these remarks are ambiguous but appear to point to a disqualifying rule grounded in considerations of public policy. Now we may add that this disqualifying rule seems to recognise that in some circumstances, religious diversity – which, as we have seen, we have reason to think is an autonomy-promoting public good – might conflict with the religious purposes of a particular person or group, and that such a conflict ought to be resolved in favour of religious diversity. More specifically, section 3(10) of the Irish Charities Act of 2009 provides that a gift is not for the advancement of religion if it is for the benefit of 'an organisation or cult ... that employs oppressive psychological manipulation'; this provision appears to be clearly directed against interference with the freedom from coercion and manipulation that is a fundamental condition of autonomy. On the other hand, in Chapters 1 and 2 we saw that in *Holmes* v. *Attorney-General*, Walton J applied a presumption of benefit to the purposes of the Exclusive Brethren, notwithstanding evidence suggesting that the Exclusive Brethren might have engaged in harmful practices.[60] To the extent that this evidence revealed that the practices of the Exclusive Brethren impaired the autonomy of members of that group, it is arguable that Walton J decided *Holmes* v. *Attorney-General* by resolving a conflict between religion and autonomy in favour of religion. From the perspective of autonomy-based liberalism, the resolution of conflicts between religion and autonomy in favour of religion is unjustified. The better response is one that vindicates the liberal ideal of autonomy, whether by refusing to make a finding of public benefit or applying a disqualifying rule such as the one alluded to in *Thornton* v. *Howe*, or by assessing evidence of harms to autonomy

[59] (1862) 31 Beav 14; 52 ER 1042 (Sir John Romilly MR), 20.
[60] *The Times* (London), 12 February 1981, 8.

and finding that these are outweighed by benefits that stand to promote the conditions of autonomy overall.[61]

D. Singling out 'advancement of religion'

As we saw in Chapter 1, in the general descriptions of charitable purpose that figure in the criteria of charity law in various jurisdictions, 'advancement of religion' is almost always singled out as a distinct type of charitable purpose. By singling out 'advancement of religion' in this fashion, decision-makers imply that certain goods are associated with religious purposes in a special or unique way that is not replicated in the case of purposes of other types. When 'advancement of religion' is contrasted with 'relief of poverty', 'advancement of education' or, indeed, many other general descriptions of charitable purpose in modern charity law, it is not usually difficult to grasp the ways in which goods associated with religious purposes are distinct from goods associated with purposes within those other descriptions. However, matters become more complicated when 'advancement of religion' is contrasted with purposes associated with the maintenance and promotion of secular belief systems, including atheism, that play a role in the lives of their adherents that is functionally similar to the role of religion in the lives of the religious. As we have seen, there are reasons to think that a variety of autonomy-promoting goods, both private and public, are associated with religion. That said, there appears to be no reason to think that, with the possible exception of faith, the various autonomy-promoting private goods associated with religion – the spiritual, emotional and intellectual resources made available by religious creeds, worldviews and doctrines, and the goods associated with practising religion, especially in communities – cannot be realised through the pursuit of purposes for the maintenance and promotion of secular beliefs and practices that are functionally similar to religion. Moreover, there seems no reason to believe that the conditions of autonomy are not maintained, indeed enhanced, in circumstances where religious diversity is accompanied by diversity in analogous beliefs and practices. All of this raises the possibility that, from the perspective of autonomy-based liberalism, decision-makers are not justified in singling out

---

[61] In this regard, the decision of the Charity Commission for England and Wales in *Preston Down Trust* has something to commend it: Charity Commission for England and Wales, *Preston Down Trust* (3 January 2014).

'advancement of religion' as a distinct type of charitable purpose, and that autonomy-based aspirations for public discourse might demand that 'advancement of religion' be replaced with a broader general description that captures all of the purposes – religious and secular – likely to generate the autonomy-promoting goods associated with religion that we considered earlier.[62]

The problem of singling out 'advancement of religion' has not gone unnoticed in charity law. At times, decision-makers seem to have responded to that problem by expressing the view that religious and analogous secular purposes should be treated in the same way because they promise to realise similar goods.[63] However, on other occasions, decision-makers seem to have denied the proposition that goods associated with religion might also be realised by secular purposes: the best-known of these cases is *Neville Estates Ltd* v. *Madden*, in which Cross J stated that '[a]s between different religions the law stands neutral, but it assumes that any religion is at least likely to be better than none'.[64] In some cases decision-makers have sought to avoid the problem by defining religion in the setting of 'advancement of religion' so as to exclude certain secular purposes, and then finding such secular purposes charitable under the 'catch-all' general description of charitable purposes that invariably completes the set of such descriptions in charity law. Such was the case in *In re South Place Ethical Society*.[65] There, Dillon J said that it was desirable in a liberal society not to draw distinctions between 'beliefs deeply and sincerely held, whether they are beliefs in a god or in the excellence of man or in ethical principles, or in Platonism or some other scheme of philosophy'; however, he also said that the purposes of a society formed for the 'study and dissemination of ethical principles and the cultivation of a rational religious sentiment' were not within the description 'advancement of religion' because they did not relate to

---

[62] For an argument for such a broader category, but not from an autonomy-based perspective: Steve T. Woodfield, 'Doing God's Work: Is Religion Always Charitable?' (1996–9) 8 *Auckland University Law Review* 25, 41–42. See also, at a greater level of generality, Gemma Cornelissen, 'Belief-Based Exemptions: Are Religious Beliefs Special?' (2012) 25 *Ratio Juris* 85.

[63] See *In re Price* [1943] 1 Ch 422 (Cohen J), 433; *Walz* v. *Tax Commission of the City of New York* 397 US 664 (1970) (US Supreme Court). Such a view may also be implied by ss 2(1)(c) and 3(3)(f) of the Charities and Trustee Investment (Scotland) Act 2005 (Scotland).

[64] [1962] 1 Ch 832 (Cross J), 853. See also *Attorney-General* v. *Becher* [1910] 2 IR 251 (King's Bench), 267–268 (Gibson J).

[65] [1980] 1 WLR 1565 (Dillon J).

'man's relation with God', and could only be charitable under the fourth 'head' of the *Pemsel* set.[66]

With autonomy-based aspirations for public discourse in view, the latter two of these strategies present certain problems. Denying the proposition that goods associated with religion might also be realised by secular purposes appears to be defensible in view of the unique value of faith, understood as a secular value in light of the contribution that it makes to the epistemic lives of the religious.[67] However, from the perspective of autonomy-based liberalism, the distinctive value of faith is almost certainly an insufficient basis for the seemingly illiberal statement that 'any religion is at least likely to be better than none'; moreover, given that almost all of the autonomy-promoting goods associated with religion are also associated with secular beliefs and practices that are analogous to religion, there is reason to think that the unique contribution of faith to religious lives may not be of sufficient weight to justify singling out 'advancement of religion' as a distinct type of charitable purpose. The strategy of defining religion in the 'advancement of religion' setting so as to exclude secular purposes and then finding secular purposes charitable under the 'catch-all' description is also not without problems in view of autonomy-based aspirations for public discourse. Assuming that a satisfactory definition of religion can be achieved – and the fact that the definition offered in *In re South Place Ethical Society* arguably excludes Buddhism indicates the difficulties in this regard[68] – the question of interest is not whether or not decision-makers can draw a conceptual line between religious and secular purposes; rather, it is whether decision-makers should draw such a line, or reach for some further conceptual category that spans both religious and secular purposes in light of the fact that religious purposes and certain secular purposes appear to stand to realise similar autonomy-promoting goods.[69]

---

[66] Ibid, 1571–1572. Contrast *Decision of the Charity Commissioners for England and Wales, Application for Registration as a Charity by the Church of Scientology (England and Wales)*, 17 November 1999, in which the purposes of the Church of Scientology were found to be neither within the description 'advancement of religion' nor within the fourth 'head' of the *Pemsel* set.

[67] Macklem, above n 11.

[68] [1980] 1 WLR 1565 (Dillon J), 1573. See also *Church of the New Faith* v. *Commissioner for Pay-Roll Tax (Victoria)* (1983) 154 CLR 120 (High Court of Australia) and *R (on the application of Hodkin)* v. *Registrar General of Births, Deaths and Marriages* [2013] UKSC 77 (UK Supreme Court) for the difficulties in defining religion.

[69] At times, decision-makers merge the question of the definition of religion with the question of the justification of treating religion differently in law from analogous secular

With autonomy-based aspirations for public discourse in view, a justification for singling out 'advancement of religion' as a general description of charitable purpose might be found in one of at least two ways. First, such a justification might emerge from reflection on the special way in which religion combines a range of autonomy-promoting goods. Michael McConnell expresses this as well as anyone could:[70]

> Religion is a special phenomenon, in part, because it plays such a wide variety of roles in human life: it is an institution, but it is more than that; it is an ideology or worldview, but it is more than that; it is a set of personal loyalties and locus of community, akin to family ties, but it is more than that; it is an aspect of identity, but it is more than that; it provides answers to questions of ultimate reality, and offers a connection to the transcendent; but it is more than that. Religion cannot be reduced to a subset of any larger category. In any particular context, religion may appear to be analogous to some other aspect of human activity – to another institution, worldview, personal loyalty, basis of personal identity, or answer to ultimate and transcendent questions. However, there is no other human phenomenon that combines all of these aspects; if there were such a concept, it would probably be viewed as a religion.

To the extent that religion uniquely combines goods in the way McConnell describes, and to the extent that this unique combination of goods makes a special contribution to the conditions of autonomy that could not be achieved otherwise, then in light of autonomy-based aspirations for public discourse, the state may be justified in singling out 'advancement of religion' as a distinct type of charitable purpose in law. Presenting religious purposes as distinct in this way is consistent with the proposition that religious purposes serve autonomy in a special way within an overall liberal conception of the good. Whether or not McConnell is right to assert that religion combines goods uniquely is a question that we will not pursue here; for now, let us simply note that if he is right, he may point to a liberal case for singling out 'advancement of religion' in charity law.

---

beliefs and practices, with arguably regrettable consequences for the definition of religion: see *Torcaso* v. *Watkins* 367 US 488 (1961) (US Supreme Court); *US* v. *Seeger* 380 US 163 (1965) (US Supreme Court); *Welsh* v. *US* 398 US 333 (1970) (US Supreme Court); *Wisconsin* v. *Yoder* 406 US 205 (1972) (US Supreme Court).

[70] Michael W. McConnell, 'The Problem of Singling Out Religion' (2000) 50 *DePaul Law Review* 1, 42. Note also Koppelman, *Defending American Religious Neutrality*, above n 5, ch 4, arguing that 'religion' denotes a 'cluster of goods' (quotation on 124).

A second way in which a liberal justification of the state practice of singling out 'advancement of religion' might be found is via an argument that autonomy-based aspirations for public discourse demand that decision-makers reason about the options that constitute the conditions of autonomy in ways that reflect all or at least a majority of citizens' beliefs about those options. Earlier, we saw that autonomy is meaningless as a personal and political ideal when it is abstracted from people's epistemic lives. If the architecture of people's beliefs entails categories that refer to religion, then to that extent, the provision of an adequate range of options in matters that have traditionally been dealt with by religion may depend on the maintenance and preservation of those categories. Now we may add that if autonomy is a meaningful ideal for people only against their epistemic horizons, respect for autonomy demands that decision-makers achieve some degree of faithfulness to those horizons. This is especially so when decision-makers are reasoning in ways that may reinforce people's options on the one hand, or change their options on the other; and *a fortiori* is it so when the state's actions constitute options that might not otherwise exist, as is the case with charity law. (Recall from Chapter 3 that via charity law the state creates options relating to the altruistic pursuit of charitable purposes.) We might further add that where the state engages with citizens' options in terms that do not reflect widespread beliefs about those options, citizens may come to be alienated from their law, with consequences for the rule of law that ought to be of concern from a liberal point of view. In light of these considerations, even if it is true that the autonomy-promoting goods associated with religious purposes are associated in the same way with analogous secular purposes, given that religion is widely believed to be a distinct phenomenon, the state has reasons when legislating with respect to religion to do so in terms that reflect that widespread belief, so long as the result of this is not an unacceptable cost to autonomy. Thus, if all else is equal and the state must choose between a general description of charitable purpose that refers specifically to religion on the one hand and a description that refers to a category wider than but including religion on the other, there may be reason for the state to choose the category that refers specifically to religion, and to deal with the non-religious purposes that would have been caught by the wider category in some other way.[71] On this view, the judgment of Dillon J in *In re South*

---

[71] The argument in the text goes beyond the more basic point made by Koppelman, 'Is It Fair to Give Religion Special Treatment?', above n 12, 597: 'All one needs to say, in order

Place Ethical Society, notwithstanding its shortcomings, might be offered as an example of sound judicial reasoning in an 'advancement of religion' case against the backdrop of autonomy-based aspirations for public discourse.

4. Conclusion

The conclusions of this chapter may be presented in the form of two broad claims. The first claim is that the treatment of religious purposes in charity law is in many, but not all, respects consistent with the commitments that animate autonomy-based liberalism. There are reasons to think that religious lives are at least in part autonomous lives, and equally there are reasons to think that religious purposes stand to realise a variety of private and public goods that contribute to the conditions under which people may lead autonomous lives. To that extent, charity law's promotion of religious purposes appears to be both justified and desirable in light of the value of autonomy. However, where religion and autonomy come into conflict, an autonomy-based account of political morality demands that the conflict be resolved in favour of autonomy, and this may require the withdrawal of the privileges of charity law in cases where religious purposes stand to harm people by diminishing their autonomy. The second claim is that the reasoning of decision-makers in the charity law setting is, to a degree, consistent with autonomy-based aspirations for public discourse. To an extent, charity law has adopted an approach to religious purposes that reflects: (a) the secularism of autonomy-based liberalism; (b) an appreciation of the links between religious purposes and autonomy-promoting goods; (c) the proposition that conflicts between religion and autonomy should be resolved in favour of autonomy; and (d) that in some respects, religious purposes may serve the conditions of autonomy in unique ways. However, such consistency with respect for autonomy as charity law has achieved in these ways is not complete, and in some ways, public discourse about religious purposes in the charity law setting may fail to live up to liberal aspirations. These conclusions suggest that many of the traditional liberal anxieties about the state promotion of religion, at least in the charity law setting, may turn out, from the perspective of autonomy-based liberalism, to be unfounded. But not all of them.

to justify distinctive treatment of religion, is that religion is a category that may be relevant to legitimate legislative purposes.'

6

Political purposes

1. Introduction

In Chapter 1, we were introduced to the disqualifying rules of charity law; perhaps the best known, and arguably the most controversial, is the rule that disqualifies political purposes from being charitable in law. In this chapter, we will consider charity law's treatment of political purposes, and specifically the rule against political purposes, in detail. We will begin by considering the history and nature of the rule against political purposes, paying particular attention to its scope. We will then turn to two defences of the rule that have been offered by the decision-makers who have endorsed and applied it. Having found these traditional defences of the rule wanting, we will consider whether a justification of the rule may be found. This will lead us to consider the question: do political purposes generate public benefit? We will see that there are strong arguments, supported by liberal political philosophy, for answering that question in the affirmative. Those arguments yield a prima facie case for rejecting the rule against political purposes as an unjustified component of charity law. However, we will conclude by pointing out that asking questions about the public benefit of political purposes focuses our attention only on what in Chapters 3 and 4 we described as the 'demand' side of the pursuit of such purposes; once we bring what we described in those chapters as the 'supply' side into view, another argument emerges – this time an argument in favour of maintaining the rule against political purposes, but only in certain circumstances and with a much narrower scope than the rule has often been thought to have.

2. The rule against political purposes

A. *The history and nature of the rule*

The starting point for identifying charity law's rule disqualifying political purposes from being charitable is often taken to be the judgment of Lord

Parker of Waddington in *Bowman* v. *Secular Society*, a judgment in which his Lordship stated that 'a trust for the attainment of political objects has always been held invalid'.[1] At the outset, it is worth pointing out that this statement was in the nature of *obiter dicta* and that in 1917, when *Bowman* v. *Secular Society* was decided, it was far from clear that trusts for political purposes had invariably or even mostly been regarded by decision-makers as invalid.[2] Indeed, the history of Victorian Britain reveals a strong tradition of charities pursuing political purposes of different types, with no suggestion that such purposes were impeded or constrained by charity law.[3] Against this backdrop, commentators have noted that Lord Parker's thinking on the status of political purposes in charity law appears to have been informed by a discussion of that topic in a late nineteenth-century text that took an idiosyncratic view of the extant case law.[4] Thus, there are reasons to think that Lord Parker's judgment in *Bowman* v. *Secular Society* did not carry the authority that has often been claimed for it. Nonetheless, as we will see shortly, the judgment, and the rule against political purposes that it recognised and endorsed, has been approved and applied many times since around the common law world.

In recognising a rule against political purposes, Lord Parker's judgment in *Bowman* v. *Secular Society* indicated in a general way that some purposes are too political in character to be charitable in law. However, that judgment gave little guidance as to the types of purpose that are to be considered 'too political' in this way. Lord Parker made reference to purposes of achieving reforms to various laws embedding Christianity in the law of England in his brief discussion of the rule against political purposes, but he went no further than that.[5] In *National Anti-Vivisection Society* v. *Inland Revenue Commissioners*, a case we encountered in

---

[1] [1917] AC 406 (House of Lords), 442 (Lord Parker).

[2] See, e.g., *Farewell* v. *Farewell* (1892) 22 OR 573 (Boyd C) and *In re Scowcroft* [1898] 2 Ch 638 (Stirling J), although note also *Haberson* v. *Vardon* (1851) 4 De G & Sm 461 (Knight Bruce VC). See generally Adam Parachin, 'Distinguishing Charity and Politics: The Judicial Thinking Behind the Doctrine of Political Purposes' (2008) 45 *Alberta Law Review* 871, 877–879.

[3] Michael Chesterman, *Charities, Trusts and Social Welfare* (Weidenfeld and Nicholson, London, 1979) ch 4.

[4] The text was A.D. Tyssen, *The Law of Charitable Bequests* (1st edn, Sweet and Maxwell, London, 1888), 177. See the discussion in Parachin, above n 2, 876–880.

[5] [1917] AC 406 (House of Lords), 442 (Lord Parker), referring to '[t]he abolition of religious tests, the disestablishment of the Church, the secularization of education, the alteration of the law touching religion or marriage, or the observation of the Sabbath'.

Chapter 2 in our discussion of the 'benefit' component of the public benefit test, the House of Lords held that the purpose of securing the repeal of legislation permitting live animal experimentation attracted the operation of the rule.[6] The *Anti-Vivisection* case thus confirmed what Lord Parker suggested in *Bowman* v. *Secular Society*: one type of purpose that is clearly too political to be charitable is a purpose of achieving law reform. And other case law has established that several further types of purpose are considered too political to be charitable as well. In *Re Hopkinson; Lloyds Bank Ltd* v. *Baker*, Vaisey J considered that the rule against political purposes applied to the purpose of supporting the maintenance of the present law.[7] In *McGovern* v. *Attorney-General*, Slade J held that the rule disqualified from being charitable purposes of furthering the interests of a political party or procuring changes in government policy or decisions.[8] And in *Human Life International in Canada Inc* v. *Minister of National Revenue*, the Canadian Federal Court of Appeal extended the operation of the rule to the purpose of advocating for an opinion on a social issue in a way that urges 'proper forms of conduct' on other members of the community.[9]

In modern charity law, then, the rule against political purposes tends to be given a range of application much broader than just purposes of achieving law reform. That said, it is important to notice that the rule applies only in cases where the dominant purpose of an organisation is political; where an organisation engages in political activities or pursues political purposes in a way that is subsidiary to a dominant non-political purpose, the rule against political purposes does not apply and the question whether or not the dominant purpose is charitable in law falls to be determined by an application of the criteria of charity law.[10] Thus,

---

[6] [1948] AC 31 (House of Lords).

[7] [1949] 1 All ER 346 (Vaisey J), 350, although note also *Public Trustee* v. *Attorney-General (New South Wales)* (1997) 42 NSWLR 600 (Santow J), 608.

[8] [1982] 1 Ch 321 (Slade J).

[9] [1998] 3 FC 202 (Canadian Federal Court of Appeal), 217–218.

[10] *McGovern* v. *Attorney-General* [1982] 1 Ch 321 (Slade J), 340–343. See also *Slee* v. *Commissioner of Internal Revenue* (1930) 72 ALR 400 (Court of Appeals, 2nd circuit); *Girard Trust Company* v. *Commissioner of Internal Revenue* (1941) 138 ALR 448 (Court of Appeals, 3rd circuit); *International Reform Federation* v. *District Unemployment Compensation Board* (1942) 131 F 2d 337 (Court of Appeals for the District of Columbia), three cases that demonstrate the difficulties for decision-makers who are called upon to ascertain whether or not the dominant purpose of an organisation is a political purpose. In Chapters 1 and 3, we encountered similar difficulties for decision-makers in ascertaining whether the dominant purpose of an organisation is a 'public' or 'private' purpose, or a 'not for profit' or 'for profit' purpose.

except in Canada, an organisation whose dominant purpose falls within an accepted general description of charitable purpose such as 'relief of poverty' and satisfies the public benefit test and other relevant require-ments of charity law may, without jeopardising its charity status or the legal privileges that attend that status, advocate for the reform of law or government policy or even lobby government, so long as these activities remain subsidiary to its dominant purpose.[11] In Canada, at least in the tax law setting, a more rigorous approach is taken to charities that engage in political activities in the pursuit of charitable purposes; there, legisla-tors have enacted specific rules stipulating that charities are entitled to income tax exemptions only where they devote 'substantially all' of their resources to charitable purposes, and the Canada Revenue Agency defines 'substantially all', in the ordinary case, as 90 per cent of a charity's resources each year.[12] It follows that, in Canada, a charity may engage in political activities in a way that is subsidiary to a dominant charitable purpose and nonetheless be denied an income tax exemption on the basis that it expends too many of its resources on those subsidiary activities.

The rule against political purposes, understood to have the wide range of application we have just considered, is endorsed and applied around the com-mon law world. It remains part of the law of Canada,[13] England and Wales,[14]

[11] See, e.g., Charity Commission for England and Wales, *Speaking Out: Guidance on Campaigning and Political Activity by Charities* (CC9, March 2008).

[12] Income Tax Act 1985 (Canada) s 149.1(6.1) and 149.1(6.2), and Canada Revenue Agency, *Policy Statement: Political Activities* (CPS-022, 2 September 2003).

[13] See *Re Knight* [1937] 2 DLR 285 (Rose CJHC); *Re Positive Action Against Pornography and Minister of National Revenue* (1988) 49 DLR (4th) 74 (Canadian Federal Court of Appeal); *Human Life International in Canada Inc* v. *Minister of National Revenue* [1988] 3 FC 202 (Canadian Federal Court of Appeal); *Alliance for Life* v. *Minister of National Revenue* [1999] 3 FC 405 (Canadian Federal Court of Appeal); *Vancouver Society of Immigrant and Visible Minority Women* v. *Minister of National Revenue* [1999] 1 SCR 10 (Supreme Court of Canada); *Action by Christians for the Abolition of Torture* v. *Canada* (2000) 225 DLR (4th) 99 (Canadian Federal Court of Appeal).

[14] *Inland Revenue Commissioners* v. *Temperance Council of the Christian Churches of England and Wales* (1926) 136 LT 27 (Rowlatt J); *In re Jones* (1929) 45 TLR 259 (Eve J); *Bonar Law Memorial Trust* v. *Inland Revenue Commissioners* (1933) 49 TLR 220 (Finlay J); *In re Strakosch* [1949] 1 Ch 529 (Court of Appeal); *National Anti-Vivisection Society* v. *Inland Revenue Commissioners* [1948] AC 31 (House of Lords); *Re Hopkinson* [1949] 1 All ER 346 (Vaisey J); *In re Shaw* [1957] 1 WLR 729 (Harman J); *Buxton* v. *Public Trustee* (1962) 41 TC 235 (Plowman J); *In re Jenkins's Will Trusts* [1966] 1 Ch 249 (Buckley J); *McGovern* v. *Attorney-General* [1982] Ch 321 (Slade J); *Southwood* v. *Attorney-General* [2000] WTLR 1199 (Court of Appeal).

Ireland[15] and New Zealand.[16] In Australia, a broad rule against political purposes was applied by decision-makers (although with some degree of reluctance)[17] until the landmark case of *Aid/Watch Inc* v. *Federal Commissioner of Taxation*, a case we first encountered in Chapter 1.[18] In *Aid/ Watch*, the High Court of Australia declared that Australian charity law ought not to disqualify many of the political purposes that have, over time, been recognised as falling foul of the rule against political purposes, viz, purposes of achieving law reform, achieving changes to government policy or decisions, or agitating for the adoption of a particular point of view on a social issue.[19] However, the Court was careful not to say that Australian law should remove restrictions on political purposes being recognised as charitable altogether, and the Australian Charities Act of 2013 has retained some such restrictions, providing that certain types of political purpose – for example, engaging in party politics – may not be recognised as charitable.[20] To this extent, there continues to be a rule against political purposes in the charity law of Australia, but its scope is radically narrower than the scope of the broad rule that has been developed by courts around the common law world since *Bowman* v. *Secular Society* was decided.

In the United States, there is a long tradition of ignoring or rejecting the rule against political purposes in cases about the validity of trusts for purposes,[21] although there are also cases, particularly from the state of Massachusetts, that endorse the rule.[22] In the tax law of the United States,

---

[15] See the discussion of the Irish position in Oonagh B. Breen, 'Too Political to be Charitable? The Charities Act 2009 and the Future of Human Rights Organisations in Ireland' [2012] *Public Law* 268.

[16] *In re Wilkinson* [1941] NZLR 1065 (Kennedy J); *Knowles* v. *Commissioner of Stamp Duties* [1945] NZLR 522 (Kennedy J); *Molloy* v. *Commissioner of State Revenue* [1981] 1 NZLR 688 (Court of Appeal); *Re Collier* [1988] 1 NZLR 81 (Hammond J); *In re Draco Foundation (NZ) Charitable Trust* CIV 2010–485–1275 (Ronald Young J); *In re Greenpeace of New Zealand Incorporated* [2012] NZCA 533 (Court of Appeal). At the time of writing, this last case had been appealed to the Supreme Court of New Zealand but no decision had been handed down.

[17] *Royal North Shore Hospital of Sydney* v. *Attorney General of New South Wales* (1938) 60 CLR 396 (High Court of Australia); *Re Inman* [1965] VR 238 (Gowans J); *Public Trustee* v. *Attorney-General (New South Wales)* (1997) 42 NSWLR 600 (Santow J).

[18] (2010) 241 CLR 539 (High Court of Australia).   [19] Ibid, [48].

[20] Charities Act 2013 (Australia) s 12(1)(l) and (2).

[21] See *Taylor* v. *Hoag* (1922) 116 A 826 (Supreme Court of Pennsylvania); *Collier* v. *Lindley* (1928) 266 P 526 (Supreme Court of California); *In re Murphey's Estate* (1936) 62 P 2d 374 (Supreme Court of California); *International Reform Federation* v. *District Unemployment Compensation Board* (1942) 131 F 2d 337 (Court of Appeals for the District of Columbia). See also US Restatement (3rd) of Trusts, § 28.

[22] *Jackson* v. *Phillips* (1867) 96 Mass 539 (Massachusetts Supreme Judicial Court); *Parkhurst* v. *Burrill* (1917) 117 NE 39 (Massachusetts Supreme Judicial Court); *Bowditch* v. *Attorney-General* (1922) 28 ALR 713 (Massachusetts Supreme Judicial Court); *In the Matter of*

there is no rule against political purposes as such; as we saw in Chapter 1, in the tax setting the charity law of the United States tends to recognise as charitable all 'not for profit' purposes so long as they do not offend public policy. That said, in the United States, the legislative strategy is to withdraw tax privileges from charities that engage in certain types of political activities – specifically, lobbying and electioneering – unless they pursue those political activities via certain structures and in accordance with certain rules.[23] These restrictions on political activity have been conceived in American jurisprudence not as matters for charity law but rather as posing questions about the scope of the protection of freedom of expression afforded by the First Amendment to the Constitution of the United States. We will return to those constitutional questions below.

B. Traditional defences of the rule

The foregoing should be sufficient to show that the rule against political purposes has been applied numerous times in a range of jurisdictions since *Bowman* v. *Secular Society* was handed down nearly a hundred years ago. However, it also reveals that the rule is not applied everywhere; notably, it is not applied for the most part in the United States even though there is a commitment in that jurisdiction to restricting state subsidies to charities that lobby government or engage in party politics in the setting of an election campaign. Moreover, the foregoing shows that in jurisdictions where the rule against political purposes is applied, the scope of the rule varies; in Canada, for example, the rule tends to be given a relatively broad range of application, whereas in Australia the state has eschewed a wide scope for the rule and instead embraces an approach to political purposes that regards many of them – including purposes of achieving law reform or changes to government policy or decisions – as charitable. This variation in approach to the rule against political purposes suggests that the considerations in favour of and against the rule are complex and difficult to balance. In order to better understand those considerations and, as a consequence, the extent to which the rule against

Killen (1925) 209 NYS 206 (Surrogate's Court, Westchester County); *Vanderbilt* v. *Commissioner of Internal Revenue* (1937) 93 F 2d 360 (Court of Appeals, 1st circuit).

[23] For discussion, see Nina J. Crimm and Lawrence H. Winer, 'Dilemmas in Regulating Electoral Speech of Non-Profit Organisations' in Matthew Harding, Ann O'Connell and Miranda Stewart (eds), *Not-for-Profit Law: Theoretical and Comparative Perspectives* (Cambridge University Press, 2014) 61–86.

political purposes might be justified, we will turn first to traditional defences of the rule offered by decision-makers who have endorsed and applied it. As we will see, those traditional defences turn out to provide little support to the rule, although their lack of justificatory force does not preclude some other, more convincing, justification being offered.

The first of the traditional defences of the rule against political purposes was raised by Lord Parker in *Bowman* v. *Secular Society* itself. Referring to purposes of achieving law reform – the core case of purposes that have been regarded as too political to be charitable according to the rule against political purposes – Lord Parker stated that such purposes must be disqualified from being charitable because 'the Court has no means of judging whether a proposed change in the law will or will not be for the public benefit'.[24] Let us leave to one side the question whether this defence of the rule against political purposes applies in the case of political purposes other than law reform purposes. Instead, let us concentrate on the more fundamental question whether the defence has justificatory force even when applied to the core case of law reform purposes. It has been noted that Lord Parker's statement might be interpreted as meaning either that courts are institutionally incapable of making findings of fact as to the public benefit of law reform, or that for constitutional reasons courts ought not to make findings of fact as to the public benefit of law reform, even though they are institutionally capable of doing so.[25] Let us consider each of these interpretations of Lord Parker's statement in turn.

If understood to mean that courts are institutionally incapable of making findings of fact as to the public benefit of law reform, Lord Parker's statement in *Bowman* v. *Secular Society* seems at odds with those cases in which courts have done precisely that.[26] The best-known

---

[24] [1917] AC 406 (House of Lords), 442 (Lord Parker). See also *Southwood* v. *Attorney-General* [2000] WTLR 1199 (Court of Appeal) and *In re Greenpeace of New Zealand Incorporated* [2012] NZCA 533 (NZ Court of Appeal), [63].

[25] Abraham Drassinower, 'The Doctrine of Political Purposes in the Law of Charities: A Conceptual Analysis' in Jim Phillips, Bruce Chapman and David Stevens (eds), *Between State and Market: Essays on Charity Law and Policy in Canada* (McGill-Queen's University Press, Montreal and Kingston, 2001) 288–315, 293–294.

[26] This point has been made many times before: see L.A. Sheridan, 'Charity versus Politics' (1973) 2 *Anglo-American Law Review* 47, 58; R.B.M. Cotterrell, 'Charity and Politics' (1975) 38 *Modern Law Review* 471, 474; C.E.F. Rickett, 'Charity and Politics' (1982) 10 *New Zealand Universities Law Review* 169, 172; G.F.K. Santow, 'Charity in its Political Voice – A Tinkling Cymbal or a Sounding Brass?' (1999) 18 *Australian Bar Review* 225, 229; Parachin, above n 2, 881–887; Jonathan Garton, 'National Anti-Vivisection Society

such case is the *Anti-Vivisection* case. There, the House of Lords found that the dominant purpose of the National Anti-Vivisection Society was a purpose of achieving law reform and therefore attracted the rule against political purposes.[27] However, as we saw in Chapter 1 when we first considered the *Anti-Vivisection* case, the House of Lords also found that the dominant purpose of the Society would, if carried out, generate considerable detriment to the public by thwarting medical research that depended on live animal experimentation. Arguments to the effect that public benefit in the form of a humane culture would result from the cessation of live animal experimentation were not rejected but the House of Lords thought that any such public benefit was clearly outweighed by detriments associated with the purpose of the Society, and therefore found that the public benefit test of charity law was not satisfied on the facts of the case.[28] In the *Anti-Vivisection* case, the House of Lords showed that courts are institutionally capable of making findings of fact as to the public benefit of law reform.[29] To the extent that Lord Parker's statement in *Bowman* v. *Secular Society* suggests otherwise, it lacks justificatory force as a defence of the rule against political purposes.

If Lord Parker's statement in *Bowman* v. *Secular Society* is taken to mean that for constitutional reasons courts ought not to make findings of fact as to the public benefit of law reform, it seems more promising as a possible justification of the rule against political purposes. After all, it might be thought, in liberal democratic states constitutional principles typically demand that the merits or otherwise of acts of parliament are first and foremost matters for parliament, not the courts, to decide. Yet while these broad demands of liberal democratic constitutional principles can scarcely be doubted, the more precise demands that such principles make of courts are less straightforwardly ascertained. In liberal democratic states, courts are often constitutionally empowered to rule on the validity of acts of parliament in accordance with human rights instruments or constitutional divisions of power in federal systems.

v. Inland Revenue Commissioners' in Charles Mitchell and Paul Mitchell (eds), *Landmark Cases in Equity* (Hart Publishing, Oxford, 2012) 529–555, 543–544.

[27] [1948] AC 31 (House of Lords), 49–51 (Lord Wright), 61–63 (Lord Simonds).

[28] Ibid, 41–49 (Lord Wright), 63–75 (Lord Simonds).

[29] Note that decision-makers other than judges – regulators and tax officials, for example – might be constrained in their fact-finding abilities in ways that judges are not. But there are no reasons to think that these constraints are any more severe when non-judicial decision-makers are considering political purposes than when they are considering non-political purposes.

If constitutional principles authorise courts to invalidate legislation in these ways, it seems difficult to accept that such principles also prohibit courts from making findings of fact about whether or not aiming to reform or maintain legislation will be of public benefit.[30] In any event, regardless of the extent to which courts are constitutionally empowered to invalidate legislation, a court that makes a finding that a purpose of achieving reform to legislation is of public benefit may make that finding while at the same time stating that whether or not to realise the reform in question is a matter for the legislature. Indeed, in the common law world it is a well-established practice for judges, especially in appellate courts, to indicate that the public would benefit from a law reform of one type or another but at the same time state that any such reform is for the parliament to realise.[31] In these circumstances, it is difficult to see how the court in question might have engaged in any constitutional overreaching.

That said, to point out that courts are constitutionally empowered to assess the public benefit of purposes of achieving law reform is to say nothing about whether decision-makers other than judges are empowered in this way. Indeed, it seems unlikely that the charity regulators and tax officials who might, in the absence of a rule against political purposes, be asked to assess the public benefit or otherwise of law reform in the setting of an inquiry into whether or not some political purpose is charitable could be constitutionally empowered to do so except with specific authorisation from the legislature. It is therefore possible that Lord Parker's traditional defence of the rule against political purposes has little justificatory force when applied to judges, but must be taken more seriously when applied to other decision-makers. However, as we will see

---

[30] See Joyce Chia, Matthew Harding and Ann O'Connell, 'Navigating the Politics of Charity: Reflections on *Aid/Watch Inc v. Federal Commissioner of Taxation*' (2011) 35 *Melbourne University Law Review* 353, 363. We might add that it is uncontroversial to assert that courts – at least appellate courts – are constitutionally empowered to assess the merits of judge-made law; thus, Lord Parker's defence of the rule against political purposes has little justificatory force when applied to cases where a purpose of reforming judge-made law is in view.

[31] For just one example, drawn from charity law, see the judgment of Lord MacDermott in *Oppenheim v. Tobacco Securities Trust Co Ltd* [1951] AC 297 (House of Lords), 319: 'for the reasons already given, I would hold the present trust charitable and allow the appeal. I have only to add that I recognize the imperfections and uncertainties of that process. They are as evident as the difficulties of finding something better. But I venture to doubt if it is in the power of the courts to resolve those difficulties as matters stand. It is a long cry to the age of Elizabeth and I think what is needed is a fresh start from a new statute.'

in the next part of this chapter, there is a way of conceiving of the public benefit associated with political purposes, including purposes of law reform, that does not require an assessment of the merits or otherwise of the purposes in question being achieved. If this approach to the question of political purposes and public benefit is adopted by a decision-maker, that decision-maker may make a finding about the public benefit of a political purpose without ever intruding into territory that is properly the province of the legislature. Thus, Lord Parker's defence of the rule against political purposes may have justificatory force, as far as it goes, with respect to non-judicial decision-makers, but those decision-makers may also have available to them conceptual tools to circumvent the defence in cases about political purposes.

A second way in which decision-makers have traditionally sought to defend the rule against political purposes is via a claim that to find that it is of public benefit to reform the law is to 'stultify' the law, or to render the law incoherent.[32] To begin with, we should note that this traditional defence applies only in cases where a purpose aims at law reform. It does not apply to cases where purposes of changing government policy or decisions are in view, nor does it apply to purposes of agitating for a point of view on a social issue, lobbying government or engaging in party politics. The second traditional defence of the rule of political purposes is thus narrow in scope. However, even within these narrow parameters, the defence lacks justificatory force.

Take first the charge of stultification. It is far from clear why recognising that there might be public benefit in law reform should stultify the law; indeed, it seems much more plausible that recognising public benefit associated with law reform might draw attention to ways in which the law's aims are frustrated by its inability to keep up with social and economic change and thus help to alleviate any stultification of the law.[33] Similarly, the charge of incoherence seems difficult to defend.

---

[32] The charge of stultification appears to have been first articulated in Tyssen, above n 4, 177, and was adopted by Lord Wright in the *Anti-Vivisection* case: [1948] AC 31 (House of Lords), 50. The charge of incoherence was expressed by Dixon J in *Royal North Shore Hospital of Sydney* v. *Attorney-General of New South Wales* (1938) 60 CLR 396 (High Court of Australia), 426 ('A coherent system of law can scarcely admit that objects which are inconsistent with its provisions are for the public welfare').

[33] See Sheridan, above n 26, 57; Santow, above n 26, 229; Parachin, above n 2, 880–881; Hamish McQueen, 'The Peculiar Evil of Silencing Expression: The Relationship between Charity and Politics in New Zealand' (2012) 25 *New Zealand Universities Law Review* 124, 139.

We should remember that to state that a particular law reform will be of public benefit is not actually to realise the reform but rather to express a view about its likely consequences; the law that stands in need of reform is unchanged by the finding of public benefit. Thus, in circumstances where a decision-maker expresses such a view, there is no legal incoherence in the sense that the demands of the law requiring reform are in some way contradicted or weakened. Moreover, the charge of incoherence seems to rest on an assumption that there is no way for decision-makers to promote coherence in the law while at the same time expressing views about the desirability of law reform. And yet there are reasons to think that sometimes decision-makers may do precisely this. According to one influential account of adjudication, judges (and other decision-makers) ought to be engaged constantly in a practice of seeking to bring legal rules into alignment with the moral principles that underpin them, all the time keeping faith with precedent and legal tradition.[34] On this view, there are circumstances in which the coherence of the legal system – understood to entail coherence of rules with underpinning principles as well as coherence of rules among themselves – demands law reform. In these circumstances, a judge (or other decision-maker) may promote coherence in the law by finding that law reform is likely to generate public benefit in light of underpinning moral principles that would be served better by the law reform in question. Finally, it cannot be assumed without argument that coherence in the law is a desideratum of first importance in circumstances where law reform will generate public benefit; it may be that, at times, coherence in the law is rightly sacrificed to other political ideals, not least the ideal of justice.[35]

3.   Political purposes and public benefit: a liberal perspective

The traditional defences of the rule against political purposes lack justificatory force. But this does not necessarily mean that some other, more convincing, justification of that rule is absent. In the remainder of this chapter, we will consider whether such a justification might be found, drawing, as we have done throughout the book, on the resources of liberal political philosophy. In this part of the chapter we will consider

---

[34] See generally Ronald Dworkin, *Law's Empire* (Fontana Press, London, 1986).

[35] For general discussion of the value of coherence in the law: Barbara Baum Levenbrook, 'The Role of Coherence in Legal Reasoning' (1984) 3 *Law and Philosophy* 355; Joseph Raz, 'The Relevance of Coherence' (1992) 72 *Boston University Law Review* 273.

whether, from a liberal perspective, it can be argued that political purposes generate public benefit. We will then turn in the final part of the
chapter to the question whether there are reasons, grounded in liberal
political philosophy, for the state to apply a rule against political purposes, regardless of whether such purposes generate public benefit.

A. Constitutional rights and the rule against political purposes

But before thinking about the question of political purposes and public
benefit, we should notice another sort of question that, from a liberal
perspective, seems an important one to ask with respect to the rule
against political purposes. In jurisdictions whose law contains constitutional guarantees of free political expression, does the rule against
political purposes represent an unconstitutional burden on such expression? Decision-makers in the United States have tackled a similar question against the backdrop of the right to freedom of expression – and
specifically the right to freedom of political expression – enshrined in the
First Amendment to the US Constitution. The traditional view has been
that in circumstances where the state withholds subsidies from charities
that engage in certain activities entailing political expression, such as
lobbying or electioneering, there is no infringement of First Amendment
rights; decision-makers have distinguished between withholding subsidies on the one hand and taking coercive steps to silence charities on the
other, ruling that only actions of the latter type are constitutionally
impermissible.[36] This approach has enabled the US government to make
the tax privileges of charity law available only to charities that engage in
political expression in certain ways and via certain structures. However,
the decision of the US Supreme Court in *Citizens United* v. *Federal
Electoral Commission* has cast some doubt on this traditional view.[37]
There, the Court ruled that laws requiring 'for profit' corporations to
engage in political expression only through specially regulated affiliated
entities constituted an impermissible burden on that expression in light
of the First Amendment; the consequences of the decision for federal

---

[36] *Taxation without Representation* v. *Regan* 461 US 540 (1983) (US Supreme Court). See
also the remarks of the Canadian Federal Court of Appeal in *Human Life International in
Canada Inc* v. *Minister of National Revenue* [1998] 3 FC 202, [18] and the New Zealand
Court of Appeal in *In re Greenpeace of New Zealand Incorporated* [2012] NZCA 533,
[59]–[60].

[37] 558 US 310 (2010) (US Supreme Court).

laws that burden the political expression of charities in similar ways remain to be seen.[38]

The question of the extent to which the rule against political purposes might represent an infringement of constitutional rights to freedom of political expression is an important one, at least in jurisdictions whose constitution enshrines a right to freedom of political expression. In order to pursue it more fully, it would be necessary to consider several subsidiary questions. For example, in what circumstances, if any, does a state withdrawal of subsidies from an organisation that pursues political purposes amount to unconstitutional interference with political expression?[39] Where a trust is declared invalid and unenforceable because it is for political purposes, is this normatively similar to the withdrawal of state subsidies for political expression or is it akin to the coercive suppression of such expression? Given that in most jurisdictions the rule against political purposes has its source in judge-made law, to what extent are constitutional rights constraints on judge-made law?[40] However, while these questions about the rule against political purposes are important from a liberal perspective that recognises the justification and significance of constitutional rights to free political expression, for two reasons they will not be our primary focus in what follows. First, they are constitutional questions, not questions for charity law; their resolution does not determine whether or not political purposes ought to be recognised as charitable in law. That question turns ultimately on whether or not political purposes stand to produce public benefit. If political purposes do not produce public benefit, then there is no reason for the state to subsidise them via charity law and no question arises as to whether or not the state is entitled to withhold the subsidies of charity law from them on account of their political character. And second, from the liberal perspective we are exploring in this book – the perspective of the autonomy-based liberalism that we first encountered in Chapter 2 – to ask questions about constitutional rights to freedom of political expression is to divert attention from a number of other questions about free political expression that seem to be of greater importance in light of the political ideal of autonomy. These questions have to do with the

---

[38] For discussion, see Lloyd Hitoshi Mayer, 'Charities and Lobbying: Institutional Rights in the Wake of *Citizens United*' (2011) 10 *Election Law Journal* 407.

[39] For some thoughts relevant to this question: Martin H. Redish and Daryl I. Kessler, 'Government Subsidies and Free Expression' (1996) 80 *Minnesota Law Review* 543.

[40] We will return to this question in Chapter 7.

propensity of free political expression to contribute to the conditions of autonomy and they demand a focus on the consequences of the pursuit of political purposes, not the rights-based constraints under which the state operates when responding to that pursuit through law. From this perspective, the question that forms naturally in the mind of the charity lawyer – do political purposes generate public benefit? – seems the right sort of question to ask.

B. Do political purposes generate public benefit?

If political purposes generate public benefit then there is a prima facie case for recognising them as charitable in law, subject to identifying further reasons why they should not be so recognised even though they generate public benefit; if political purposes do not generate public benefit, then not even a prima facie case for recognising them as charitable can be made out. In the latter circumstances, the rule against political purposes would seem to be justified, all else being equal. In considering the extent to which political purposes generate public benefit, our starting point is to remember from Chapter 1 that in some cases, decision-makers are prepared to make findings of public benefit based on the fact that the pursuit of purposes entailing the provision of private goods to a private class of persons nonetheless stands to produce incidental public goods. Thus, the provision of health care to a private class has been regarded as charitable on the basis that that provision relieves the burden of health care otherwise borne by the state,[41] and private worship has been found to be of public benefit because of incidental public goods that decision-makers perceive to flow from the mixing of the worshippers with the wider public.[42] Political purposes do not always, or even perhaps typically, aim at benefiting a private class of persons. Nonetheless, the key to answering the question whether or not political purposes generate public benefit is to adopt the same strategy with respect to political purposes as decision-makers have occasionally adopted in cases where they have recognised incidental public goods flowing from the pursuit of private purposes. According to this strategy, the answer to the question whether or not political purposes generate

[41] *Re Resch's Will Trusts, Le Cras v. Perpetual Trustee Co Ltd* [1968] 1 AC 514 (Privy Council).
[42] *Neville Estates Ltd v. Madden* [1962] 1 Ch 832 (Cross J), 853; Charity Commission for England and Wales, *Preston Down Trust* (3 January 2014), [51].

public benefit is not to be found in an examination of the likely consequences of particular political purposes being achieved; it is to be found
in the incidental public goods generated by the pursuit of political
purposes, irrespective of the consequences of those purposes being
achieved.

We may now reformulate our question, so that we ask ourselves: does
the pursuit of political purposes generate incidental public goods? Over
the years, many academic commentators have argued that this is the
case,[43] but it was not until the decision of the High Court of Australia in
2010 in the *Aid/Watch* case that the proposition gained judicial acceptance in a charity law setting.[44] Aid/Watch had been formed to monitor
and evaluate Australian government agencies' delivery of foreign aid to
the developing world. It engaged in political activities of the type that
have traditionally caused concern in light of the rule against political
purposes. A majority of the High Court found that the dominant purpose
of Aid/Watch was 'the generation by lawful means of public debate ...
concerning the efficacy of foreign aid directed to the relief of poverty',
and ruled that this purpose was charitable under Australian law.[45]
Whether or not this truly was the dominant purpose of Aid/Watch is
an interesting question, but we will leave it to one side here.[46] Of present
interest is what the majority said about why the purpose of generating
public debate about foreign aid delivery satisfies the public benefit test of
charity law. The majority did not take the view that generating such
debate is of public benefit because of any effect that the debate might
have on law or government action; rather, the majority thought that
generating public debate about foreign aid delivery is apt to produce

---

[43] See, e.g., Elias Clark, 'The Limitation on Political Activities: A Discordant Note in the Law
of Charities' (1960) 46 *Virginia Law Review* 439, 457; Rickett, above n 26, 173–174;
Chesterman, above n 3, 343–349; Santow, above n 26, 231–233; Mayo Moran, 'Rethink-
ing Public Benefit: The Definition of Charity in the Era of the Charter' in Jim Phillips,
Bruce Chapman and David Stevens (eds), *Between State and Market: Essays on Charities
Law and Policy in Canada* (McGill-Queen's University Press, Montreal and Kingston,
2001) 251–287, 266; Parachin, above n 2, 884–885.

[44] (2010) 241 CLR 539 (High Court of Australia), although note Lord Reid's dictum in
Inland Revenue Commissioners v. *Baddeley* [1955] AC 572 (House of Lords), 604: 'I think
that it would generally be agreed that in a democratic country political purposes are
among the most important, and perhaps the most important, of all public purposes.'

[45] (2010) 241 CLR 539 (High Court of Australia), [46]–[47].

[46] In his dissenting judgment, Heydon J found that the dominant purpose of Aid/Watch
was to have government and others yield to its views on foreign aid delivery: ibid, [52]–
[62]. We will return to this interpretation of the case below at 196–197.

public benefit because of its effects on political culture. The majority pointed out that the Australian Constitution contains an implied freedom of political communication to the extent necessary to ensure the maintenance of a system of representative and responsible government.[47] According to the majority, by recognising and protecting this implied freedom, Australian law also recognises that political communication generates public benefit; the public benefit thus recognised is an incidental public benefit, arising not because of the particular ends sought via acts of political communication but rather because of the contribution that such acts make to the 'operation of . . . constitutional processes'.[48]

From a perspective informed by liberal political philosophy, the reasoning of the majority of the High Court of Australia in *Aid/Watch* is attractive. That reasoning suggests that in some ways a culture of free political expression is a public good because of the special contribution that such a culture makes to democratic government. From a liberal perspective that prizes democratic government as a great good, the proposition that a culture of free political expression serves democratic government in important ways seems difficult to doubt.[49] Democratic government depends for its effectiveness on factors such as the government being responsive to the wishes of citizens and not acting corruptly or in the service of vested interests; it also depends on the government not manipulating the desires and wishes of citizens, and on citizens being able to disseminate, access and evaluate information about the government so as to hold the government to account.[50] Democratic government

---

[47] Ibid, [44]. For recognition and discussion of the implied freedom of political communication: *Australian Capital Television Pty Ltd* v. *Commonwealth* (1992) 177 CLR 106 (High Court of Australia); *Nationwide News Pty Ltd* v. *Wills* (1992) 177 CLR 1 (High Court of Australia); *Theophanous* v. *Herald & Weekly Times Ltd* (1994) 182 CLR 104 (High Court of Australia); *Stephens* v. *West Australian Newspapers Ltd* (1994) 182 CLR 211 (High Court of Australia); *Lange* v. *Australian Broadcasting Corporation* (1997) 189 CLR 520 (High Court of Australia); *Levy* v. *Victoria* (1997) 189 CLR 579 (High Court of Australia); *Coleman* v. *Power* (2004) 220 CLR 1 (High Court of Australia); *Mulholland* v. *Australian Electoral Commission* (2004) 220 CLR 181 (High Court of Australia); *Wotton* v. *Queensland* (2012) 246 CLR 21 (High Court of Australia).

[48] (2010) 241 CLR 539 (High Court of Australia), [45].

[49] See generally Alexander Meiklejohn, *Free Speech and its Relation to Self-Government* (Harper and Brothers, New York, 1948); Frederick Schauer, *Free Speech: A Philosophical Inquiry* (Cambridge University Press, 1982) ch 3; Joseph Raz, 'Free Expression and Personal Identification' in his *Ethics in the Public Domain: Essays in the Morality of Law and Politics* (Clarendon Press, Oxford, 1994) 146–169, 151–153; Eric Barendt, *Freedom of Speech* (2nd edn, Oxford University Press, 2007) ch 5.

[50] Raz, 'Free Expression and Personal Identification', above n 49, 151–153.

is further enhanced by a culture in which, absent extraordinary circumstances, no citizens are denied full membership of the political community through being silenced or having their speech interfered with or marked out for disapproval in one way or another.[51] All of these factors depend on the culture of free political expression that was recognised as being of public benefit in *Aid/Watch* and their service to democratic government helps to illuminate the ways in which such a culture is a significant public good.

If the pursuit of political purposes tends to produce a culture of free political expression and therefore tends to sustain and augment conditions under which democratic government can flourish, there are reasons to think that the pursuit of such purposes by 'not for profit' organisations tends to make a distinctive contribution to such a culture. Although it cannot be doubted that some 'not for profit' organisations pursue political purposes in order to serve powerful interests in society,[52] it is also true that many such organisations pursue political purposes in order to advocate on behalf of people whose voices might not otherwise be heard or taken seriously in political circles. Organisations whose dominant purpose is a political one but whose political interest extends to advocating on behalf of the poor, or the disabled, or refugees might be offered as examples. Democratic government flourishes only when government is as responsive to the marginalised voices of groups such as these as it is to the voices of the powerful. Thus, to the extent that 'not for profit' organisations facilitate government responsiveness to the marginalised by bringing their needs and interests to the attention of government and urging government to place due weight on those needs and interests, those organisations contribute to a democracy-promoting culture of free political expression in a way that might not be achieved in their absence.[53]

The contribution that a culture of free political expression makes to democratic government has to do with the ways in which such a culture ensures that government remains responsive and accountable to citizens; it is this government responsiveness and accountability that is the

---

[51] Ibid, 152. See also James W. Nickel, 'Freedom of Expression in a Pluralistic Society' (1988–1989) 7 *Law and Philosophy* 281, 289–290.

[52] For example, consider the use for campaign financing purposes of 'not for profit' organisations formed under § 527 of the US Internal Revenue Code.

[53] This point is made in Eleanor Burt, 'Charities and Political Activities: Time to Re-Think the Rules' (1998) 69 *Political Quarterly* 23.

distinguishing feature of democracy. From the perspective of the autonomy-based liberalism that we are exploring in this book, government responsiveness and accountability to citizens serves the political ideal of autonomy in important ways; given the central importance of government in the life of the political community, it is scarcely possible to conceive of circumstances in which citizens could live self-determining lives except where government achieves some sufficient degree of sensitivity to their wishes. Moreover, once the political ideal of autonomy is brought into view, a culture of free political expression contributes to the conditions of autonomy in ways that go beyond what is necessary to sustain democratic government.[54] Such a culture enables citizens to articulate and publicise their preferences, beliefs and commitments in political matters, testing them for plausibility and subjecting them to the scrutiny of others in public debate. As Jonathan Gilmore has suggested, this sort of critical engagement with one's own preferences, beliefs and commitments is important to the self-determining engagement with options that is central to an autonomous life.[55] Moreover, a culture of free political expression facilitates the constitution and development of different ideas, doctrines and worldviews about political matters, and these in turn play a role in informing the various options that are available to citizens in choosing ways in which to engage with the life of their political community.[56] The options of being a communist, or adhering to liberation theology, or belonging to the Tea Party movement all depend in part on a culture in which citizens are free to propound principles and teachings of a political character and to associate in order to learn, understand and realise those principles and teachings in different ways.

---

[54] Of course, there are reasons to think that personal autonomy demands freedom of political expression quite apart from the contribution that such freedom makes to an autonomy-promoting culture: see the discussion of Mill's thinking in Owen Fiss, 'A Freedom Both Personal and Political' in David Bromwich and George Kateb (eds), *On Liberty: John Stuart Mill* (Yale University Press, New Haven, 2003) 179–196. However, for present purposes we are concentrating on the cultural effects of freedom of political expression because we are interested in the question whether political purposes generate public benefit.

[55] Jonathan Gilmore, 'Expression as Realization: Speakers' Interests in Freedom of Speech' (2011) 30 *Law and Philosophy* 517.

[56] Thus T.M. Scanlon Jr, 'Freedom of Expression and Categories of Expression' (1979) 40 *University of Pittsburgh Law Review* 519, 527 ('The central audience interest in expression, then, is the interest in having a good environment for the formation of one's beliefs and desires').

C.   *When are political purposes inconsistent with democracy and autonomy?*

In short, then, from a liberal perspective that prizes democratic government, the case for claiming that political purposes generate public benefit is both straightforward and strong once it is accepted as a general proposition that a finding of public benefit might depend on the acknowledgement of incidental public goods; from such a perspective, political purposes contribute to an incidental public good in the form of a political culture that serves democratic government. From the perspective of autonomy-based liberalism, the case for the public benefit of political purposes is even stronger; from that perspective, the culture that is generated by the pursuit of political purposes serves autonomy in several ways that go beyond what is necessary to support democratic government. Indeed, the liberal case for recognising the public benefit of political purposes is so strong that the interesting question from a liberal perspective seems to be not whether the pursuit of political purposes can ever generate public benefit – of course it can – but rather whether there are any circumstances in which the pursuit of political purposes is likely *not* to generate public benefit. In other words, are there circumstances in which the pursuit of political purposes is likely not to contribute to cultural public goods that support democracy and promote autonomy?

The pursuit of political purposes is most obviously unlikely to contribute to a democracy- and autonomy-promoting culture where that pursuit entails political expression that undermines democracy or the institutions and values that sustain it, or that is directed against the political ideal of autonomy. A trust for the purpose of overthrowing by force a democratically elected government or advocating the subordination of women in public life might be offered by way of example. Similarly, democracy and autonomy are likely to be undermined by purposes that entail hateful political expression that is likely to cause the citizens against whom it is directed to withdraw from political life and debate out of fear. From a liberal perspective, the question of when the state ought to respond to political expression that undermines liberal values and ideals by refusing to tolerate it is a difficult one: on the one hand, those liberal values and ideals seem to demand the suppression of such expression;[57] on the other, there are reasons to doubt that the state is likely to act in a

---

[57] See Larry Alexander, *Is There a Right of Freedom of Expression?* (Cambridge University Press, 2005) ch 8.

justifiable way, all things considered, where it seeks to silence political expression, and these reasons support a state posture of tolerance towards at least some such expression.[58] That said, the state can tolerate political expression directed against liberal values while at the same time propounding the view that the political expression in question stands to undermine those values,[59] and this points to an argument for decision-makers to refuse to recognise the public benefit of political purposes where those purposes entail political expression that undermines democracy or autonomy, whether or not an argument is made out for the state to suppress the expression in question.

Difficult questions arise with respect to purposes entailing acts of political expression that are intemperate or emotive, or take the form of stunts or gimmicks designed to capture public imagination or attract media interest. To what extent do these purposes contribute to a democracy- and autonomy-promoting culture? There is a line of liberal thought that ascribes value to expressive acts insofar as they tend to facilitate a true understanding of the requirements of reason in a given situation; according to this line of thought, some unreasoned, intemperate or emotive expressive acts may lack value to the extent that they do not invite engagement with reason. For those who adhere to this view, the famous liberal argument for freedom of expression based on the value of the 'marketplace of ideas'[60] as a means of ascertaining truth does not demand freedom to engage in the widest range of expressive acts consistent with public safety, but rather is an argument for freedom to engage in those expressive acts that are to some sufficient degree reasoned and measured in character.[61]

---

[58] See Schauer, above n 49, ch 6, describing (at 86) the 'argument from governmental incompetence' as perhaps the most persuasive argument for a free speech principle, and Raz, 'Free Expression and Personal Identification', above n 49, 160–164.

[59] See Cory Brettschneider, *When the State Speaks, What Should It Say?* (Princeton University Press, Princeton, 2012).

[60] Even though the phrase 'marketplace of ideas' comes from the judgment of Justice Douglas in the First Amendment case of *United States* v. *Rumely* 345 US 41 (1953) (US Supreme Court), 56, the argument from the 'marketplace of ideas' is usually attributed to John Stuart Mill, *On Liberty* (Longmans, Green & Co, London, 1865), 10 ('But the peculiar evil of silencing the expression of an opinion is, that it is robbing the human race; posterity as well as the existing generation; those who dissent from the opinion; still more those who hold it. If the opinion is right, they are deprived of the opportunity of exchanging error for truth; if wrong, they lose, what is almost as great a benefit, the clearer perception and livelier impression of truth, produced by its collision with error').

[61] See generally Schauer, above n 49, ch 2, and Ronald Dworkin, *Sovereign Virtue: The Theory and Practice of Equality* (Harvard University Press, Cambridge, MA, 2000), 380–382.

It may be that a 'marketplace of ideas' as a means of ascertaining truth is a public good and is best served by expressive acts that are reasoned and measured as opposed to unreasoned, intemperate or emotive. However, in some ways the public good of a democracy- and autonomy-promoting culture may depend on the sorts of unreasoned, intemperate and emotive acts of political expression that, on one view at least, undermine the functioning of a 'marketplace of ideas' as a means of ascertaining truth. If the key to democracy is government responsiveness and accountability to citizens, then there is a case for recognising the value of unreasoned, intemperate and emotive contributions to political debate insofar as these ensure that government takes notice of citizens who might otherwise be ignored. In a more general sense, the value of acts of political expression is in part determined by prevailing social conditions, and in circumstances where political influence and voice is possessed disproportionately by powerful elites, it might be appropriate to ascribe value to unreasoned, intemperate and emotive acts of political expression by which marginalised groups can be heard.[62] Moreover, once we turn our attention to the ways in which free political expression serves the political ideal of autonomy, we have further reasons for ascribing value to at least some unreasoned, intemperate or emotive acts of political expression. Such expressive acts may help to facilitate self-determination and to constitute options with which citizens may engage autonomously in participating in political life. Joining a street protest or burning the national flag can be options of the greatest significance to autonomous citizens who wish to be politically involved, and such acts take their place alongside structured debating and writing argued submissions to government departments as valuable acts of political expression.

If a wide range of political expression is valuable because it serves a democracy- and autonomy-promoting culture, then from the perspective of autonomy-based liberalism, decision-makers have reasons to recognise the public benefit of political purposes whether those purposes entail the presentation of reasoned argument, the intemperate expression of points of view on political matters or attention-seeking stunts and gimmicks.[63] In this regard, it is interesting to note that while decision-makers have,

---

[62] See the important discussion in Schauer, above n 49, 202–203. And note more generally Owen M. Fiss, 'Free Speech and Social Structure' (1986) 71 *Iowa Law Review* 1405.

[63] For a view along these lines, see Perri 6 and Anita Randon, *Liberty, Charity and Politics: Non-Profit Law and Freedom of Speech* (Dartmouth, Aldershot, 1995) ch 8.

via the rule against political purposes, refused to recognise the public benefit of unreasoned, intemperate and emotive acts of political expression,[64] they have tended to recognise, via other paths, the public benefit of purposes entailing political expression of a reasoned and measured kind. For example, in some cases purposes that relate to political matters, but entail reasoned and measured acts of political expression, have been brought within the general description 'advancement of education'. An excellent example is *In re Koeppler Will Trusts*, in which a testamentary trust was set up to further the work of a unique institution – Wilton Park – that facilitated high-level discussions among European governments and policy-makers.[65] The trust was construed as one for educational purposes and upheld, even though the discussions to be facilitated were unquestionably political in character.[66] Decision-makers have also made more specific accommodations of reasoned argument and debate; for example, the Charity Commissioners for England and Wales once adhered to the view that charities in that jurisdiction were permitted to engage in political expression in pursuit of their charitable purposes only where that expression took the form of a 'reasoned memorandum'.[67]

Given the history of decision-makers showing a preference for reasoned and measured political expression in charity law, the recognition of the purposes of Aid/Watch as charitable in the *Aid/Watch* case was remarkable. In finding that the dominant purpose of Aid/Watch was the generation of public debate about foreign aid delivery and that this purpose stood to generate public benefit, the majority of the High Court of Australia was not concerned that Aid/Watch sought to generate such debate by intemperate and emotive means, for example arranging to have ironic birthday gifts delivered to the headquarters of the World Bank on the occasion of its 60th birthday along with a request to the Bank to

---

[64] See, e.g., *Human Life International in Canada Inc* v. *Minister of National Revenue* [1998] 3 FR 202 (Canadian Federal Court of Appeal), where the political purpose in question was carried out by sending postcards to members of parliament containing images of aborted foetuses.

[65] [1986] 1 Ch 423 (Court of Appeal).

[66] Ibid, 435–439. Note also *Jackson* v. *Phillips* (1867) 96 Mass 539 (Massachusetts Supreme Judicial Court) and *Parkhurst* v. *Burrill* (1917) 117 NE 39 (Massachusetts Supreme Judicial Court), both cases in which purposes entailing political expression were construed as being for the advancement of education.

[67] See the discussion in Francis Gladstone, *Charity, Law and Social Justice* (Bedford Square Press NCVO, London, 1982), 109–114. Contrast the more accommodating approach of the present Charity Commission for England and Wales, above n 11.

retire.[68] In contrast, Heydon J in his dissenting judgment made much of the fact that Aid/Watch did not seek to persuade government and others of its views by reasoned argument and debate, but instead sought to force government and others to its point of view, adopting means that were characterised by 'rancour' and 'asperity' to do so.[69] In Aid/Watch, then, we find reflected in charity law the tension in liberal political philosophy between the view that political expression is of value only when it is reasoned and measured and the view that political expression can be of value, in light of the demands of democratic government and the political ideal of autonomy, even when it lacks those qualities. And in light of the liberal arguments relating to the value of political expression that we considered above, there are reasons to prefer the approach taken by the majority in Aid/Watch to that of Heydon J.

4. Political purposes and altruism

Given that the traditional defences of the rule against political purposes lack justificatory force, and given that strong liberal arguments can be made for the public benefit of political purposes, it might be thought perplexing that a broad rule against political purposes persists in many jurisdictions. Indeed, as Elias Clark noted many years ago, it seems as though the rule against political purposes is indifferent to the substantial public benefit that is produced by the pursuit of a wide range of political purposes.[70] What could be the reason for such indifference, in the setting of a body of law like charity law that is oriented to promoting the production of public benefit? One possibility is that there is no reason for charity law's indifference to the public benefit generated by political purposes, and that once we apprehend the ways in which political purposes generate public benefit we must accept the conclusion that a broad rule against political purposes is unjustified and should be removed from charity law, in much the way that the High Court of Australia did in Aid/Watch.[71] This line of argument raises some difficult questions that require further consideration. For example, if political purposes generate public benefit to the extent that their pursuit

---

[68] Aid/Watch Incorporated and Commissioner of Taxation [2008] AATA 652 (Justice Downes), [35].

[69] (2010) 241 CLR 539 (High Court of Australia), [59].   [70] Clark, above n 43, 440.

[71] See, e.g., Chia, Harding and O'Connell, above n 30. As will be clear from the text, the author no longer adheres to some of the arguments made in that article.

contributes to a democracy- and autonomy-promoting culture, then presumably it must be accepted that, all else being equal, the purposes of political parties generate public benefit.[72] In these circumstances, should party political purposes be recognised as charitable in law? For the charity lawyer, the intuitive response to this question is no. But it is difficult to justify this intuition once we focus on the public benefit generated by the pursuit of political purposes.

In this last part of the chapter, we will consider another possible explanation for charity law's indifference towards public benefit in the setting of the rule against political purposes. This explanation comes into view once we cease to consider the consequences of the pursuit of political purposes, consequences in the form of the promotion of a certain political culture, and turn instead to the means by which political purposes are carried out. This shift in focus demands that we turn away from what in Chapters 3 and 4 we called the 'demand' side of the pursuit of charitable purposes and towards what in those chapters we called the 'supply' side of the pursuit of those purposes. In those earlier chapters, we focused on the 'supply' side in the course of arguing that, via charity law, the state takes an interest in altruism and seeks to promote altruism by facilitating its successful exhibition in human interactions. Thus, via the 'public' component of the public benefit test and the 'not for profit' requirement, the state creates a public meaning for legal charity that aligns it with selfless and detached motivations for human action; at the same time, charity law distinguishes legal charity from the normative world of the bargain and the duties and attachments associated with virtues such as loyalty and trustworthiness. A whole mode of social interaction – the altruistic pursuit of charitable purposes – is thus created, sustained and promoted. This mode of social interaction is constituted less by the outcomes it produces than by the virtues and norms that are entailed in it.

Can it be that the rule against political purposes, just like the 'public' component of the public benefit test and the 'not for profit' requirement, performs a function of ensuring that the public meaning of legal charity remains aligned with altruism? In exploring this possibility, we must begin by noting that the mode of social interaction that is politics is not invariably, or even often, inconsistent with the selfless and detached character of altruism. In other words, politics can be altruistic. A trust

---

[72] See Rickett, above n 26, 173.

for the purpose of repealing laws permitting slavery,[73] or pressuring governments to release political prisoners,[74] or advocating for nuclear disarmament[75] is perfectly consistent with altruistic motivations; indeed, it seems plausible to suggest that such a trust is more likely to be motivated altruistically than non-altruistically. More generally, we might say that where purposes of seeking law reform or changes to government policy or decisions, or advocating for particular viewpoints on social issues, are oriented to realising public goods associated with the law reform, governmental action or viewpoint in question, the purposes in question are likely to be pursued altruistically.[76] Self-interested or partisan people tend not to work for the production of public goods, as opposed to private goods for themselves or those whom they care specially about. Moreover, it is arguable that to the extent that political purposes entail the use of political means in the service of an aim of producing public goods, political purposes are likely to be interpreted as motivated by altruism. To the extent that politics is consistent with altruism in these ways, for the state to invoke a rule disqualifying political purposes from being charitable is unlikely to assist, and may indeed frustrate, any overarching state aim of aligning the public meaning of legal charity with altruism. These considerations point to an argument for the state not to invoke the rule against political purposes in a variety of cases where it has traditionally been invoked.

A 'supply'-side case for a rule against political purposes seems plausible only to the extent that the pursuit of political purposes is unlikely to be motivated in the selfless and detached way that is characteristic of altruism. In this regard, two types of political purpose stand out. First, there are purposes associated with political parties. In one sense, political parties – in particular via the development of the policies that they formulate and present to voters at elections – unquestionably pursue purposes that aim at the production of public goods, and to this extent they, and their members, are likely to be motivated by altruism.[77] But it

---

[73] *Jackson v. Phillips* (1867) 96 Mass 539 (Massachusetts Supreme Judicial Court).

[74] *McGovern v. Attorney-General* [1982] 1 Ch 321 (Slade J).

[75] *In re Greenpeace of New Zealand Incorporated* [2012] NZCA 533 (NZ Court of Appeal).

[76] See Alison Dunn, 'Charity Law as a Political Option for the Poor' (1999) 50 *Northern Ireland Legal Quarterly* 298, 300 ('There is much common ground between the political and charitable spheres, most particularly in that they are unified by their concern with public benefit, or the common good').

[77] Consider, for example, the US Republican and Democratic Party Platforms for 2012: http://www.gop.com/wp-content/uploads/2012/09/2012GOPPlatform.pdf and http://www.democrats.org/democratic-national-platform

seems implausible to suggest that political parties are animated entirely or even largely by altruism, as opposed to a self-interested desire for political power or a partisan desire to promote the interests of one or another group in society. And even if political parties are animated largely by altruism, political culture and popular beliefs about party politics are such that many citizens do not interpret the actions of political parties as motivated by altruism as opposed to self-interest, loyalty or worse.[78] If the purposes of political parties bear a public meaning that diverges from altruism, then it follows that purposes of supporting or promoting political parties are likely to bear this divergent public meaning as well. To the extent that the purposes of party X are motivated and understood to be motivated non-altruistically, then a trust to promote party X is likely to be motivated and understood to be motivated non-altruistically as well.[79]

A second type of political purpose whose public meaning is likely to diverge from altruism is a purpose of pressuring or lobbying government in order to secure some private advantage for oneself or for a person or group with whom one is associated. A trust formed to advocate for the maintenance of a government subsidy to a particular industry might be offered as an example. There are reasons to think that such a purpose might make a contribution to a political culture that ensures government responsiveness and accountability to citizens; thus, there is an argument that the purpose stands to produce public benefit. On the other hand, there are reasons to think that pressuring or lobbying government in order to secure private advantage tends to corrupt political processes and undermines democratic government as a consequence. But irrespective of such effects on the 'demand' side, on the 'supply' side a purpose of pressuring or lobbying government in the service of a private interest is likely to be motivated by self-interest or in a partisan way, and it is equally likely to be interpreted as motivated non-altruistically. Its public meaning is thus likely to diverge from altruism. Of course, in part the public meaning of this purpose depends on how a decision-maker construes it. If it is construed as a purpose of raising awareness of the

---

[78] See generally Russell J. Dalton, *Democratic Challenges, Democratic Choices: The Erosion of Political Support in Advanced Industrialised Democracies* (Oxford University Press, New York, 2004).

[79] Two possible examples of such trusts are *Bonar Law Memorial Trust* v. *Inland Revenue Commissioners* (1933) 49 TLR 220 (Finlay J); *Re Hopkinson; Lloyds Bank Ltd* v. *Baker* [1949] 1 All ER 346 (Vaisey J).

importance to the national economy of the industry in question and, at the same time, arguing that the maintenance of a government subsidy to the industry is a way of generating public goods, then its public meaning might align with altruism. However, if it is construed as a purpose of promoting the interests of the businesses within the industry without regard to the public effects of that promotion, its public meaning is likely to diverge from altruism. In part, as we saw with respect to political parties, the likely public meaning of a purpose in light of its construction is a function of prevailing culture and beliefs; thus, against a backdrop of widespread cynicism about the motivations of those who own and manage businesses, a purpose of promoting business interests is not likely to be interpreted as altruistic.

In a general and qualified way, then, we may assert that the public meaning of purposes associated with political parties and pressure and lobby groups is not aligned with altruism. Now we may add that for the state to recognise purposes associated with political parties and the purposes of pressure and lobby groups as charitable would be at odds with its strategy, evident in the 'public' component of the public benefit test and the 'not for profit' requirement, of aligning the public meaning of legal charity with altruism.[80] When directed against purposes that are pursued and understood to be pursued non-altruistically, there are reasons to think that the rule against political purposes serves the state's overarching project of promoting altruism by enabling citizens to successfully exhibit altruism in the pursuit of charitable purposes. To the extent that it ensures that one class of purposes that are likely to be motivated non-altruistically is not recognised as charitable, a rule against political purposes plays a role in bolstering the association of altruism and those purposes that are recognised as charitable. This is an argument for maintaining a rule against political purposes even though such purposes stand to produce public benefit. Note, however, that it is not an argument for the broad rule against political purposes that decision-makers have developed and applied in most jurisdictions since *Bowman* v. *Secular Society* was handed down; it is, rather, an argument for a narrow rule disqualifying purposes associated with political parties and purposes entailing lobbying for private interests, along the lines of the rule now applied in Australia in light of the High Court's decision

---

[80] See generally Brian Galle, 'Charities in Politics: A Reappraisal' (2013) 54 *William and Mary Law Review* 1561.

in *Aid/Watch* or informed by the same considerations as inform the US tax law's treatment of charities that engage in political activities.

Even if the rule against political purposes rightly disqualifies non-altruistic purposes associated with political parties and pressure and lobby groups from being charitable in law, it nonetheless tolerates the deployment of non-altruistic political means in the service of charitable ends. This is because, as we saw earlier, the rule against political purposes applies only to the dominant purpose of an organisation and not to subsidiary purposes or activities. In Chapter 3, we saw that the 'not for profit' requirement of charity law likewise applies only to the dominant purpose of an organisation, enabling the pursuit of charitable purposes via means that entail bargaining and therefore are typically interpreted as non-altruistic. We saw that as long as these means are clearly subsidiary to charitable purposes, the alignment of the public meaning of legal charity with altruism is unlikely to be jeopardised, although there has been pressure in recent years to relax the 'not for profit' requirement in ways that might erode such alignment of the public meaning of legal charity with altruism as has been achieved through that requirement. Similar pressures may be detected in respect of non-altruistic political means serving charitable ends; for example, such pressures seem to underlie the Canada Revenue Agency's requirements in respect of the proportion of total resources that a charity is permitted to spend each year on political activities that are subsidiary to its charitable purpose.[81] As in the case of the 'not for profit' rule, a rule against political purposes can withstand some degree of pressure arising from the toleration of non-altruistic political means subsidiary to dominant charitable ends. After a point, however, such pressure may obscure the public meaning of legal charity, with the consequence that the alignment of that public meaning with altruism is undermined. There is, then, a case for decision-makers to carefully monitor the extent to which non-altruistic political means are to be permitted in the service of charitable ends, in addition to monitoring the scope and application of the rule against political purposes itself.

---

[81] Although, as Galle points out, rules that fix on the proportion of resources spent may be ill-suited to an objective of aligning the public meaning of legal charity with altruism. Galle writes, 'If the Gates Foundation decided to spend $500 million to push for a carbon tax, it's doubtful that public perception of them as "partisan" would be dampened by the fact that the Foundation still had another $39.5 billion to throw around': ibid, 1621.

In Chapter 3 it was argued that, in light of a liberal commitment to the plurality in modes of social interaction that helps to constitute the conditions of autonomy, there are reasons for the state to act so as to ensure that the altruistic pursuit of charitable purposes is preserved as a viable mode of social interaction. These reasons gain strength in light of the inexorable shift towards market norms that seems recently to have characterised social life in many countries. It is arguable that just as market norms have grown more prevalent in recent times, so, in some respects, has a politics of self-interest and partisanship come increasingly to replace a politics oriented to the public good. The extent to which such a trend may be detected is a matter of some debate among observers of political life.[82] However, to the extent that the trend may be detected, it presents a threat to diversity in modes of social interaction similar to the threat presented by the encroachment of market norms onto an ever-larger slice of social life. Where the public life of a polity is widely conceived to be more a competition between private interests for resources than a collective deliberation about what is good for all, the successful expression of altruism in perhaps the most important sphere of all – the political sphere – is likely to be frustrated. To the extent that – via a rule against political purposes – charity law can help to promote altruistic engagement with politics, it may play some role in sustaining conditions under which citizens may conceive of the political community, as well as the problems and challenges that it creates and may resolve, in selfless and detached ways. As we have seen throughout this book, the ideal of personal autonomy is largely constituted by the value of self-determination in a world whose meaning is created by the people who inhabit it. To the extent that law, including charity law, enables and encourages people not only to sustain and engage with their political communities but also to imagine those communities in multiple ways, opening up new options for sustaining and engaging with them, law serves autonomy and its conditions in significant ways.

---

[82] See Dalton, above n 78 and Theda Skocpol, *Diminished Democracy: From Membership to Management in American Civic Life* (University of Oklahoma Press, Norman, 2003), presenting evidence that in some respects the politics of the common good has been replaced by the politics of self-interest; but contrast Leif Lewin, *Self-Interest and Public Interest in Western Politics* (Oxford University Press, 1991), arguing that there is insufficient evidence to support such findings in respect of voting behaviour, politicians' priorities and the behaviour of bureaucrats.

5.   Conclusion

The rule against political purposes, understood as having the broad scope that it is typically given in modern charity law, seems indefensible. Traditional defences of the rule fail to stand up to close scrutiny. There are strong liberal arguments for recognising the public benefit of political purposes via the recognition of an incidental public good in the form of a culture of free political expression that serves democratic government and also promotes autonomy in other ways. Thus, the liberalising step that the High Court of Australia took in *Aid/Watch*, in declaring that a broad rule against political purposes has no place in Australian law, has much to commend it when contrasted with the rigorous application of a broad rule against political purposes in cases such as *McGovern* v. *Attorney-General*. However, if there is one lesson to take away from this chapter, it is that an evaluation of the rule against political purposes is incomplete except in light of all the arguments for and against that rule on both the 'demand' and the 'supply' sides of the pursuit of charitable purposes. To focus entirely on the 'demand' side, asking questions about the public benefit of political purposes and neglecting the differences between the modes of social interaction that we call 'charity' and 'politics' respectively, is bound to lead to puzzlement about the fact that charity law retains a rule against political purposes at all. However, once the 'supply' side is brought into view, and the state's project of promoting altruism via charity law with it, we can begin to see why a rule against political purposes might be desirable even against the backdrop of the powerful liberal case grounded in the public benefit of a culture of free political expression. In setting the scope of the rule against political purposes, then, the liberal state must seek to strike the right balance between the democracy- and autonomy-promoting consequences of the pursuit of political purposes on the one hand, and altruism on the other. The balance struck by a broad rule against political purposes is not the right one, but the competing considerations are best served by a rule against some political purposes, albeit one that is narrow in scope.

7

Charity and discrimination

1. Introduction

In this concluding chapter, we will turn to some of the difficult questions posed by cases of discrimination in the pursuit of charitable purposes.[1] What is the proper legal response when a community association expels a volunteer because she is a Muslim? Should the state enforce a trust for the purpose of educating 'Caucasian' children? Can a priest lawfully refuse to administer the sacraments to homosexual people? In liberal political philosophy, questions such as these are often thought to raise fearsome problems, implicating as they do both state and non-state action, public and private spheres, the demands of equality and liberty. In this chapter, we will look at the topic of charity and discrimination from the perspective of the autonomy-based liberalism first introduced in Chapter 2. We will begin with some taxonomy, distinguishing between varieties of discrimination that might be encountered in the pursuit of charitable purposes. We will then turn to current legal approaches to charity and discrimination; these approaches may be found in constitutional and statutory anti-discrimination law of general application, and in the public benefit test and the public policy rule that may be found in the traditional core of charity law. We will see that only one of these current approaches is desirable in light of autonomy-based liberalism. Finally, we will abstract from charity and discrimination to consider discrimination as a matter of political morality in light of the demands of autonomy, before returning to charity and discrimination and suggesting the outlines of a principled approach to the varieties of

---

[1] As we will see, in some cases where purposes entail discrimination they may fail to satisfy the public benefit test or the public policy rule of charity law, or both, and thus are charitable only putatively. However, for ease of expression, in this chapter references to 'discrimination in the pursuit of charitable purposes' should be taken to include discrimination in the pursuit of purposes that would be charitable except for the fact that they entail discrimination.

discrimination in the pursuit of charitable purposes, informed by autonomy-based liberalism. Throughout, our focus will be on discriminatory acts that pick out elements of group identity, whether explicitly or implicitly, as a basis for unfavourable treatment; less direct forms of discrimination and so-called 'affirmative action' discrimination will not be our focus, although many of the arguments of this chapter should apply, mutatis mutandis, to those types of discrimination as well.

2. Varieties of discrimination in the pursuit of charitable purposes

Different varieties of discrimination might be encountered in the pursuit of charitable purposes. Some of these varieties of discrimination are of interest in light of the public benefit test and the public policy rule of charity law; some are of interest in light of anti-discrimination law of general application that affects those who pursue charitable purposes either because it imposes upon such persons anti-discrimination norms or because it exempts such persons from anti-discrimination norms that would otherwise apply to them. (In passing, note that we may regard rules of anti-discrimination law invoking the category of 'charity' in the legal sense as a basis for exemptions from anti-discrimination norms as part of charity law, even if, generally speaking, anti-discrimination law is not part of charity law.) All are of interest to a study of charity law and the liberal state. But they are of interest to such a study in different ways, and so we should begin our discussion of charity and discrimination by noting distinctions between the varieties of discrimination in the pursuit of charitable purposes.

A. Discriminatory purposes and discriminatory activities

The first distinction to be drawn is between discriminatory purposes on the one hand, and discriminatory activities in the pursuit of non-discriminatory purposes on the other. As an example of the former, consider a trust for the purpose of providing medical care to 'white babies';[2] as an example of the latter, consider a faith-based school that refuses to hire homosexual teaching staff. As we saw in Chapter 1, discriminatory purposes are a matter for the public benefit test and the

---

[2] The example is taken from *Kay v. South Eastern Sydney Area Health Service* [2003] NSWSC 292 (Young CJ in Eq).

public policy rule of charity law; now we may add that such purposes are also a matter for anti-discrimination law in various jurisdictions.[3] Discriminatory activities in the pursuit of non-discriminatory purposes, on the other hand, are typically thought to be a matter for anti-discrimination law rather than charity law (except insofar as rules of anti-discrimination law invoke the legal category of 'charity' and thus fall within charity law). So, where charities adopt discriminatory employment practices, this is typically dealt with by anti-discrimination law; such law often exempts charities from relevant anti-discrimination norms.[4] Similarly, discrimination by charities against volunteers or potential trustees is usually not conceived as a charity law problem;[5] in perhaps the most celebrated case of volunteer discrimination in recent times – *Boy Scouts of America* v. *Dale* – the US Supreme Court framed the case as one in which provisions of the anti-discrimination law of New Jersey were trumped by a charity's constitutional right to expressive association, making it lawful for the charity to discriminate against a volunteer on the basis of his sexual orientation.[6] And in cases where the pursuit of non-discriminatory purposes entails the provision of services to the public, and this service provision is organised in a discriminatory way, it is – in the ordinary case, at least – anti-discrimination law that will be engaged, not the public benefit test or the public policy rule of charity law.[7]

---

[3] See, e.g., Equality Act 2010 (UK) ss 193 and 194. Note also *Catholic Care (Diocese of Leeds)* v. *Charity Commission for England and Wales* [2012] UKUT 395 (Upper Tribunal), in which, on the basis of anti-discrimination law, a charity was not permitted to amend its constituent documents so as to articulate a purpose entailing discrimination against homosexual couples. The question whether or not that discriminatory purpose would satisfy the public benefit test or the public policy rule of charity law was hardly considered.

[4] Relatively wide exemptions may be found in Australian anti-discrimination legislation, e.g., Racial Discrimination Act 1975 (Australia) s 8; Sex Discrimination Act 1984 (Australia) s 36; Disability Discrimination Act 1992 (Australia) s 49; Age Discrimination Act 2004 (Australia) s 34. The Equality Act 2010 (UK) contains narrower exemptions: see s 193(2), (4) and (9).

[5] For a discussion of the phenomena of 'volunteer discrimination' and 'trustee discrimination', see Debra Morris, 'Charities and the Modern Equality Framework: Heading for a Collision?' (2012) 65 *Current Legal Problems* 295.

[6] 530 US 640 (2000) (US Supreme Court). For a detailed study of the case, see Andrew Koppelman and Tobias Barrington Wolff, *A Right to Discriminate? How the Case of* Boy Scouts of America *v* James Dale *Warped the Law of Free Association* (Yale University Press, New Haven, 2009).

[7] In the *Catholic Care* case, the charity had historically pursued the non-discriminatory purpose of facilitating the adoption of hard-to-place children, but it had also engaged in discriminatory activities in the pursuit of that non-discriminatory purpose, viz, refusing to

The qualification – 'in the ordinary case' – is necessary because some-times decision-makers seem to assume that if an organisation engages in discriminatory activities in the pursuit of a non-discriminatory purpose, that organisation fails in some relevant sense to satisfy the criteria of charity law and is not a charity as a result. In Chapter 1 we encountered the case of *Bob Jones University* v. *US*, in which the US Supreme Court ruled that a university that adopted racially discriminatory admissions and student conduct policies failed to satisfy the public benefit test, or the public policy rule, or (most likely) both.[8] In *Bob Jones University*, the university lost its charitable status notwithstanding that, as Rehnquist CJ pointed out in his dissenting judgment in the case, its purpose appeared to be a non-discriminatory purpose within the description 'advancement of education'.[9] The ruling in *Bob Jones University* might be interpreted as resting on an inference that the true purpose of the university was in fact discriminatory, an inference drawn from the university's dis-criminatory activities; however, there is little textual support for such an interpretation, and it seems more likely that it was the university's discriminatory activities themselves that caused it to lose its charitable status. If this interpretation is correct, it puts the reasoning of the Supreme Court at odds with the well-established principle of charity law – a principle that we noted in Chapter 1 – that organisations stand or fall as charities depending on the character of their purposes, not their activities. Thus, the discriminatory activities in *Bob Jones University* may not have been appropriately addressed by an application of the public benefit test and the public policy rule of charity law; the more fitting way to address those activities might have been to consider whether or not some anti-discrimination norm of general application was engaged by the facts of the case, as was done in *Boy Scouts of America* v. *Dale*.[10]

---

place children with homosexual couples. These discriminatory activities attracted provisions of anti-discrimination law, but one such provision exempted the charity's activities from the purview of the relevant anti-discrimination norm. The exempting provision was time-limited, and when it expired the charity sought to amend its objects to articulate a discrimin-atory purpose, so as to attract a different exempting provision. The decision of the Upper Tribunal confirmed that the purpose of providing adoption services to all but homosexual couples could not be pursued consistently with the anti-discrimination law of England and Wales, and held that the Charity Commission was right to refuse to accede to an amendment of the charity's objects. See generally [2012] UKUT 395 (Upper Tribunal).

[8] 461 US 574 (1983) (US Supreme Court).   [9] Ibid, 623.

[10] This is not to say that such a norm was available; nor is it to say that in *Boy Scouts of America* v. *Dale* the Court was right to rule that the engaged anti-discrimination norm

B. *Discriminatory purposes and discriminatory motivations*

A second distinction may be drawn between purposes that are discrim-inatory regardless of the motivations that animate them, and purposes that are motivated by a desire to discriminate but are not themselves discriminatory. A trust for the purpose of providing university scholarships to 'white Protestant men' may be motivated by bigotry, or (perhaps less likely) by a benign sense of commitment to white Protestant men as a class, or indeed (less likely still) by caprice, but it is unnecessary to inquire into the motivations underpinning the trust to understand the sense in which its purpose is discriminatory. The discriminatory character of the purpose is a matter of the public meaning of that purpose, not the private meaning that the purpose has for the trust's settlor, a matter to which we will return in more detail below. Now consider a trust for the purpose of 'promoting the music of Richard Wagner', and imagine that its settlor is motivated to pursue this purpose by a bigoted admiration for Wagner's anti-Semitism, coupled with a belief that promoting Wagner's music is a way of promoting anti-Semitism. In asking whether or not the purpose of this trust is discriminatory, it is irrelevant that the settlor has a discriminatory motivation. Once again, the public and private mean-ings of this purpose diverge, and only the public meaning is relevant in ascertaining whether or not the purpose is discriminatory. As we saw in Chapter 3, motivations are, generally speaking, irrelevant when determining the character of a purpose in accordance with the criteria and disqualifying rules of charity law. Thus, charity law draws a distinction between discriminatory purposes and discriminatory motiv-ations, and concerns itself only with discriminatory purposes. It has been said that decision-makers should show greater sensitivity to discriminatory motivations when applying the public benefit test and the public policy rule of charity law;[11] however, as we will see later in this chapter, an argument can be made that charity law's adherence to the distinction between discriminatory purposes and discriminatory motivations is justifiable from the perspective of autonomy-based liberalism.

was trumped by the constitutional right to expressive association. It is simply to suggest that the criteria and disqualifying rules of charity law may not be appropriate tools for dealing with discriminatory activities in the pursuit of non-discriminatory purposes.

[11] Ontario Law Reform Commission, *Report on the Law of Charities* (1996), 217–218.

C.   *The purpose of discrimination and purposes entailing discrimination*

Finally, we may draw a distinction between the purpose of discriminating against a class of persons and a purpose that is not plausibly construed in that way but nonetheless necessarily entails discrimination against a class of persons. As an example of the purpose of discrimination, imagine a trust whose purpose is 'to promote the suppression of women'. Although there are no cases dealing directly with a purpose like this, the very gist of which is the discrimination that it contemplates, there can be no doubt that such a purpose fails the 'benefit' component of the public benefit test of charity law and falls foul of the public policy rule. There is simply nothing to be said for the benefit of a purpose whose content is exhausted by its discriminatory character. In this regard, it is interesting to note that there is authority in charity law for the proposition that promoting the elimination of discrimination is a purpose that satisfies the 'benefit' component of the public benefit test.[12] If this is the case, then it seems to follow that charity law must regard the purpose of discrimination as lacking in benefit to a degree sufficient to attract the operation of the public policy rule.

In contrast, a purpose that is not plausibly construed as a purpose of discriminating against a class of persons, but nonetheless necessarily entails such discrimination, raises more complex questions for charity law. In some cases, such a purpose will entail discrimination because it is a purpose of benefiting only a certain class. Take, for example, a trust for the purpose of educating 'children of European descent'. The most plausible interpretation of this purpose is that it is a purpose of educating the class of 'children of European descent', not a purpose of discriminating against those who fall outside that class; on this interpretation the purpose stands to generate whatever benefit flows from purposes within the general description 'advancement of education'. Nonetheless, there is no way of pursuing the purpose of educating 'children of European descent' except by discriminating against children outside that class and to this extent the purpose necessarily entails discrimination, notwithstanding that it stands to generate benefit. In other cases, a purpose will entail discrimination, even if it is not an instance of the purpose of

---

[12] *Jackson* v. *Phillips* (1867) 96 Mass 539 (Massachusetts Supreme Judicial Court); *Lewis* v. *Doerle* (1898) 25 OAR 206 (Ontario Court of Appeal); and see the discussion of the English law in Morris, above n 5, 299–300.

discrimination, because a certain class is excluded from its benefits. Consider a trust for the purpose of educating 'children, except for Muslim children'. Here again, the purpose is most naturally understood as a purpose within the general description 'advancement of education' – a purpose that stands to generate benefit – but at the same time it is a purpose that necessarily discriminates against the class of Muslim children.

In some cases where a purpose is either a purpose of benefiting a certain class or excludes a certain class from its benefits, the entailed discrimination may be so blatant as to suggest that the purpose is actually best construed as an instance of the purpose of discrimination.[13] But in most such cases, a conclusion that the purpose is one of discrimination will be unavailable, and decision-makers in the charity law setting will have to deal with purposes that, although they necessarily entail discrimination, are most plausibly construed as purposes that aim to produce benefits of some type. In such cases, decision-makers will most likely have to attempt some weighing of detriments associated with the discrimination against the benefits that the purpose in question aims to produce, in order to determine whether the 'benefit' component of the public benefit test is satisfied and/or whether the public policy rule should be invoked. The weighing of detriments against benefits in deciding whether or not a purpose satisfies the 'benefit' component of the public benefit test is mandated by charity law,[14] but if this sort of weighing exercise is to be undertaken in respect of purposes entailing discrimination then decision-makers must have some sense of the nature of detriments associated with discrimination, as well as some sense of how to weigh such detriments against any benefits that purposes entailing discrimination aim to generate. In the last part of this chapter we will consider how best to understand the detriments associated with discrimination, and how those detriments might be weighed against any benefits that purposes entailing discrimination aim to produce, in light of liberal aspirations for public discourse grounded in the value of autonomy.

[13] The purposes in *Re Canada Trust Co* v. *Ontario Human Rights Commission* (1990) 69 DLR (4th) 321 (Ontario Court of Appeal) and *Kay* v. *South Eastern Sydney Area Health Service* [2003] NSWSC 292 (Young CJ in Eq) seem to have come close to having this character.

[14] *National Anti-Vivisection Society* v. *Inland Revenue Commissioners* [1948] AC 31 (House of Lords). See also Charities Act 2013 (Australia) s 6(2) and Charities and Trustee Investment (Scotland) Act 2005 (Scotland) s 8(2).

3. Current approaches to charity and discrimination

A review of cases arising against a backdrop of constitutional or statutory anti-discrimination law of general application and in the charity law setting, along with a review of scholarly literature, reveals several current approaches to charity and discrimination. From the perspective of autonomy-based liberalism, only one of these current approaches is desirable and should be utilised in developing a principled approach to charity and discrimination that is justifiable in light of the value of autonomy. We will consider each of the approaches in turn, before identifying the desirable one and considering why it alone is desirable in light of autonomy-based liberalism.

A. Public norms and public institutions

In some cases, it has been thought that the question whether or not an anti-discrimination norm applies to a charity depends on whether or not that charity is a public institution either because it is properly viewed as an institution of the state or because, in some relevant way, it is analogous to a state institution. The idea animating this line of thought is the uncontroversial idea that anti-discrimination norms, whether found in a constitutional setting or in anti-discrimination statutes, apply to state and analogous action and in this sense are public norms. Thus, in *Pennsylvania* v. *Board of Directors of City Trusts of the City of Philadelphia*, the US Supreme Court determined that the trustee of a testamentary trust for the purpose of establishing an educational college for 'white male orphans' was not permitted to deny black children entry to the college in accordance with the terms of the trust; the basis of the Court's determination was that the trustee was the City of Philadelphia and therefore an agency of the state, subject to the public anti-discrimination norm enshrined in the Equal Protection Clause of the Fourteenth Amendment to the US Constitution.[15] Perhaps more controversial is the associated idea that constitutional and statutory

---

[15] 353 US 989 (1957) (US Supreme Court). Following the Supreme Court's decision, the trustee was replaced by private individuals; in a subsequent appeal, it was held that for the state to endorse this replacement, thus enabling the new trustees to pursue the discriminatory purpose, would itself violate the Equal Protection Clause: *Pennsylvania* v. *Brown* 392 F2d 120 (1968) (Court of Appeals, 3rd Circuit). See also *Evans* v. *Newton* 382 US 296 (1966) (US Supreme Court) and the discussion of *Shelley* v. *Kramer* 334 US 1 (1948) (US Supreme Court) below at 218–219.

anti-discrimination norms do not, in the ordinary case, apply to the actions of institutions that are neither state institutions nor analogous to state institutions and are therefore in some relevant sense private. In *Boy Scouts of America* v. *Dale*, the anti-discrimination norm that was invoked against the charity was one that applied only to 'public accommodations' in New Jersey; in ruling that the charity's constitutional right to expressive association trumped the anti-discrimination norm, the Supreme Court effectively determined that the charity was a private association and thus beyond the reach of that anti-discrimination norm.[16] In the United Kingdom, organisations pursuing charitable purposes might, depending on their circumstances, be subject to the anti-discrimination norm of the European Convention on Human Rights where they are 'public authorities' under section 6 of the Human Rights Act.[17] That said, ascertaining when and why a charity might be a public authority for the purposes of the Human Rights Act is no easy matter, and the extent to which charities might be subjected to Convention norms on the basis that they are public authorities within the meaning of section 6 remains to be seen.[18] In any event, in the United Kingdom, as elsewhere, inquiries into whether or not charities should be subjected to anti-discrimination norms because they are in some relevant sense public institutions are unusual; this is because, as we saw earlier, anti-discrimination law in many jurisdictions exempts charities from its requirements, whether charities are public institutions or not.

B. Public norms and public purposes

According to another line of argument, in appropriate cases, those who pursue charitable purposes ought to be subjected to anti-discrimination norms because: (a) anti-discrimination norms are in some relevant sense public norms; (b) charitable purposes are in some relevant sense public purposes; and (c) the pursuit of public purposes ought to be subject to the

---

[16] 530 US 640 (2000) (US Supreme Court).

[17] The anti-discrimination norm is contained in Article 14 of the Convention, which must be read in conjunction with other provisions of the Convention: see Lord Lester of Herne Hill QC, Lord Pannick QC and Javan Herberg, *Human Rights Law and Practice* (Lexis, London, 2009), [4.14.2]–[4.14.4].

[18] For discussion, see Leslie Turano, 'Charitable Trusts and the Public Service: The Public Accountability of Private Care Providers' (2007) 18 *King's Law Journal* 427; Ian Alderson, '*R (Weaver) v London and Quadrant Housing Trust*' (2013) 16 *Charity Law and Practice Review* 129.

demands of public norms.[19] This line of argument does not depend on the proposition that charities are public institutions because they are agencies of the state or analogous to such agencies; it relies instead on the notion that when private citizens, either individually or collectively, pursue purposes that stand to generate public benefit, those citizens become subject to public norms. Importantly, it also implies that when private citizens pursue purposes of a private character, for example by settling trusts for individuals or identified classes of persons, public norms do not apply to them – a point to which we will return shortly. Neither does the argument from public norms and public purposes depend on the proposition that anti-discrimination norms are public norms to the extent that they apply to state and analogous action; rather, it views anti-discrimination norms as public in a different way. Again, we will return to this point below.

One clear statement of the argument from public norms and public purposes is to be found in the judgment of Tarnopolsky JA of the Ontario Court of Appeal in *Re Canada Trust Co* v. *Ontario Human Rights Commission*, a case that we touched on briefly in Chapter 1.[20] The Leonard Foundation had been created by trust deed in 1923 to fund a range of scholarships in schools and universities; it was, and remains, a well-known scholarship provider in Canada.[21] The trust deed excluded from the benefits of the trust 'all who are not Christian of the White Race, all who are not of British Nationality or of British Parentage, and all who owe allegiance to any Foreign Government, Prince, Pope or Potentate or who recognize any such authority, temporal or spiritual'.[22] The trust deed also stipulated that only one quarter of available funds each year

---

[19] This line of argument may be found in L.S.A. Lamek, 'Case Comment: *In re Lysaght*' (1966) 4 *Osgoode Hall Law Journal* 113; Lorraine E. Weinrib and Ernest J. Weinrib, 'Constitutional Values and Private Law in Canada' in Daniel Friedman and Daphne Barak-Erez (eds), *Human Rights and Private Law* (Hart Publishing, Oxford, 2001) 43–72; Peter Benson, 'Equality of Opportunity and Private Law' in Daniel Friedman and Daphne Barak-Erez (eds), *Human Rights and Private Law* (Hart Publishing, Oxford, 2001) 201–243; James W. Colliton, 'Race and Sex Discrimination in Charitable Trusts' (2002–2003) 12 *Cornell Journal of Law and Public Policy* 275; Nicholas A. Mirkay, 'Is It "Charitable" to Discriminate? The Necessary Transformation of Section 501(c)(3) Into the Gold Standard for Charities' (2007) 45 *Wisconsin Law Review* 45.

[20] (1990) 69 DLR (4th) 321 (Ontario Court of Appeal).

[21] See further Bruce Ziff, *Unforeseen Legacies: Reuben Wells Leonard and the Leonard Foundation Trust* (University of Toronto Press, Toronto, 2000).

[22] *Re Canada Trust Co* v. *Ontario Human Rights Commission* (1990) 69 DLR (4th) 321 (Ontario Court of Appeal), 327. That class of persons was also excluded from management of the trust.

should be paid out in scholarships to female candidates.[23] The trustee of the Leonard Foundation sought directions as to the validity of the trust and the Ontario Court of Appeal ordered a *cy-pres* scheme varying the terms of the trust so that it no longer discriminated on grounds of race, sex, nationality or religion.[24] A majority of the Court based its decision on the proposition that an anti-discrimination norm informs the considerations of public policy that partly determine the content of Canadian private law;[25] we will return to the majority's reasoning shortly. In a concurring judgment, Tarnopolsky JA took a different approach.[26]

> Historically, charitable trusts have received special protection. ... This preferential treatment is justified on the ground that charitable trusts are dedicated to the benefit of the community. It is this public nature of charitable trusts which attracts the requirement that they conform to the public policy against discrimination. Only where the trust is a public one devoted to charity will restrictions that are contrary to the public policy of equality render it void.

Tarnopolsky JA also made clear that 'the public policy against discrimination' does not apply to trusts for named individuals or classes of persons because such trusts lack a sufficiently public character.[27]

As Tarnopolsky JA's judgment suggests, the argument from public norms and public purposes is typically accompanied by one or both of two assumptions. The first assumption is that, because the state extends privileges to charity – most notably the tax privileges that we first encountered in Chapter 1 – it is only fair that those who pursue charitable purposes be required to adhere to public norms; this assumption appeals to a principle of reciprocity as the basis for the imposition of public norms on public purposes.[28] The second assumption is that those who choose to pursue charitable purposes choose to pursue public purposes and must therefore be taken to choose to be regulated by public norms.[29] The concomitant of this second assumption, articulated most clearly in the work of Lorraine Weinrib and Ernest Weinrib, is that those who choose to pursue private purposes do not choose to be

---

[23] Ibid, 328.

[24] Interestingly, other provisions of the trust that discriminated on grounds of parental occupation were left undisturbed: ibid.

[25] Ibid, 333–335.   [26] Ibid, 353.   [27] Ibid.

[28] See, e.g., Lamek, above n 19, 116–117; Mirkay, above n 19, esp 85–86.

[29] See, e.g., Weinrib and Weinrib, above n 19, esp 67–68 ('Because public benefit constitutes the entire range of application for testamentary freedom in charitable trusts, that freedom has no application inconsistent with [public norms]' (at 68)); Benson, above n 19.

regulated by public norms and therefore should not be bound by such norms.[30] Later in this chapter we will see that from the perspective of autonomy-based liberalism, we have no reason to accept the assumptions underpinning the argument from public norms and public purposes and, consequently, no reason to accept the argument from public norms and public purposes itself.

C. Public norms and private purposes

A third current approach to the question of charity and discrimination begins by assuming that charitable purposes are private purposes even though they stand to produce public benefit. In this way, the third approach is inconsistent with, and an alternative to, the second approach which assumes that charitable purposes are public purposes. (Note, however, that the first approach and the third approach can coexist without fear of inconsistency. It is possible to argue that public institutions can pursue private purposes; indeed, *Pennsylvania* v. *Board of Directors of City Trusts*, a case we considered earlier, seems to provide an example of this phenomenon.[31]) On the basis of the assumption that charitable purposes are private purposes, the third approach asks whether or not anti-discrimination norms that are in some sense public should regulate the pursuit of charitable purposes *qua* private purposes.[32] The third approach to charity and discrimination thus leads to a consideration of the broader topic of the extent to which public anti-discrimination norms should play some role in regulating the pursuit of private purposes of all types and not only the pursuit of charitable purposes.[33]

On one view, public anti-discrimination norms should play no role in regulating the pursuit of private purposes. In *Re Lysaght*, a charity law case, the Royal College of Surgeons refused a testamentary gift to be held on trust for the purpose of providing scholarships to a class that excluded Roman Catholics and Jews; the College was prepared to accept the gift only if the discriminatory condition of the

---

[30] Weinrib and Weinrib, above n 19, 68.   [31] 353 US 989 (1957) (US Supreme Court).

[32] For a particularly insightful statement of this approach: Adam Parachin, 'Public Benefit, Discrimination and the Definition of Charity' in Darryn Jensen and Kit Barker (eds), *Private Law: Key Encounters with Public Law* (Cambridge University Press, 2013) 171–206.

[33] See generally Matthew Harding, 'Some Arguments against Discriminatory Gifts and Trusts' (2011) 31 *Oxford Journal of Legal Studies* 303.

trust was excised.[34] Buckley J stated that 'it is going much too far to say that the endowment of a charity, the beneficiaries of which are to be drawn from a particular faith or are to exclude adherents to a particular faith, is contrary to public policy',[35] even though he went on to approve a *cy-pres* scheme removing the discriminatory condition so as to ensure that the donor's intention, which was that the College would be the trustee, was carried out.[36] In *Blathwayt* v. *Baron Cawley*, which was not a charity law case, the House of Lords was asked to consider the validity of a testamentary settlement that discriminated on grounds of religion.[37] Lord Wilberforce arguably acknowledged the existence of a public anti-discrimination norm in the English law of the time, but he denied that it had any application to the private disposition before him: '[d]iscrimination is not the same thing as choice: it operates over a larger and less personal area, and neither by express provision nor by implication has private selection yet become a matter of public policy.'[38] And as we saw earlier, in his judgment in *Canada Trust*, Tarnopolsky JA took the view that public norms do not apply to the pursuit of private purposes, and that a public anti-discrimination norm applied to the pursuit of the purposes of the Leonard Foundation only because, being charitable purposes, they were public in character.

Contrasting with these views are arguments to the effect that public anti-discrimination norms can and should play some role in regulating the pursuit of private, including charitable, purposes. We may break down arguments of this sort into two types: first, arguments that where the source of a public anti-discrimination norm is the constitution, the norm's constitutional source causes it to have some particular regulatory effect in relation to the pursuit of private purposes; and second, arguments that an anti-discrimination norm can inform the considerations of public policy to which decision-makers often appeal in developing private law. These two types of argument are not always clearly distinguishable from each other; for example, with respect to a jurisdiction whose constitution contains an anti-discrimination norm, it might be argued

---

[34] [1966] Ch 191 (Buckley J).   [35] Ibid, 206.

[36] Ibid, 209. Other instances of decision-makers exhibiting sympathy for trustees who are unwilling to carry out discriminatory trusts include *Re Dominion Students' Hall Trust* [1947] Ch 183 (Evershed J); *Re Mere's Will Trusts*, The Times, 4 May 1957, 10 (Wynn-Parry J).

[37] [1976] AC 397 (House of Lords).   [38] Ibid, 426.

that decision-makers should use the public policy doctrine so as to give effect to that norm in cases, say, about trusts for discriminatory purposes.[39] Nonetheless, for analytical purposes it will be helpful to consider the two types of argument separately, not least because not all jurisdictions have constitutions that contain relevant anti-discrimination norms.[40]

The general notion that constitutional anti-discrimination norms should regulate the pursuit of private purposes is capable of informing several more specific approaches. One such approach begins with the thought that, as we saw in Chapter 3, via the law of trusts the state makes available to citizens power-conferring rules that enable the pursuit of private, including charitable, purposes. On this approach, where settlors utilise those power-conferring rules to pursue discriminatory purposes, they implicate the state in that discrimination; moreover, where state institutions enforce rights and duties arising out of discriminatory arrangements that are facilitated by power-conferring rules, in a sense those state institutions themselves engage in discrimination. Thus, it is argued, in jurisdictions where there is a constitutional anti-discrimination norm that applies to state action, the state may be constitutionally barred from recognising and enforcing trusts for discriminatory purposes or, for that matter, the discriminatory pursuit of other private purposes, say through contracts or the institutions of property law. Such an argument swayed the US Supreme Court in the celebrated case of *Shelley* v. *Kraemer*.[41] Land was subject to a restrictive covenant forbidding its sale to non-Caucasians; the covenant was upheld by a Missouri court and the matter was then appealed to the Supreme Court, which found that the anti-discrimination norm of the Equal Protection Clause had established a constitutional bar against racially discriminatory state action and that the Missouri court's action in upholding the covenant had violated that bar.[42] The 'state action' doctrine from *Shelley* v. *Kraemer* has potential application, in the US at least, in any case where a court is called on to recognise or enforce a

---

[39] See Harding, above n 33, 304–316 for some arguments as to how the public policy doctrine might be used in this way.

[40] For instance, Australia's federal constitution does not.

[41] 334 US 1 (1948) (US Supreme Court).

[42] Ibid, 13–19. But see also *Evans* v. *Abney* 396 US 435 (1970) (US Supreme Court), in which a court order enforcing a racially discriminatory will was not regarded as 'state action' for the purposes of the Equal Protection Clause.

trust for a discriminatory purpose, and this has implications for charity law in that jurisdiction.[43]

A different sort of argument does not go so far as to assert that state action to facilitate and enforce discriminatory private purposes is constitutionally barred, but instead develops the thought that decision-makers are under an institutional duty or, at the least, have reasons to develop private law so as to bring it into alignment with constitutional anti-discrimination norms.[44] In Canada, the Supreme Court has stated that the rights enjoyed by citizens under the Canadian Charter of Rights and Freedoms are not actionable in private law, but that the values enshrined in the Charter – including, most relevantly for present purposes, the anti-discrimination norm enshrined in section 15 – properly guide the development of that body of law.[45] In England and Wales, notwithstanding considerable debate and disagreement about the extent to which the norms of the European Convention on Human Rights affect private law, it is fair to say that there is substantial judicial authority for the proposition that Convention norms – including the anti-discrimination norm in Article 14 – do and should guide and shape the development of private law, even if those norms do not function as the source of rights of action enjoyed by citizens against each other.[46] Similar developments may be detected in other jurisdictions whose constitutions contain

---

[43] See Colliton, above n 19.

[44] An argument of this type accompanies the argument from public norms and public purposes in Weinrib and Weinrib, above n 19, esp 48–51 ('The constitution, as society's authoritative repository of legally supreme and publicly accessible values concerning human dignity, is a pre-eminent source from which public reason can draw as it gives concrete meaning to the categories that comprise private law' (at 49)). See also Mayo Moran, 'Authority, Influence and Persuasion: *Baker*, Charter Values and the Puzzle of Method' in David Dyzenhaus (ed), *The Unity of Public Law* (Hart Publishing, Oxford, 2004) 389–429; Mayo Moran, 'Influential Authority and the Estoppel-Like Effect of International Law' in Hilary Charlesworth et al. (eds), *The Fluid State: International Law and National Legal Systems* (Federation Press, Annandale, 2005) 156–186; Mayo Moran, 'Inimical to Constitutional Values: Complex Migrations of Constitutional Rights' in Sujit Choudry (ed), *The Migration of Constitutional Ideas* (Cambridge University Press, Leiden, 2007) 233–255.

[45] *Retail, Wholesale and Department Store Union, Local 580, Al Peterson and Donna Alexander* v. *Dolphin Delivery Ltd* [1986] 2 SCR 573 (Supreme Court of Canada); *Hill* v. *Church of Scientology* [1995] 2 SCR 1130 (Supreme Court of Canada).

[46] See *Campbell* v. *MGN Ltd* [2004] 2 AC 457 (House of Lords); *Douglas* v. *Hello! Ltd* [2006] QB 125 (Court of Appeal); *HRH Prince of Wales* v. *Associated Newspapers Ltd* [2008] Ch 57 (Court of Appeal).

anti-discrimination norms.[47] In these jurisdictions, part of the answer
to the question of charity and discrimination is likely given by constitutional law.

The second type of argument to the effect that public anti-discrimination norms can and should play some role in regulating the
pursuit of private purposes is that an anti-discrimination norm can
inform considerations of public policy in private law. This argument
may be found in the judgment of the majority of the Ontario Court of
Appeal in *Canada Trust.*[48] Earlier we saw that, in his concurring judgment in that case, Tarnopolsky JA appealed to the argument from public
norms and public purposes. The majority, led by Robins JA (Osler JA
agreeing), also appealed to public norms, and also appeared to view the
purposes of the Leonard Foundation as public purposes.[49] However, the
majority ultimately determined the case on the basis that public norms
appropriately regulate the pursuit of both public and private purposes,
via the notion of public policy as it is understood in the private law
setting:[50]

> The freedom of an owner of property to dispose of his or her property as
> he or she chooses is an important social interest that has long been
> recognized in our society and is firmly rooted in our law ... That interest
> must, however, be limited in the case of this trust by public policy
> considerations. In my opinion, the trust is couched in terms so at odds
> with today's social values as to make its continued operation in its present
> form inimical to the public interest.

Apart from a passing reference to constitutionally guaranteed rights of
equality, Robins JA did not refer to the values of the Canadian Charter of
Rights and Freedoms in his application of public norms to private
purposes in this passage.[51] In this way, his judgment belongs to a long
tradition of appealing to public policy, understood in general terms and
not as the outworking of constitutional principles, in developing the
common law with reference to what decision-makers have taken to be
prevailing public norms; such appeals may be detected in numerous cases

---

[47] See, e.g., *Du Plessis* v. *De Klerk* 1996 (3) SA 850 (Constitutional Court of South Africa)
(decided under the Interim Constitution of 1994); Andrew Geddis, 'The Horizontal
Effects of the New Zealand Bill of Rights Act, as Applied in *Hosking v Runting*' [2004]
New Zealand Law Review 681.

[48] *Re Canada Trust Co* v. *Ontario Human Rights Commission* (1990) 69 DLR (4th) 321
(Ontario Court of Appeal).

[49] Ibid, 333.   [50] Ibid, 334.   [51] Ibid.

dealing with the validity of trusts seeking to interfere with the institutions of marriage and the family,[52] and – less frequently – in cases in which private law institutions are deployed for discriminatory ends.[53]

D. Evaluating current approaches

In evaluating current approaches to the question of charity and discrimination, two points are worth bearing in mind. The first is that the argument from public norms and public institutions and the argument from public norms and public purposes assume that public norms should regulate only the public sphere. So does any argument to the effect that charitable purposes are private purposes and for that reason beyond the reach of public norms. For the argument from public norms and public institutions, the public sphere is defined with reference to the character of the institutions that occupy it; for the argument from public norms and public purposes, as well as the argument that public norms are not applicable to charitable purposes *qua* private purposes, the public sphere is defined with reference to the character of the purposes that are pursued in it. But although these arguments define the public sphere in different ways, they all depend on some notion of the public sphere and draw a distinction between that sphere, in which public norms operate, and the private sphere, which is beyond the reach of public norms. The second point to note is that an argument to the effect that public norms apply to the pursuit of private purposes, whether on constitutional grounds or via some public policy doctrine that is indigenous to private law, effectively collapses the distinction between the public and private spheres on which the other arguments depend. Such an argument does this by insisting that in a sense there is no private sphere beyond the reach of public norms.[54]

---

[52] See, e.g., *Long* v. *Dennis* (1767) 4 Burr 2052; *Westmeath* v. *Westmeath* (1831) 1 Dow & Cl 519; *Lloyd* v. *Lloyd* (1852) 2 Sim (NS) 255 (Kindersley VC); *In re Moore* (1888) 39 Ch D 116 (Court of Appeal); *In re Sandbrook* [1912] 2 Ch 471 (Parker J); *In re Boulter* [1922] 1 Ch 75 (Sargant J); *In re Borwick* [1933] 1 Ch 657 (Bennett J); *In re Tegg* [1936] 2 All ER 878 (Farwell J); *In re Caborne* [1943] 1 Ch 224 (Simmonds J); *Re Piper* [1946] 2 All ER 503 (Romer J); *Newcastle Diocese (Church Property Trustee)* v. *Ebbeck* (1960) 104 CLR 394 (High Court of Australia); *Re Johnson's Will Trusts* [1967] 1 All ER 553 (Buckley J).

[53] See, e.g., *In re Borwick* [1933] 1 Ch 657 (Bennett J); *In re Tegg* [1936] 2 All ER 878 (Farwell J); *In re Drummond Wren* [1945] 4 DLR 674 (Mackay J); *Trustees of Church Property of the Diocese of Newcastle* v. *Ebbeck* (1960) 104 CLR 394 (High Court of Australia).

[54] See further Dawn Oliver, 'The Human Rights Act and Public/Private Divides' [2000] *European Human Rights Law Review* 343; Mayo Moran, 'The Mutually Constitutive

The idea that public norms should regulate only the public sphere is one that is sometimes associated with John Rawls's theory of justice, a theory that we first encountered in Chapter 2. As we saw in that chapter, in describing the scope of his principles of social justice, Rawls draws a distinction between the 'basic structure' of society and the dimensions of human endeavour and co-operation that do not fall within the basic structure. For Rawls, citizens' pursuit of their purposes individually or in associations other than the political community is not, except where it takes place in the basic structure, a matter for social justice and, depending on the character of the purposes in question, may not even be a matter for justice at all.[55] Rawls's distinction between the basic structure of society, to which principles of social justice apply, and arrangements and institutions outside the basic structure, to which such principles do not apply, can be understood as, in essence, a distinction between the public and private spheres.[56]

Given that Rawls's conception of social justice entails anti-discrimination norms,[57] his thinking on the non-applicability of principles of social justice to arrangements and institutions insofar as they are in the private sphere seems to be echoed in approaches to charity and discrimination that seek to identify charities either as public institutions and therefore susceptible to public anti-discrimination norms, or as private institutions and therefore beyond the range of application of such norms. Thus, we may detect Rawlsian commitments in cases like *Pennsylvania v. Board of Directors of City Trusts* and *Boy Scouts of America v. Dale*, perhaps unsurprisingly given that Rawls's political philosophy is

---

Nature of Public and Private Law' in Andrew Robertson and Tang Hang Wu (eds), *The Goals of Private Law* (Hart Publishing, Oxford, 2009) 17–45.

[55] For a sense of Rawls's thinking on these points: John Rawls, *A Theory of Justice* (rev. paperback edn, Oxford University Press, 1999), 7; John Rawls, *Political Liberalism* (expanded edn, Columbia University Press, New York, 2005), 261, 268–269; John Rawls, *The Law of Peoples with "The Idea of Public Reason" Revisited* (Harvard University Press, Cambridge, MA, 1994), 156–164; Rawls, *Justice as Fairness, A Restatement* (Belknap Press, Cambridge, MA, 2001), [4.2], [50.2]–[50.4]. See also the critique in Susan Moller Okin, *Justice, Gender, and the Family* (Basic Books, New York, 1989) ch 5.

[56] We must take care here because Rawls conceives of the basic structure and the public sphere functionally. Thus, an institution may be in the public sphere in certain respects and in the private sphere in others: 'the spheres of the political and the public, and of the not-public and the private, take their shape from the content and application of the conception of justice and its principles. If the so-called private sphere is a space alleged to be exempt from [social] justice, then there is no such thing'. Rawls, *Justice as Fairness*, above n 55, [50.4].

[57] Rawls, *A Theory of Justice*, above n 55, 266.

aligned in many ways with American constitutional traditions. We should acknowledge that it is open to debate whether or not, from a Rawlsian perspective, the US Supreme Court reached the right conclusions in those cases.[58] That said, what is important to note for present purposes is not the outcome in cases such as *Pennsylvania* v. *Board of Directors of City Trusts* and *Boy Scouts of America* v. *Dale* but rather that, from a Rawlsian perspective that seeks to confine the operation of social justice – including anti-discrimination norms – to only the public sphere, the Court in each of those cases was asking itself the right questions about the range of application of the public anti-discrimination norm in view.

A similar liberal perspective informs the assumptions underpinning the approach from public norms and public purposes, and the associated argument that public norms should not regulate the pursuit of private purposes. We saw earlier that those who make the argument from public norms and public purposes tend to make one or both of two assumptions. The first of these assumptions is that, because of the tax and other privileges that the state extends to charity, it is only fair that those who pursue charitable purposes be required to adhere to public norms. The second is that those who choose to pursue charitable purposes choose to pursue public purposes and must therefore be taken to choose to be regulated by public norms. The first assumption points to a reason for the state to insist on adherence to public norms in the pursuit of purposes that attract a certain type of public support; however, it stops short of identifying any reason for the state to refrain from applying public norms to the pursuit of purposes that do not attract that type of support, including purposes that attract state support of some other type (e.g., purposes that are facilitated by power-conferring rules even though they do not attract tax privileges). Similarly, the second assumption nominates a moral reason for subjecting the pursuit of public purposes to public norms, but it does not, in the absence of further argument, nominate any moral reason for refraining from subjecting the pursuit of private purposes to public norms. In order for the argument from public norms and public purposes – and the associated argument that charitable purposes *qua* private purposes should not be subject to public norms – to work, this rational deficit must be addressed.

---

[58] 'It is not always clear which institutions or features thereof should be included [in the basic structure]': ibid, 8.

One effort to address the rational deficit associated with the argument from public norms and public purposes is that of Ernest Weinrib in his well-known book on the theory of private law.[59] For Weinrib, the law regulating the pursuit of private purposes is a distinctive moral practice whose form is determined exhaustively by norms of corrective justice.[60] Such norms, according to Weinrib, derive their content from the demands of Kantian right, understood as the outworkings of the moral freedom and equality of all citizens.[61] Thus, private law may regulate the pursuit of private purposes only by enforcing claims of right, understood in the Kantian sense, via norms of corrective justice. From a perspective informed by Weinrib's work, anti-discrimination norms are norms of distributive justice whose content cannot be understood in terms of the demands of Kantian right in relation to citizens' pursuit of their private purposes;[62] it is in this sense that, from a perspective inspired by Weinrib's work, anti-discrimination norms are public norms that ought to play no role in the regulation of private purposes. The vision of political morality that Weinrib puts forward in his theory of private law is one in which citizens may pursue their individual conceptions of the good in their dealings with each other, within boundaries established by the demands of Kantian right but unfettered in any other way by laws grounded in social considerations. It is in essence the same liberal vision that animates the Rawlsian notion that there is a division of labour between the social justice that regulates the basic structure of society and the ethical considerations that constrain and guide interpersonal and associational activity outside the basic structure. Indeed, given that – in *A Theory of Justice*, at least – Rawls bolsters the case for his theory of justice by appealing to Kantian moral theory,[63] we might say that while

---

[59] Ernest Weinrib, *The Idea of Private Law* (2nd edn, Oxford University Press, 2012).

[60] Weinrib's understanding of the formal character of corrective justice is inspired by Aristotle, *The Nicomachean Ethics* (ed Roger Crisp, Cambridge University Press, 2000) bk V. See also Alan Beever, *Forgotten Justice: The Forms of Justice in the History of Legal and Political Theory* (Oxford University Press, 2013).

[61] On Kantian right as the basis for legal rights and duties, see also Arthur Ripstein, *Force and Freedom: Kant's Legal and Political Philosophy* (Harvard University Press, Cambridge, MA, 2009).

[62] On the character of anti-discrimination norms as norms of distributive justice: see John Gardner, 'Liberals and Unlawful Discrimination' (1989) 9 *Oxford Journal of Legal Studies* 1; John Gardner, 'Discrimination as Injustice' (1996) 16 *Oxford Journal of Legal Studies* 353.

[63] Rawls, *A Theory of Justice*, above n 55, 221–227. Contrast Rawls, *Political Liberalism*, above n 55, 89–129.

Rawls specifies the demands of Kantian right for public law (including an anti-discrimination norm that applies in the public sphere), Weinrib specifies those demands for private law (governing a private sphere in which anti-discrimination norms play no role). In this sense we might regard the two theories as complementary contributions to the liberal tradition of political philosophy, each depending in critical ways on a public/private distinction.

We are now in a position to see that those who find Rawlsian liberalism or Kantian corrective justice accounts of private law appealing are likely to be drawn to approaches to charity and discrimination that seek to distinguish between public and private spheres. In contrast, from the perspective of the autonomy-based liberalism that we are exploring in this book, such approaches are difficult to accept. Once we endorse the proposition that autonomy is the key personal and political value, the notion that autonomy might ground principles of action in one sphere of human activity but not in another is perplexing. Rather, as we saw in Chapter 2, autonomy grounds reasons for action for everyone, in respect of individual conduct, interpersonal dealings, associational life and the collective action mediated by state institutions that characterises political community. A division of labour between the basic structure of society, in which citizens are constrained by social justice, and activity outside the basic structure, in which citizens are constrained only by their individual conceptions of the good, is not part of this vision of political morality. Neither is the notion that the moral practice of private law is formally and substantively different from the moral practice of public law. Thus, from the perspective of autonomy-based liberalism, the most desirable of the current approaches to charity and discrimination is the approach that argues for the application of public anti-discrimination norms to the pursuit of purposes not only in the public sphere but also in the private sphere, and thereby effectively collapses the public/private distinction that is associated with Rawls's theory of justice and Weinrib's theory of private law. This approach is capable of facilitating inquiry into the right sorts of questions about the problem of charity and discrimination: questions about the demands of autonomy and the implications of those demands for the actions of state and citizens alike.

4. Charity, discrimination and autonomy

With these thoughts in mind, we may now set aside questions about public and private spheres in favour of an approach to charity and discrimination that is sensitive to the demands of autonomy in all aspects of social life. The task of the remainder of this chapter is to explore such an approach. First, we will abstract from current approaches to charity and discrimination to consider discrimination as a matter of political morality in light of autonomy-based liberal principles. We will consider the implications of the harm principle for anti-discrimination law, before thinking about how the liberal state might deal with discrimination in non-coercive ways in the setting of a broad project of promoting the conditions of autonomy. Finally we will return briefly to the charity law setting to sketch the outlines of a new approach to the varieties of discrimination that might be encountered in the pursuit of charitable purposes, an approach informed by autonomy-based liberalism.

A. Discrimination and the harm principle

In Chapter 2, we were introduced to the harm principle as a constraint on state action. We saw that, from the perspective of autonomy-based liberalism, the harm principle specifies that the state may deploy coercive power against an unwilling citizen only where this is necessary either in order to prevent that citizen from diminishing the autonomy of others or, in certain cases, in order to compel that citizen to take actions that are necessary to improve the conditions of autonomy for others; in this way, the harm principle operates on the basis that one can harm another by making her worse off through impairing her autonomy, or by failing to make her better off by furthering her autonomy when one has a duty to do so. The harm principle, thus understood, may have significant implications for anti-discrimination law, for if there are harms to autonomy associated with discrimination then, all else being equal, the coercive measures entailed in anti-discrimination law are justified as a matter of political morality.[64] Moreover, those measures are justified whether aimed at action in the public or in the private sphere. But in order to better understand the implications of the harm principle for anti-discrimination law, we must consider more carefully the question whether there are harms to autonomy associated with discrimination and, if so, what they look like. This requires that we consider the likely effects of discrimination both on individuals who are directly affected by discriminatory acts and also on members of groups who are indirectly

---

[64] See Gardner, 'Liberals and Unlawful Discrimination', above n 62, 18–19 for a discussion of the implications of the harm principle for anti-discrimination law.

affected by such acts because some element of their shared identity is picked out as the basis for discrimination by the acts in question.[65]

Perhaps the clearest way in which discrimination harms the autonomy of individuals who are directly affected by discriminatory acts is by interfering with their options in fashioning their lives. Such interference might be thoroughgoing, diminishing a person's options by radically curtailing her possible life paths; this might be the effect of widespread systematic and sustained discrimination such as the discrimination that once characterised legal and political institutions in South Africa and parts of the United States. In contemporary societies organised according to liberal principles, however, this sort of state-organised discrimination tends to be unusual. More commonplace is discrimination in interpersonal dealings and associational life, and this sort of ad hoc discrimination tends to occasion interference with options in a relatively narrow and unsystematic way. It is worth remembering that, as we saw in Chapter 2, autonomy depends on the existence only of what Joseph Raz calls an 'adequate range' of options to choose from in life;[66] it is not a demand of autonomy that the widest possible range of options be available. It follows that in some circumstances, ad hoc discrimination may interfere with options only in a morally insignificant way; if a person is refused service at one restaurant on the grounds of race but has a hundred other restaurants to choose from, the contraction of that person's dining options is trivial.[67] In other cases, though, ad hoc discrimination may interfere with options of such overall importance to a person's life that the interference may be said to harm the autonomy of the person in question. Again, an example should serve to illustrate.[68] A homosexual couple wish to adopt a child; in doing so, they must approach an adoption agency to take them on as clients and place a suitable child with them. There is an appropriate agency in the district where the

---

[65] Some philosophical discussions of discrimination insist that a focus on effects is misplaced: see, e.g., Deborah Hellman, *When Is Discrimination Wrong?* (Harvard University Press, Cambridge, MA, 2008). Any consideration of discrimination and the harm principle must at some point depart from these non-consequentialist discussions, and we will do so here to the extent necessary.

[66] Joseph Raz, *The Morality of Freedom* (Clarendon Press, Oxford, 1986), 372–373.

[67] This is not to say that this act of racism generates only trivial harms; as we will see below, there are reasons to think that the restaurant owner's act harms the autonomy of the person refused service, and the autonomy of the racial group to which that person belongs, in ways that ought to be of great moral concern.

[68] The example is inspired by the *Catholic Care* case, but the facts of that case differed in significant ways from the example.

couple live, but this agency discriminates against homosexual couples by refusing to take them on as clients. There are other adoption agencies in other districts, but they serve only local residents. The couple will be compelled to move to a new district so as to be in a position to adopt a child. In having to move to a new district in order to become parents, this couple stands to lose a range of options connected with living in the district that they have moved from; if the couple have developed close ties in their local community, or work locally, or have a strong sense of local identity, this loss may amount to the loss of options to pursue relationships and goals of central importance to the couple's life. As a consequence, the options left to them may no longer be adequate if they are to live autonomously.

Moreover, even if the autonomy of the couple is not harmed by the fact that they lose options as a consequence of the adoption agency's discrimination against them, their autonomy may be harmed in a more subtle way by that discrimination. Given the adoption agency's discrimination against them, the couple must move to a new district and engage the services of another adoption agency if they are to become parents. In deciding where to move and which new agency to approach, the couple will not be able to think about their options just as a couple who wish to become parents; rather, they will be forced to make their choices as a consciously *homosexual* couple who wish to become parents. They cannot do otherwise because they know that at least one adoption agency discriminates against homosexual couples, and they will want to know whether or not any other agencies discriminate in this way before deciding where to move. That the couple will be constrained to deliberate about their options with their sexual orientation in mind ought to be of concern in view of the demands of autonomy. Among the conditions of autonomy is freedom to abstract from elements of one's identity in making choices in life, especially where those elements of identity are not obviously of relevance to the choices in question – and the fact that one is homosexual is not obviously of relevance to one's decision about where to live or how best to adopt a child. Where people are compelled to have regard to elements of their identity when making choices, their autonomy is diminished in a way that ought to be of concern in light of the harm principle, even if their options are not reduced.[69]

---

[69] For thoughts along these lines, see the discussion of 'deliberative freedom' in Sophie Moreau, 'What is Discrimination?' (2010) 38 *Philosophy and Public Affairs* 143.

Of course, whether or not the state should coercively prevent harms to the autonomy of individuals who are directly affected by discrimination depends on more than just the identification of such harms. To illustrate this point, imagine that our adoption agency discriminates against homosexual couples because of religious convictions.[70] If anti-discrimination law coercively forces this agency to deal with a homosexual couple despite those religious convictions, then anti-discrimination law seems to interfere with the autonomous pursuit of valuable options, consistent with religious convictions, on the part of those responsible for the agency.[71] How can harms to the autonomy of the couple be prevented in these circumstances without, at the same time, occasioning harms to the autonomy of those responsible for the agency?[72] At least two points may be raised in response to this question. First, recall once again that it is not a demand of autonomy that the widest possible range of options be available. With this general point in mind, it seems plausible to suggest that facilitating the autonomous pursuit of religion does not necessarily demand making available the option of running an adoption agency on religious principles; religious people who feel unable to run a non-discriminatory adoption agency consistent with their religious convictions are free to choose to pursue other options in order to express their faith in action. If this is the case, then the non-availability of the option of running an adoption agency that discriminates against homosexual couples should not be viewed as a harm to the autonomy of religious people at all. (In contrast, given the centrality of worship to religion, preventing religious people from running a church or a temple on religious principles may amount to a harmful interference with their options.) Second, harms to the autonomy of individuals discriminated against are not necessarily the only harms that are associated with discrimination. It may be that, once all the harms associated with discrimination are brought into view, any harm to the autonomy of those who would discriminate that is occasioned by the coercive application of anti-discrimination law is outweighed by the harms prevented by that body of law.

---

[70] This was in fact the case in *Catholic Care*: [2012] UKUT 395 (Upper Tribunal), [1]–[2].

[71] Recall from Chapter 5 that religious lives can be autonomous lives in significant ways.

[72] If our adoption agency discriminates against homosexual couples because of bigotry, the agency's discriminatory practices are not worthy of any legal protection or concern. As we saw in Chapter 2, the autonomous pursuit of valueless options itself lacks value; thus, interference with such pursuit can hardly be said to harm autonomy.

This brings us to the likely effects of discrimination on members of groups who are indirectly affected by discriminatory acts. That discrimination is of concern because of its effects on members of groups is widely acknowledged in the philosophical literature on discrimination.[73] From the perspective of autonomy-based liberalism, we may see the ways in which those effects amount to harms to members of groups by thinking about the effects in terms of autonomy. The starting point is to see that a discriminatory act picks out, explicitly or implicitly, some element of the shared identity of a group as the basis for discrimination. When the shared identity of a group is picked out as the basis for discrimination in this way, members of the group other than those who are directly affected by the discriminatory act in question are implicated.[74] In order to see how this is so, we must focus attention on the expressive dimension of discrimination – another aspect of discrimination that has been much traversed in the philosophical literature on the subject.[75]

Picking out elements of shared group identity as the basis for discrimination can express a variety of public meanings. These public meanings depend on the complex of social understandings and practices that engage in some way with elements of group identity and thus help to constitute what it means, in a particular society, to be 'black', or 'a woman', or 'Jewish', and so forth.[76] Some of these social understandings and practices are respectful of the elements of group identity with which they engage; others are disrespectful of such elements, as the depressing history of human intolerance of difference attests. In some cases, the public meaning of discrimination is in accord with social understandings and practices that are respectful of group identity; in these cases, discrimination is not likely to have harmful consequences for members of

---

[73] See, e.g., Owen M. Fiss, 'Groups and the Equal Protection Clause' (1976) 5 *Philosophy and Public Affairs* 107; Cass R. Sunstein, 'The Anticaste Principle' (1994) 92 *Michigan Law Review* 2410; Tarunabh Khaitan, 'Prelude to a Theory of Discrimination Law' in Deborah Hellman and Sophie Moreau (eds), *Philosophical Foundations of Discrimination Law* (Oxford University Press, 2014) 138–162.

[74] On the ways in which individual and group identities are intertwined: Fiss, above n 73, 148–151.

[75] See, e.g., Deborah Hellman, 'The Expressive Dimension of Equal Protection' (2000) 85 *Minnesota Law Review* 1; Hellman, above n 65, ch 1; Tarunabh Khaitan, 'Dignity as an Expressive Norm: Neither Vacuous Nor a Panacea' (2012) 32 *Oxford Journal of Legal Studies* 1.

[76] See Robert Post, 'Prejudicial Appearances: The Logic of American Antidiscrimination Law' (2000) 88 *California Law Review* 1, esp 16–17.

the group whose shared element of identity is the basis for the discrimination. Thus, the public meaning of a law that prohibits children from voting because they are children is not likely to entail harms to children as a group because the law is consistent with respectful social understandings of childhood, understandings that are based on a rational belief that children lack certain capacities required in order to discharge civic duties. In other cases, however, the public meaning of discrimination is aligned with social understandings and practices that are disrespectful of elements of group identity. Consider a law that prohibits women from voting. Unless the law is enacted in exceptional circumstances, its public meaning is likely to be informed not by contemporary respectful understandings of gender equality, but rather by the sorts of disrespectful understandings of women's role in society, all too familiar from history, that place women alongside children as lacking in capacity and fit objects of paternal concern. A law carrying this public meaning stands to harm women as a group.

Now consider another example, drawn from a charity law case.[77] Imagine that a settlor establishes a trust in South Africa for the purpose of funding scholarships for university students to study abroad, and stipulates that the class of students eligible for scholarships is limited to 'white' students. The public meaning of this discrimination cannot be understood except by considering what it signals against the backdrop of South Africa's history of apartheid. In a country where racism and race-based exclusion and disadvantage were key elements of a centrally organised way of life for many years, the framing of a charitable trust so as to limit its benefits to 'white' people is likely to bear the public meaning of endorsing and seeking to perpetuate that racism, exclusion and disadvantage, irrespective of the motivations behind it and irrespective of how it directly affects individuals within the excluded class.[78] There

---

[77] *BoE Trust Limited NO* [2012] ZASCA 147 (Supreme Court of Appeal of South Africa). See also *Ex parte President of the Conference of the Methodist Church of Southern Africa: In re William March Will Trust* 1993 (2) SA 697 (C); *Minister for Education* v. *Syfrets Trust Ltd* 2006 (4) SA 205 (C), and the excellent discussion in Francois du Toit, 'Constitutionalism, Public Policy and Discriminatory Testamentary Bequests: A Good Fit Between Common Law and Civil Law in South Africa's Mixed Jurisdiction' (2010) 27 *Tulane European and Civil Law Forum* 97.

[78] Indeed, in *BoE Trust*, the settlor stipulated that scholarship recipients must return to South Africa to work upon completion of their studies, and thus may have been motivated less by bigotry than by a desire to address the problem of 'bright flight' among young educated South Africans of European ancestry: [2012] ZASCA 147, [14].

is no way, given South Africa's history, to discriminate in that country so as to exclude people who are not 'white' and not invoke the deeply disrespectful understandings and practices of the past.[79]

The point of these examples is to show some ways in which discrimination can *demean* groups by endorsing and reinforcing social understandings and practices that are disrespectful of group identity. Where such social understandings and practices are both profoundly disrespectful and have caused severe historical disadvantage, discrimination that endorses or reinforces them is likely to be demeaning in a striking way; thus, racial discrimination – associated as it is with practices such as slavery that are so disrespectful as to deny even the humanity of certain races – is often marked out as a particularly offensive type of discrimination.[80] That said, discrimination can demean a group by affirming social understandings and practices that are disrespectful of group identity in less dramatic ways. Imagine that a charity declines the services of a Muslim volunteer, because he is a Muslim, in a role that will be highly visible in the community; part of the public meaning of this act is that it reinforces disrespectful understandings of Muslims – that 'they are not to be trusted', even that 'they are dangerous' – that have figured in the public discourse of Western societies since the events of 11 September 2001. Insofar as the act bears this public meaning, it demeans Muslims as a group.

With this account of how discrimination can demean groups in view, let us now consider how demeaning a group might generate harms to the autonomy of members of that group. The key is in seeing that, just as a person's autonomy may be harmed where she is compelled to have regard to some element of her identity when making choices in life, so a person's autonomy is harmed where she does not enjoy self-respect in relation to some element of her identity.[81] The possession of self-respect

---

[79] See also the discussion of discrimination against Roman Catholics in testamentary settings in Northern Ireland in Sheena Grattan and Heather Conway, 'Testamentary Conditions in Restraint of Religion in the Twenty-First Century: An Anglo-Canadian Perspective' (2005) 50 *McGill Law Journal* 511, 543–547.

[80] This seems to be reflected in anti-discrimination law, which sometimes treats racial discrimination more severely than discrimination on other grounds. See, e.g., Equality Act 2010 (UK) ss 193(2) and 194(2).

[81] Some have sought to make an argument of this type by appealing to the notion of dignity and drawing a connection between dignity and autonomy. See, e.g., the work of Denise Réaume: 'Harm and Fault in Discrimination Law: The Transition from Intentional to Adverse Effect Discrimination' (2001) 2 *Theoretical Inquiries in Law* 348; 'Discrimination and Dignity' (2003) 63 *Louisiana Law Review* 1; 'Dignity, Equality and Comparison' in

is among the fundamental conditions of autonomy; a lack of self-respect can impede the acquisition and development of many of the inner capacities on which autonomous living depends, and it can prevent a person from grasping that certain options are available to and rational for her.[82] The woman who feels that she is worthless because she is a woman, and the homosexual man who believes that because of his sexual orientation he is unsuited to important roles (like the role of parent) in his community, are alienated from their options because in significant ways they lack self-respect. The same is true of the Indigenous person who believes that a university education is for other people and the Muslim who hides his faith as he makes his way in the world. Social understandings and practices that are disrespectful of women, homosexual men, Indigenous people and Muslims take their place among the causes of this lack of self-respect and the alienation from options that accompanies it. In short, the maintenance of self-respect as a member of a group depends on a cultural backdrop which is respectful of the group's identity. Where discrimination reinforces and endorses disrespectful social understandings and practices, and thereby demeans groups, it plays its role in undermining the conditions of autonomy in the development and maintenance of self-respect on the part of members of such groups.[83] It thereby harms members of groups in a way that ought to be of interest in light of the harm principle.

B. Discrimination, autonomy and state action

The notion that discrimination, in its expressive dimension, can demean groups and thereby harm the autonomy of members of those groups should not be taken too far. The idea that people whose group identity is demeaned by discrimination might come to lack self-respect as a result

---

Deborah Hellman and Sophie Moreau (eds), *Philosophical Foundations of Discrimination Law* (Oxford University Press, 2013) 7–27. For present purposes, we may accept that the concept of dignity can assist in illuminating connections between discrimination and harms to the autonomy of members of groups.

[82] For some related thoughts specific to the position of women: Timothy Macklem, *Beyond Comparison: Sex and Discrimination* (Cambridge University Press, 2003).

[83] A point echoed in the famous passage from *Brown* v. *Board of Education* 374 US 483 (1954) (US Supreme Court), 494: 'To separate [children] from others of similar age and qualifications solely because of their race generates a feeling of inferiority as to their status in the community that may affect their hearts and minds in a way unlikely ever to be undone.'

seems plausible enough, but we should not forget those who, far from lacking self-respect on account of discrimination, take pride in their identity and on that basis feel the outrage of discrimination especially keenly. Nor should we forget that discrimination does not invariably demean groups – recall the law prohibiting children from voting – and that, even where it does demean groups, how it does so, and therefore the likely consequences of discrimination for the autonomy of members of groups, depends on many variables. In the end, while it seems plausible that – in general terms – discrimination entails harms to the autonomy of members of groups by undermining their self-respect, when it comes to identifying specific connections between discriminatory acts and harms to the autonomy of members of groups occasioned by such acts, it seems necessary to speak in a cautious, qualified way. That said, the expressive dimension of discrimination may be understood, from the perspective of autonomy-based liberalism, in a way that frees us from having to identify group – or indeed any – harms associated with discrimination, but still enables us to say something about discrimination with reference to the demands of autonomy.[84] To view the expressive dimension of discrimination in this way we must depart from the harm principle and consider discrimination and its effects in light of reasons for state action grounded in the value of autonomy.

In Chapter 2, we saw that cultural public goods make a substantial contribution to constituting the adequate range of valuable options on which living autonomously depends. Such cultural public goods range from institutions such as the family and marriage, to goods associated with excellence in science and the arts, to goods such as an educated society. Among the cultural public goods that support autonomy in significant ways is a culture characterised by attitudes of empathy, trust and respect. A culture in which these quintessentially liberal attitudes are present contributes to the conditions of autonomy in several ways; we touched on those ways briefly in Chapter 5, in our discussion of the value of religious diversity. There, we saw that attitudes of empathy, trust and respect dispose their holders to grasp and respond to the value in different options, and thus contribute to the development of autonomy-enhancing capacities. A culture in which such attitudes are prized and promoted helps to create conditions under which citizens may come to appreciate the value in the attitudes and come to hold them; in

---

[84] See Gardner, 'Liberals and Unlawful Discrimination', above n 62, 19–20.

this regard institutions, for instance schools and universities, play a central role in developing and maintaining the necessary culture. Moreover, we saw in Chapter 5 that a culture characterised by attitudes of empathy, trust and respect helps to ensure that in a given society a diversity of beliefs, practices, cultures and understandings can flourish, along with the multiplicity of valuable options for autonomous choice that are entailed in such diversity. Citizens who empathise with each other, who trust each other and who respect each other are more likely to tolerate and even support each other's different ways of pursuing value than citizens who engage with each other on less positive terms.

In the liberal project of building a society characterised by an autonomy-promoting culture, anti-discrimination norms can play a key role.[85] This is because discrimination, in its expressive dimension at least, tends to undermine a culture characterised by attitudes of empathy, trust and respect. We have just seen the ways in which discrimination demeans groups by endorsing and reinforcing disrespectful social understandings and practices that engage with elements of group identity; where the state either demeans groups in this way, or remains unmoved while others engage in such demeaning conduct, the state expresses indifference at best and endorsement at worst in relation to the demeaning conduct in question. This tends to undermine a culture of respect. Associated attitudes of empathy and trust are undermined too: for groups who are demeaned by discrimination, trust in the state and in fellow citizens may be impaired where discrimination goes unchecked; moreover, other citizens may lose empathy for groups who are demeaned by discrimination. Indeed, these effects are part of what it means to be demeaned.

None of this is to say that the state must coercively compel citizens to refrain from discrimination so as to bring about an autonomy-promoting culture. In the absence of specific harms to autonomy, there may be no case for coercion. However, it is worth remembering that the range of options available to the liberal state in dealing with the inconsistency of discrimination and liberal values is not limited to coercive options.[86] Autonomy gives the state reasons to utilise anti-discrimination norms in

---

[85] Ibid.

[86] See Simone Chambers and Jeffrey Kopstein, 'Bad Civil Society' (2001) 29 *Political Theory* 837, 855 (making the case for state incentives to promote 'good civil society'); Cory Brettschneider, *When the State Speaks, What Should It Say?* (Princeton University Press, Princeton, 2012) (arguing for liberal toleration of illiberal practices coupled with expressions of disapproval with reference to liberal values).

non-coercive ways in order to promote an autonomy-promoting culture. This brings us back to charity law for, as we saw in Chapter 2, in exploring the facilitative, incentive and expressive strategies of charity law, that body of law is not typically coercive. Charity law therefore offers the liberal state non-coercive options in the project of achieving sensitivity to the demands of autonomy when responding to discrimination, at least when that discrimination occurs in the pursuit of charitable purposes. With this thought in mind, and not forgetting the scope of the harm principle in justifying coercive interference with discrimination, we may now turn again to the problem of charity and discrimination, and consider in outline how charity law might respond to the varieties of discrimination in the pursuit of charitable purposes in keeping with the commitments of autonomy-based liberalism.

C.   Charity and discrimination: a principled approach

In sketching the outlines of a principled approach to charity and discrimination in light of the demands of autonomy, we may begin with two related propositions. The first proposition is that the coercive application of anti-discrimination norms against those who discriminate in the pursuit of charitable purposes is justified where it is necessary to prevent harms to autonomy associated with discrimination. As we saw earlier, discrimination does occasion harms to the autonomy of those who are directly affected by it and to the members of groups whose shared identity is picked out as the basis for discrimination. Thus, all else being equal, we have reasons to think that a state practice of coercively applying anti-discrimination norms to those who discriminate, including in the pursuit of charitable purposes, is justified. Such a practice is justified even to the extent that it entails the application of anti-discrimination norms to the pursuit of purposes in the private sphere; as we saw earlier, a public/private distinction does little analytical or evaluative work in the setting of autonomy-based liberalism. The appropriate vehicle for the coercive application of anti-discrimination norms to discrimination in the pursuit of charitable purposes is anti-discrimination law, a body of law that contemplates the deployment of coercive strategies in the pursuit of its aims.

The second, related, proposition is that where discrimination in the pursuit of charitable purposes occasions harms to autonomy, the state is not justified – again, all else being equal – in withholding anti-discrimination norms in responding to that discrimination. Thus, a state practice of creating broad exemptions from the requirements of anti-discrimination law for those who pursue charitable purposes seems difficult to justify. We should, of course, remember that in certain circumstances the state may be justified in not applying anti-discrimination norms coercively even though harmful discrimination occurs in the pursuit of charitable purposes. Where coercively preventing discrimination would occasion harms to those who would discriminate, because it would interfere with their autonomous pursuit of options of central importance to their lives, there may be an argument for tolerating harmful discrimination in the pursuit of charitable purposes. For example, it may be appropriate for the state to tolerate the Roman Catholic Church's discrimination against women who want to become priests in that church, given the centrality of the priesthood to Roman Catholic beliefs and practices. However, cases in which the coercive application of anti-discrimination law would occasion morally significant harms to those who would discriminate in the pursuit of charitable purposes seem unlikely to be sufficiently numerous as to justify the sorts of blanket exemptions from anti-discrimination norms that are sometimes made for charities.

The proper treatment of charity and discrimination in the public benefit test and the public policy rule of charity law stand to be analysed in a different way. Because charity law operates via non-coercive strategies, the deployment of anti-discrimination norms in the setting of the public benefit test and the public policy rule need not satisfy the harm principle. A finding that a discriminatory charitable purpose fails the public benefit test or falls foul of the public policy rule will be justified, as a matter of political morality, in circumstances where refusing to facilitate, incentivise pursuit of or endorse the purpose in question contributes in some way to the conditions of autonomy, even though the purpose is not likely to cause specific harms to autonomy, and even though coercively applying an anti-discrimination norm against those who would pursue the purpose would harm their autonomy. We saw earlier that the state's interest in building an autonomy-promoting society gives the state reasons to deploy anti-discrimination norms in non-coercive ways; one such way is to withhold support from discriminatory purposes in circumstances where supporting those purposes would tend to undermine a liberal culture characterised by empathy, trust and respect. Withholding such support is not the same thing as withdrawing options altogether; the risk of harm to those with discriminatory purposes is thus minimised.[87] These are reasons supporting a state practice of finding that discriminatory purposes fail the public benefit test; they also support invocations of the public policy rule against such purposes.

Thus, at a general level it would appear that the use of the public benefit test and the public policy rule to respond to discrimination in the pursuit of charitable purposes, as has occurred in cases like *Bob Jones University* and *Canada Trust*, is both justified and desirable in light of the demands of autonomy. Moreover, in some more specific ways those elements of charity law are likely to facilitate outcomes consistent with the demands of autonomy in cases of charity and discrimination. For example, as we have seen, the public benefit test and the public policy rule are directed at the character of discriminatory charitable purposes, and not at the character of motivations that animate the pursuit of such purposes. This focus is appropriate, given that the harms to autonomy and the tendency to undermine an autonomy-promoting culture that are associated with discrimination are, as we have seen, largely a matter of the public meaning of pursuing discriminatory purposes and not the private meaning of such purposes for those whose purposes they are. If charity law were to focus on motivations in the setting of charity and discrimination, decision-makers might be led not to endorse purposes even though they stood to produce public benefit and were thus autonomy-promoting, and even though they stood to produce no detriments in the form of harms to autonomy or the undermining of the cultural conditions of autonomy.

The elements of charity law are apt to facilitate appropriate outcomes in light of the demands of autonomy in another way, too. The 'benefit' component of the public benefit test and the public policy rule (which is also directed at questions of 'benefit' in the way discussed in Chapter 1) direct the attention of decision-makers, in appropriate cases, to both benefits and detriments that are likely to be occasioned by the pursuit

---

[87] It might be argued that where the state withdraws the power-conferring rules of the law of trusts from those who would pursue discriminatory purposes, by declaring invalid trusts for such purposes, the effect of the withdrawal of support is the same as the effect of coercion: the purposes may not be carried out. Chapter 3 explored some of the reasons for thinking that the state would harm the autonomy of citizens if it withdrew from them altogether the power-conferring rules that make possible the pursuit of charitable purposes via trusts; it seems less plausible that citizens' autonomy is harmed where the state withdraws those rules in particular circumstances so as to promote autonomy in other ways; *a fortiori* where the state renders a discriminatory charitable trust non-discriminatory via a cy-pres scheme.

of some purpose.[88] As we saw earlier, such an inquiry into benefits and detriments enables decision-makers, when considering discrimination in the pursuit of charitable purposes and especially in cases where purposes that stand to produce benefit also entail discrimination, to focus attention on the nature of the detriments associated with discrimination, and to weigh such detriments against any benefits that the purposes in question stand to produce. In considering detriments associated with discrimination in the pursuit of a charitable purpose, a decision-maker has an opportunity to reflect on the harms to autonomy associated with discrimination, as well as the propensity of discrimination to undermine an autonomy-promoting culture. This is not to say, of course, that where such detriments are identified, the decision-maker will find that the public benefit test is not satisfied or the public policy rule applies: benefits produced by a purpose entailing discrimination might outweigh those detriments. But to ask questions about detriments associated with discrimination is, from the perspective of autonomy-based liberalism, to ask questions of the right sort – questions that are interested in the harmful effects of discrimination.

That said, at present, in cases where discriminatory purposes are found not to satisfy the public benefit test or the public policy rule of charity law, decision-makers tend to cast their decisions in general terms, appealing to a broad notion of public policy and not seeking to give content to that notion beyond gesturing on occasion to constitutional imperatives and social change. A good example of this phenomenon is *Canada Trust*, where the majority of the Ontario Court of Appeal referred to constitutional protections of equality and prevailing social views, but did not feel constrained to go much further in justifying its finding that the trust in that case infringed the public policy rule, stating that 'to say that a trust premised on ... notions of racism and religious superiority contravenes contemporary public policy is to expatiate the obvious'.[89] While this may be true, if, in cases about discriminatory purposes, decision-makers are to realise the potential of the public benefit test and the public policy rule to deliver outcomes consistent with the demands of autonomy, they may need to engage in more detailed and specific reasoning about the detriments associated with discrimination along the lines we considered above. In Chapters 2 and 5, we developed

---

[88] The problem of discriminatory purposes is properly dealt with under the 'benefit' component of the public benefit test, not the 'public' component: see further Parachin, above n 32.

[89] (1990) 69 DLR (4th) 321 (Ontario Court of Appeal), 334.

the thought that decision-makers may promote autonomy by expressing respect for it in their reasoning about whether or not to recognise some purpose or type of purpose as charitable in law; this thought grounds liberal aspirations for public discourse in the charity law setting. Such aspirations lend support to an argument that decision-makers should reason carefully about *why* discriminatory purposes occasion detriments so as to fail the public benefit test and fall foul of the public policy rule, and not simply assert that they do. From this perspective, while cases like *Canada Trust* were rightly decided, they were insufficiently reasoned in some respects.

5. Conclusion

Two broad themes emerge from a study of charity and discrimination in light of autonomy-based liberalism. First, approaches to discrimination in the pursuit of charitable purposes that depend in some way on a distinction between public and private spheres introduce a conceptual framework for analysis and evaluation that is both difficult to maintain and unnecessary. The better approach is one that either assumes that charitable purposes are private purposes or is uninterested in whether they are public or private purposes, and then considers the extent to which anti-discrimination norms may be applied, either via the 'benefit' component of the public benefit test or via the public policy rule of charity law, in cases where charitable purposes entailing discrimination are in view. Second, the problem of charity and discrimination can and should be addressed by the deployment of at least two complementary strategies. Where the state is justified, according to the harm principle, in coercively interfering in discriminatory practices in the charity law setting, rules of anti-discrimination law may be brought to bear on the discriminatory practices in question. And whether or not the harm principle demands coercive state action, in any case where discrimination in the pursuit of charitable purposes will tend to undermine the cultural conditions of autonomy, the state is justified in deploying anti-discrimination norms non-coercively via the criteria and disqualifying rules of charity law. Charity law and its non-coercive strategies thus represent important means by which the liberal state may respond to discrimination in light of the political ideal of autonomy.

schools (cont.)
  racial discrimination by, 208
  trustees, 126
Scotland, 4–5, 11, 37
*Scottish Burial Reform and Cremation
    Society Ltd* v. *Glasgow
    Corporation*, 87–8
secularism, 158–63
  advancement of religion and, 169
  autonomy-based liberalism and,
    158–9, 174
  deference and, 163
  hostility to religion and, 158–9
  public discourse and, 159–60
'self help' arrangements, 16–17, 88–9,
    94, 101
self-determination, 49
  autonomy and, 50–1
  Damascene conversion and, 149–50
  options for, 52
  political expression and, 195
self-disclosure, 49
self-interest
  altruism distinguished from, 89–90
  common good and, 203
  gift giving and, 91–2
  incentive strategies and, 103–4
  'member benefit' arrangements and,
    94
self-respect, 232–3
self-transformation, 49
sexual orientation, 207, 227–9
Shelley v. *Kraemer*, 218–19
shunning, 157
similarity, principle of, 87
social equality, 111, 114
social justice, 43–5, 110, 222–3
social order, 154
social services, 15
society
  basic structure of, 45, 134, 222
  tax burden across, 135–6
South Africa, 231–2
spiritual edification, 167
state
  autonomy and, 114
  discrimination by, 227

distributive justice as constraint on,
    116–17
funding of charities, 79
night watchman, 83
non-neutrality of, 48
state action, 2–3, 5, 43
  autonomy and, 233–6
  autonomy-based, 50
  coercive, 63, 226
  constraints on, 55
  discrimination and, 233–6
  doctrine, 218–19
  harm principle and, 63
  limits on, 55, 63
  manipulation and, 64–6
  non-coercive, 63
state promotion
  of altruism, 103
  of autonomy, 50
  of autonomy-promoting purposes,
    failure of, 86–7
  of charitable purposes, 39–41, 43–5
    distribution and, 45
    justice and, 45
    neutrality and, 48
    political morality of, 49, 76
    reasoning and, 68
  constraining of, 130
  direct, 79
  disqualifying rules and, 81–2
  distributive justice as constraint on,
    117
  by facilitative, incentive and
    expressive strategies, 139–40
  of 'for profit' purposes, 109
  indirect, 79–81
  of religious purposes, 145, 153
  tax and spend means of, 78–9
state subsidies
  effect of, 140–1
  income tax exemptions and, 132
  political purposes and, 187
  tax privileges as, 133
  withdrawal of, 187
Statute of Elizabeth, 9–10, 86
stultification, 184
superstitious uses, 161